Anthony J. Kuzniewski, S.J., is a historian and is currently a campus minister at Loyola University of Chicago.

Faith and Fatherland

Notre Dame Studies
in American Catholicism

Number 3

Number 1: *The Brownson-Hecker Correspondence,*
edited by Joseph Gower and Richard Leliaert

Number 2: *The Survival of American Innocence:
Catholicism in an Era of Disillusionment, 1920-1940,*
by William M. Halsey

Sponsored by the
Center for the Study of American Catholicism

Faith and Fatherland
is the winner of the
Kosciuszko Foundation
Doctoral Dissertation Award
for 1973

FAITH AND FATHERLAND

The Polish Church War
in Wisconsin, 1896-1918

Anthony J. Kuzniewski

UNIVERSITY OF NOTRE DAME PRESS

NOTRE DAME   LONDON

Copyright © 1980 by
University of Notre Dame Press
Notre Dame, Indiana 46556

Library of Congress Cataloging in Publication Data

Kuzniewski, Anthony J
  Faith and fatherland.

  (Notre Dame studies in American Catholicism; v. 3)
  Bibliography: p.
  Includes index.
  1. Catholics—Wisconsin—History. 2. Polish
Americans—Wisconsin—History. 3. Wisconsin—Church
history. I. Title. II. Series.
BX1415.W6K89   282'.775   80-233
ISBN 0-268-00948-1

Manufactured in the United States of America

For My Parents

Contents

Preface   ix

Introduction   1

1. The Setting   7

2. The Model Community   18

3. The Emergence of Factions   36

4. The Promise   52

5. From Resistance to Revolt   70

6. The Archbishop's Counteroffensive   90

7. The Aftermath   109

8. In Retrospect   124

Appendix: *Text of the Pastoral Letter of February 1912*   129

Notes   135

Bibliography   154

Index   161

Preface

THE ELECTION OF KAROL Wojtyła as pope has been a noticeable cause for celebration among Polish-American Catholics. On the night of his election, network broadcasters and newspaper editors vied with each other to present pictures and statements of delighted members of that ethnic community. Not long afterward, when the pope visited Poland, a *New York Times* editorialist summarized in his title the popular perception of a special connection between the pontiff and Polish-Americans: "A Papal Visit Revives Long Memories and Ethnic Pride." Amid this flurry of descriptions about the awakening (or reawakening) of ethnic pride among Polish-Americans, however, there has been a lack of adequate analysis of why these people have been so deeply stirred by the unexpected turn of events at the Vatican; perhaps the descendants of the Polish immigrants do not fully understand the reasons themselves. But as almost everybody has pointed out, they have sensed them.

Besides the obvious explanation that members of a group (particularly one conscious of an unfavorable image) enjoy the success of a person associated with themselves, there is the subtler historical influence of the Polish-American experience with the Catholic Church in the United States. They are the one Catholic immigrant group to have propagated an important schism here—a fact which still accounts for some defensiveness on both sides. For those who have remained loyal to Rome, particularly many of the leaders, one lasting problem has been the failure to achieve proportionate recognition in the hierarchy. With the exception of a few German areas, American Catholicism has been, and to some extent remains, a bulwark of Irish Catholicism. There are, of course, a number of historical reasons for this development; and many of them reflect positively on the dedication and sacrifice of those who have maintained the Hibernian standard. But from the Polish-American perspective, the fact remains that the Church in their adopted country has in some ways seemed Catholic only in a formal sense. Some have even suggested that its four traditional marks be redesignated "one, holy, Irish, and apostolic." Whether or not the judgment is completely fair, it implies that the catholicity which is supposed to characterize the Church has too often been restricted to the level of lay membership, while the unity has been achieved in limiting the ethnic composition of the hierarchy. Having a Polish pope, therefore, seems to restore a little of the balance.

The situation is less critical for Polish-Americans today because American Catholicism has evolved from a rather strict ethnic compartmentalization to a broader acceptance of diversity of leadership and a lessening of the ethnic edge through assimilation and intermarriage. Vatican II, if anything, has accelerated the process by modifying some of the structures of government and reemphasizing the participation of the laity. At the turn of the century, however, when Poles were beginning to make a significant impact upon the history and destiny of the Church in the United States, the point was crucial. In those days, leadership was understood in the context of an ecclesiology which magnified the importance of the priests and bishops and promoted structures which were openly monarchical. The theology of the Church concentrated on the lines of authority; and church membership, for the lay person, was associated with the idea that the faithful depend upon the clergy for the means of salvation. Thus the bishop issue was highly significant for the first generation of Polish-Americans. To be sure, campaigning for Polish bishops was a means of expressing national pride and requesting acceptance from other Catholics. But it was also a matter of obtaining leaders who were as firmly bound by sympathy and understanding to the Polish newcomers as they were presumed to be to God. Much was at stake in the matter and this helps account for the emotional nature of the dispute, for the schism, and for the scars of old wounds which still trouble Polish-Americans.

My purpose in writing this book is to examine a particular facet of the religious experience of the Polish-Americans, the "Polish Church War" in Wisconsin. It is a unique chapter in church history because it encompasses the one successful campaign for hierarchical recognition by Roman Catholic Poles in the first generation of their life in America. That the movement achieved temporary success is largely the result of the participants themselves—the lay people, priests, and bishops who struggled with each other and with their beliefs to find an acceptable resolution of the tension which always exists between the unity and the catholicity of their Church. That the movement ultimately failed points to the fragility of the solution and to the vulnerability of persons and institutions to influences from unexpected sources. To gain an understanding of the success and failure of this experience of hierarchical "equality" of Polish-Americans, it has been necessary to take into account the backgrounds of the participants, as well as their methods, values, and personal qualities. Like the experiment they attempted, they, too, were unusual. They demonstrated some possibilities of religious and human fellowship which, in the face of serious difficulties, upheld important points. Although they could not sustain the effort, their experience has its implications for today.

An objection might be offered that while the book's title promises a discussion of the experience of the Poles in Wisconsin, it focuses rather narrowly on the happenings in Milwaukee. This, it seems to me, is an unavoidable consequence of the irregularity of the available data. Milwaukee has most of the historical records; yet the Green Bay Diocesan Archives, for instance, contains statistical records and personal comments from pastors on the effects of the Pastoral Letter of 1912 which I have not found elsewhere. Despite the metropolitan emphasis, therefore, I have tried, where possible, to include the experiences of out-state communities because of the additional light they shed on the controversy.

A second objection could be that the book concentrates more on the actions of the leaders than on the persons in the pew during the Church War. Partly, this is a result of the ecclesiology and the records of the period. My assumption is that the people were aware of the issues and chose sides in a partisan fashion. The evidence points to a substantial following on both sides. Beyond that, it has not been my purpose to develop a statistical breakdown of the support for the various contestants.

"Krakow," a Polish proverb runs, "was not built all at once." The point applies equally to the preparation of books, and I am deeply grateful to the friends and associates who contributed their knowledge, interest, and encouragement. Among them, the late Peter McCormick of the Milwaukee Public Library and Rev. Robert Sampon, Chancellor of the Milwaukee Archdiocese, were exceptionally generous in making resources available. Thanks are also due to Msgr. Chester Ropella for his help with the Green Bay Diocesan Archives; to Revs. Constantine Klukowski and Felician Tulko, O.F.M., for serving as hosts and guides through the Franciscan resources in Wisconsin; to Joseph Frymark, Sr., and David Kozikowski for their assistance in researching the Portage County Poles; to William J. Galush for his introduction to the holdings of the Immigrant Archives at the University of Minnesota; to Rev. Leo Neal, O.F.M. Conv., for hospitality and assistance at St. Anthony's Monastery in Detroit; to the late Rev. Joseph Swastek and Rev. Leonard Chrobot for their generous help with the materials at St. Mary's College in Orchard Lake, Michigan; to Very Rev. Andrzej Tolcz of the Savanarola Theological Seminary in Scranton for his kindness and aid with materials relating to the history of the Polish National Catholic Church; to Pat Whelan for opening the files of the *Times-Review* of La Crosse; and to Dr. Greg Harrington for his help with photographic work.

Szymon Deptuła shared his private collection and his knowledge of the Poles in Wisconsin. Enith Vardaman, Barbara Hoyt, and Nelson Minnich lent their assistance with the translation of troublesome passages; and John Fontana and Gary Buseck were invaluable comrades in the thankless job of checking successive drafts for errors. Revs. F. Paul Prucha and Robert Bireley, S.J., are entitled to honorable mention for their help and interest over the years.

Several persons proved to be friends in need in the difficult passage from dissertation to book. The most important was Rev. Joep van Beeck, S.J., whose gentle criticism and strong encouragement have been a *sine qua non* of the entire process. Paul Hass, Irving Rockwood, and James Flynn merit thanks for their valuable suggestions. A host of other friends and relatives, including Susan Reifsnyder, David O'Brien, the faculty and students of Kirkland House at Harvard, the members of St. Andrew Bobola House, and the faculty and students of Holy Cross College, the Jesuit School of Theology in Chicago, and Loyola University of Chicago, contributed support and encouragement at critical times. To all of them I offer warm thanks.

I owe particular gratitude to Notre Dame's Center for the Study of American Catholicism, especially Jay Dolan and Philip Gleason, and to the Kościuszko Foundation and its former president, Eugene Kusielewicz, for the awards and financial support which help make possible the publication of this book.

Deep thanks are also due to Professor Oscar Handlin for first interesting me in a project on Polish immigration and for providing his experienced direction during the years in which it has evolved.

Finally, my parents have helped me by their patience and understanding to shoulder the joys and the burden of a long formal education and the preparation of a first book. To them, with love, I dedicate this work.

Introduction

IN 1899, WHEN WENCESLAUS Kruszka began to write the first comprehensive history of Polish-Americans, he grouped the settlements by Catholic dioceses.[1] Few have questioned his method, for, with the exception of Jews who associated with coreligionists in America, most immigrants from the Polish areas of central Europe were Catholics. To a large extent, they centered their religious and social activity on parishes, which became important reference points in the development of their common life. These congregations, however, were more than interconnected islands of Polishness in the New World; they were also the most tangible sign of Polish presence within the institutional Church. Through them the bishops controlled and regulated the relationship of Poles to Catholics of similar and divergent backgrounds. Thus the diocese was an appropriate and convenient way for the young priest-historian to organize into larger units the data he had collected on each locality.

But Kruszka had more than convenience in mind as he prepared the Polish history. He was, even then, initiating a campaign to increase his countrymen's participation in Catholic affairs by securing episcopal appointments for their clergy. The record of achievement, he reasoned, spoke for itself. Those who had participated in building up the Church should also help govern it. And governance rested firmly in the hands of the bishops.

The immigrant Church was just beginning to recover from the fifteen-year crisis of attempting to balance the claims of ethnic preference against the demands of unity. Germans and Irish had battled to a standoff; tne Church was in transition to a more peaceful era. Scarred warriors on both sides fervently hoped that ethnic questions could be laid to rest. Under the circumstances, the efforts of Kruszka and his associates to secure Polish bishops were greeted with suspicion and resistance. Nobody denied the record of accomplishment which the thirteen-volume history enthusiastically proclaimed. But those in authority did disagree over whether that record justified the increasingly strident claims of Poles for episcopal preferment. In his book, Kruszka

1

explicitly challenged Catholic leaders, particularly in his home province of Wisconsin, to share their authority for the good of the whole. But it was not easy to agree on the common good. Soon the high emotions and questionable tactics of both sides attracted wide attention. Observers began to call the imbroglio the Polish Church War. They would doubtless be amazed that so little has been written about it since its conclusion.

The search for common ground is seldom easy. Especially was this true for American Catholics during the century of immigration which followed the Napoleonic Wars. At first there was no generally agreed-upon set of practices to determine what the Church in America should resemble. Conditioned by custom and experience in the homeland to regard certain practices and standards as normative, ethnic groups often conflicted in America in the effort to impose upon all a particular expression of Catholicism. Even Rome at times seemed to vacillate and to tolerate a range of activities which threatened the fragile unity among the competing groups. Between 1884 and 1899, hostility between Irish and Germans shook the Church, the former favoring an "American face" for the Church while the latter envisioned a more pluralistic institution. In the 1880s, German petitions won full and equal status from Rome for national language parishes, but Peter Paul Cahensly's proposal for national dioceses was rejected. Irish churchmen, in turn, gained endorsement for experimental cooperation with civil authorities in running parochial schools; but the Vatican condemned the concept of "Americanism," the belief, sometimes attributed to Irish-Americans, that doctrine and practice could be altered in the interest of gaining greater appeal in a nation which was self-consciously republican. After these limits were set, neither militantly American nor aggressively hyphenated Catholicism was to be allowed. The new century brought an uneasy truce as Germans and Irish began to concentrate on greater cooperation.

This much of the story is known. Competent historians have studied the Cahensly and Americanist controversies.[2] Their efforts have resulted in a standard interpretation of American Catholic history, propounded by such scholars as John Tracy Ellis, Will Herberg, Winthrop Hudson, and Sydney Ahlstrom, that the Church has been a means of moderately rapid Americanization for its members.[3] Irish Catholics, it is assumed, favored this policy because they had no language barrier to overcome and because the struggles they had fought with nativists spurred them to demonstrate that their Church was not un-American. German Catholics, mellowed by several generations of American life and embarrassed by the political alignments of World War I, soon dropped the hyphenated aspect of German-American life.

In this way the Church rather rapidly lost its immigrant flavor and grew into an institution which increasingly reflected American attitudes and practices, even as it continued to foster the special characteristics arising from its Roman allegiance and overwhelmingly Irish leadership.

But groups other than the Germans and Irish contributed to this evolutionary process and were affected by it. As later arrivals, they found a considerably less fluid situation in the Church. Their efforts to win concessions, therefore, were harder to sustain, but the stakes were high. Of those who tested Catholic priorities after 1900, the Poles were the most determined. Well over two million of them came to the United States between 1870 and 1914. Under foreign rule in their homeland, they had been the victims of religious pressure used for nationalistic ends. Transported to the New World, their sensitivity to such subjection frequently generated misunderstanding in Catholic circles. Friction led to division. Schismatic Polish churches grew up in Chicago, Buffalo, Scranton, and elsewhere, eventually to be united as the Polish National Catholic Church. The movement grew slowly but steadily, reaching a membership of about a quarter million by 1940. Poles who remained loyal to Rome were called upon to justify their allegiance to ecclesiastical leaders in America, contemptuously identified as "Ayrish," who didn't appear to care what happened to Polish Catholics. Thus defensiveness and embarrassment reinforced national pride in the quest for bishops.

The Polish position in American Catholic history has only begun to be examined. Parish life has received the greatest attention. Most historians have accepted the hypothesis, first advanced by sociologists Florian Thomas and William Znaniecki, that the parish filled a social function in the life of the transplanted peasants that was as important as its religious dimension. For, if faith supplied meaning in a confused and uprooted existence and ornate structures provided the appropriate setting for the solemn moments of life, the atmosphere of individuals grouped together in a congregation re-created to a substantial extent the social life of the Old World commune.[4] Differentiated from other Americans and even from other Catholics by their language, customs, and values, Polish immigrants often kept to themselves by developing autonomy at the parish level. Daniel Buczek's study of the long pastorate of Lucyan Bójnowski in New Britain, Connecticut, exemplifies this tendency. The Polish school, orphanage, newspaper, home for the elderly, religious fraternities, social and cultural organizations, all provided sufficient outlets for individuals at various stages of life. Within the first generation, Bójnowski was largely able to mediate the relationship of New Britain's Poles to the larger world.[5]

The effort to transmit Polish values and attitudes centered on the parish school. A study of Catholic education in America by Andrew Greeley and Peter Rossi shows that Poles were loyal and consistent in their support of parochial education.[6] It was hard to find adequate facilities and competent teachers in the early days, but the curriculum posed no great difficulty. Religion, Polish history and grammar, American history, English, and arithmetic generally filled the student's day. Only after World War I did reliance on Polish as a language of instruction and as a subject of study begin to wane. Thus, according to Józef Miaso, who has done the most extensive work on the topic, the school was largely a reflection of parish life. Children were not so much educated to achieve spectacular success in the broader community as to form a new generation of participants in the specifically Polish-American religious and social structures.[7]

Within the Polish parish, and ultimately outside it, national feeling intensified. Traditionalists in Polish ethnic studies have regarded the campaign for Polish bishops as a reaction to relatively unsympathetic treatment from ecclesiastical leaders. Perceiving their low status in the Church as a form of persecution, they reacted with passionate intensity in defense of the legitimacy of their aspirations. That was Wenceslaus Kruszka's position,[8] and many interpreters have followed his lead.[9] Buczek maintains that the fight for equality in the Church was an issue of justice.[10] Historians of the Polish National Catholic Church have reached similar conclusions. Paul Fox and Hieronim Kubiak have cited as causes of the ruptures legitimate but insensitive actions by the American bishops which alienated some of their Polish constituents.[11]

Recently, Victor Greene challenged this interpretation. Immigrants from Poland, he says, arrived in America with only a vague idea of their national identity. As Catholics, they were greeted warmly by American bishops; but division among the intellectual leaders over the priorities to be assigned to religion and nationality surfaced early in the life of their communities. The debate whether the Church was primarily Catholic or Polish eventually attracted the attention of all the Poles in America, elevating their sense of ethnic differentiation. In this context, Poles either declared their independence from the local bishop or embarked upon a stormy course of confrontation. Either way, the impetus came from within the group.[12]

Whatever its sources, ethnic awareness among Poles was a phenomenon to be reckoned with as early as the 1880s. Its emergence and growth ultimately affected Catholic history. Those who have studied the matter have tended to emphasize its effect on the campaign for Polish bishops. Kruszka started the process by describing his own efforts to influence prelates and pope.[13] Karol Wachtl continued the process in 1944. Poles, he said in his history, were acceptable as bishops in this country only to the extent that they were fully American.[14] The

issue was picked up again by Victor Greene, who has called Paul
Rhode's appointment in 1908 as the first Polish-American bishop a
symbolic reassurance that America's Polish Catholics were being
accepted by American bishops as hyphenates within the Church.[15]
Andrew Greeley has praised the farsightedness of Archbishop James
Quigley for supervising the appointment of Rhode as his auxiliary. This
action, Greeley implies, was a realistic and constructive acceptance of
the Church as it was.[16]

Preoccupation with the first bishop and with tabulating subsequent
appointments from the Polish community has tended to blur the differences between the various Polish-American settlements and the
distinctiveness with which each reacted to the bishop question. The
most obvious difference is the age of the ethnic community. Most of the
Poles from the German Partition, for example, arrived in America
before 1890. Many settled in the Midwestern states. Their institutions
were well established before many of their compatriots from Russia and
Austria embarked for America. Education and the degree of national
consciousness also varied among the three partitions: immigrants from
the eastern marches of Germany had the lowest rate of illiteracy, for
instance, and newcomers from Hapsburg Galicia had not been subject to
anti-Catholicism.[17] The differences associated with the origins of the
Poles were compounded by the fact that diocesan organizations in
America still reflected the nationality conflict of the late nineteenth
century. Past experiences influenced the actions and policies of
hierarchical authorities no less than those of Polish-American Catholics
in the Polish campaign for recognition.

In Wisconsin, the overwhelming reality of Catholic life was its
German character. From the erection of the Diocese of Milwaukee in
1843 to the beginning of the equality campaign, every episcopal
appointment in the state's three dioceses had come from the German
Catholic community (including Austrians and Swiss-Germans). Ardent
defenders of the pluralistic view of Catholicism during the 1880s and
1890s, these prelates had fended off several attempts by Irish
churchmen to have non-Germans appointed to Wisconsin sees.[18] At
first, the hierarchy reflected the overwhelmingly German makeup of
Wisconsin Catholicism, but by the turn of the century the influx of about
100,000 Polish immigrants made the constituency more diverse.

Wisconsin's Poles were also unusual. To a remarkable extent, they
were a homogeneous group which traced its origins to the German areas
of Poznania and West Prussia. Steeled by the *Kulturkampf* and decrees
banning Polish from the schools, they were more aware of national
identity than Poles in the other partitions. Experience under German
rule had taught them that religion and nationality must walk hand in
hand, and although some of their conclusions may have been tentative,

their memories furnished potential for anti-German feelings in America. Early arrival also distinguished Wisconsin's Poles; the movement was largely complete by 1890, and from that time the community generated most of its own growth. Thus by the turn of the century the group was relatively settled, organized, and self-conscious.

These factors supplied confidence in making a strong plea for bishops. Articulate spokesmen emerged. Wenceslaus Kruszka, the Jesuit-trained historian, priest, and Polish advocate, kept the issue constantly in the public eye after the turn of the century. His half-brother Michael, publisher of the nation's first successful Polish daily in Milwaukee, supported the effort with the printed word. Rhetoric recalling the *Kulturkampf* in Germany inflamed popular sentiments. Although they were badly divided over the choice of methods, the state's Polish leaders rarely argued about the goal, and the campaign placed the bishops in a quandary. At first advocates of a pluralistic Catholicism, they became moderate assimilationists after the turn of the century. And so their first strategy was to encourage the moderates within the Polish leadership, hoping in this way to tie appointment of a Pole to the degree to which Poles accepted their communality with other American Catholics. The effort ultimately failed and the range of choices narrowed: yield to the Poles or risk escalation of the ill will which was poisoning the state's Catholic life.

In other places, when faced by opposition, bishops were content to retaliate with excommunication and to counsel loyalty in the face of dissidence. But in Wisconsin things were different. Authority, to be sure, was employed. Wenceslaus Kruszka was silenced for a while, and Michael Kruszka's papers were put under the ban; but Polish-speaking bishops were eventually appointed—three between 1911 and 1915. One, a Czech-American, was rejected by Milwaukee's Polish priests and transferred. The second was named auxiliary bishop in Milwaukee in an unprecedented effort to restore unity and retain the loyalty of the state's Poles. And the third, as ordinary of the Green Bay Diocese, was the first Polish-American to be accorded full authority over an American diocese. The outbreak of World War I and the Americanism campaign of the postwar period brought a sudden end to Polish gains. The next bishop was not appointed from that group until 1926, and then not in Wisconsin. Infrequent appointments again became the norm.

Therefore, the Polish Catholic experience in Wisconsin in the years immediately preceding the First World War is a unique chapter in American history. Concessions to pleas for national bishops were exceedingly rare in those days, but in Wisconsin, remarkably, they were granted. For five years, Polish aspirations were acknowledged and favored, however reluctantly. The circumstances and personalities in the story have occupied an obscure corner of history until now.

1. The Setting

"AS LONG AS THE WORLD continues whole," runs an old proverb, "a German will not be brother to a Pole." Whatever its relevance for the antagonisms in Central Europe, the saying was tested in the New World. For although "becoming American" obliged one to live in harmony with persons of different backgrounds, older preferences invariably strained that idealism. The possibility to cooperate or clash was nowhere stronger than in Wisconsin, where Germans and Poles encountered one another with particular intensity as Catholics. There the Church had been guided from the start by bishops who had established a center of German Catholic life. Assailed by Irish coreligionists for being un-American, the prelates had defended their special view of the faith in an emotional, fifteen-year long controversy. Wisconsin's Poles arrived after participation in the *Kulturkampf,* and German rule imbued them with strong feelings about the relationship of Catholicism to their peoplehood. The times and the setting, therefore, were unusual. Fellowship or national antagonism, catholicity or ethnic insularity: the alternatives were crucial. As always, the past helped to explain the present.

The most important element in the institutional development of American Catholicism in the nineteenth century was the centralization of authority in the hands of the bishops. The Third Baltimore Council completed the process in 1884. Lay trusteeship, long a source of friction, was finally eliminated, leaving bishops the supreme heads of church properties in each diocese. Pastors were to act as episcopal representatives, and lay persons who assisted with parish administration were subject to the approval of the chancery office. Also, the council fathers regularized the manner of filling vacant sees; after 1884, the nomination of candidates was restricted to the bishops of the province (an archdiocese and the suffragan dioceses attached to it) in which a vacancy occurred. Diocesan consultors and irremovable rectors were given an advisory role, but the bishops alone submitted three candidates to Rome on a preferential list, a *terna* (Latin for "threesome"). Because the United States was considered a missionary country until 1908, the American Church was under the jurisdiction of the Vatican's Congrega-

7

tion for the Propagation of the Faith (or, simply, "the Propaganda").
Rome worked especially through the archbishop of Baltimore, the
unofficial primate of American Catholics. The office was held by James
Gibbons from 1877 to 1921.[1]

Implementation of the conciliar decrees presented few difficulties
in Wisconsin, where the Church was headed by the archbishop of
Milwaukee. The diocese was created in 1843 and made a metropolitan
see in 1875, with suffragan sees in Wisconsin, Upper Michigan,
Minnesota, and Dakota Territory. A provincial synod, held in Milwaukee, had obtained legislation from the state to permit bishops to
incorporate their holdings, thereby closing the question of lay control
over parish administration. With a few exceptions, legal incorporation
of the parishes was accomplished throughout Wisconsin in 1883 and
1884. When St. Paul, Minnesota, received metropolitan status in 1888,
the Wisconsin Province was reduced to the Archdiocese of Milwaukee
and the dioceses of La Crosse, Green Bay, and Marquette, Michigan.
The creation of a new see at Superior in 1905 expanded the number of
episcopal districts in the province to five.[2]

Lay persons were admonished to accord appropriate respect to
their religious leaders. The *Handbook for Catholic Parishioners of the
Archdiocese of Milwaukee,* issued in 1907, warned that "lay government even in the temporal affairs of the Church is an essentially
Protestant principle." The freedom accorded to religious institutions in
the United States permitted the Church to exercise appropriate control
over its own affairs. Thus, despite the temptation to apply the principle
of popular sovereignty to matters ecclesiastical, lay persons were
advised to draw a sharp distinction:

> It is . . . necessary that American Catholics understand clearly the
> teaching of their faith, namely, that the Church is not a republic or
> democracy, but a monarchy; that all her authority is from above
> and rests in her Hierarchy; that while the faithful of the laity have
> divinely given rights to receive all the blessed ministrations of the
> Church, they have absolutely no right whatever to rule and govern.

Even when lay persons did participate in ecclesiastical affairs, their role
was to be largely passive; the bishop had to approve the individuals in
each instance.[3] The lines, therefore, were rigid and clear. Catholicism
chose a strongly clerical orientation. Bishops, whatever their policies,
exercised authority in the name of God.

Episcopal leadership came to Wisconsin before statehood. When
John Martin Henni assumed his duties in the new Diocese of Milwaukee
in 1844, he presided over an area which was just being settled.
Centralization, therefore, could be instituted from the start. But nationality conflicts were another matter; they surfaced with Henni's

appointment and continued to haunt Milwaukee's bishops for seventy-five years. The new prelate, a native of Switzerland, had engaged in journalistic and pastoral work among the German Catholics of the Cincinnati area, and his Ohio constituents were disappointed when he was appointed to Wisconsin. It seemed to some that Henni was being exiled by Irish prelates to the wilderness because he had advocated a special seminary for German-speaking priests at the Fifth Provincial Council at Baltimore in 1843.[4] However, the real reason for his appointment was the expectation that Wisconsin and Milwaukee would become a center of German immigration. Henni, German speaking and proven in his pastoral and executive abilities, was a good choice. By 1850 he had given the diocese a reputation for catering to the needs of German-speaking newcomers. Their traditional Catholicism flourished linguistically and culturally under Henni's guidance.[5]

This orientation, however, was not without its problems. In time the fears of non-Germans, particularly the Irish, came to the surface. Objections to founding a bilingual diocesan seminary in the mid-1850s almost ruined the project. Michael Heiss, a Bavarian-born priest designated by Henni as first rector, exercised considerable tact to assure the Irish and Germans that the institution would respect the needs of each.[6] But the bishop's preference for appointing Germans to positions of authority, especially after he became an archbishop in 1875, made the Irish uneasy. In 1878, when Henni's health began to fail, the question of his successor brought the misgivings into the open. Henni's choice was Michael Heiss, who had left the seminary to become Bishop of La Crosse. The bishops of the province ratified this choice, but the protests of the Irish clergy, that the Church in Wisconsin was overly German, were forwarded to Rome by Gibbons. In the stalemate which ensued, Henni remained adamant. Only the intervention of Cardinal Joseph Hergenroether at the Vatican resolved the impasse in favor of Heiss, who succeeded to the See of Milwaukee at Henni's death in 1881.[7]

The second archbishop's nine-year reign was stormier than his predecessor's. The bitterness which had attended his nomination persisted. Several Irish priests withdrew from the archdiocese during his tenure, and Heiss postponed his required visit to Rome because there was no one he could trust with administration during his absence.[8] The basic issue was cultural, not dogmatic. The Irish feared that the Church in Wisconsin was assuming a foreign flavor, thereby jeopardizing its chance to prosper in the United States. The Germans held that language was the basis of faith and argued that immigrants would be lost to Catholicism if they were forced to assimilate too quickly.[9] The treatment of every Catholic nationality was thereby involved.

Despite determination to foster tolerance for the various cultural manifestations of Catholicism, the Wisconsin approach was identified as the German position in the conflicts which followed. A crisis erupted in 1884 with the allegations of St. Louis German Catholics that they were being treated as inferiors by Archbishop Peter Kenrick. Peter Abbelen, a Milwaukee priest, endorsed their charges and supported them with a statement he presented in Rome with the approval of Heiss. The Abbelen Memorial asserted that improper treatment of Germans by Irish prelates was widespread and asked the Vatican to put German Catholics on an equal footing. Irish churchmen opposed the allegations. Bishops John Ireland of St. Paul and John Keane of Richmond issued a strong countermemorial.[10] Rome's response, delivered in 1887, granted the request of full status for national-language parishes, even when several parishes were located in one area.[11] The dispute exacerbated German-Irish tensions so greatly that Bishop Ireland and others began to keep careful watch on Wisconsin's bishops.

Heiss's death in 1890 afforded an opportunity for intervention in Wisconsin Catholicism. Following the procedures which had been adopted at Baltimore, the bishops of the province nominated Bishops Frederick Katzer of Green Bay, Kilian Flasch of La Crosse, and Henry Richter of Grand Rapids. Angered because the names of three German-Americans were on the *terna,* Irish liberals intervened. John Ireland wrote Gibbons that Katzer was "a man thoroughly German and thoroughly unfit to be an archbishop."[12] Gibbons, in July, put the matter on the agenda of the first annual meeting of American archbishops. The prelates voted to set aside Katzer's nomination and proposed, instead, appointment of John Lancaster Spalding of Peoria. Although Spalding spoke German, his pro-Irish approach in writing about the Church in America was a handicap in Wisconsin.[13] Eventually Katzer received the appointment.

Like Heiss, Katzer favored pluralistic Catholicism in America. Half of his letter of farewell to Green Bay Catholics was a plea for unity among the nationalities. The success of his tenure, he wrote, came "because we were one, because all the people and priests and the bishop were one in spirit."[14] Unity, however, was not to be. In the end, Katzer was responsible for guiding this German province through the turmoil of the Cahensly and Americanist controversies and the early stages of the campaign for a Polish bishop.

The Cahensly dispute broke out early in 1891, after St. Rafaelsverein, a German immigrant-aid society led by Peter Paul Cahensly, presented Leo XIII with a memorial that was passed at its meeting in 1890. The document expressed concern over the apparent loss of immigrants to the Church. Its eight recommendations requested special attention to the needs and distinct religious traditions of the immigrants and urged that bishops of various nationalities be assigned to areas where immigrants from several countries had settled. Liberal churchmen seized this opportunity to protest the interference of outsiders in American church affairs and to denounce the threat to diocesan unity which the proposal for multiple bishops represented. Although Wisconsin's prelates attempted to dissociate themselves from the document, they were in an awkward position because of its origins.[15] Word of the proposal's defeat reached America in July 1891, but the liberals continued to exploit their victory for some time. In August, when Gibbons was invited to Milwaukee to confer the *pallium* on Katzer, he preached a stern warning against national division in the Church. Years later the cardinal remembered that his audience had been aghast at his open and uncompromising stand.[16]

At the height of the Cahensly controversy, the death of Bishop Flasch and the promotion of Katzer left two of the province's four sees vacant. John Ireland preferred the appointment of non-Germans, but Gibbons refused to intervene again in Wisconsin. The result was the selection of James Schwebach, a native of Luxembourg, to the Diocese of LaCrosse, and Sebastian G. Messmer, of German-Swiss origins, to Green Bay. Both men assumed their offices in the spring of 1892, and the German predominance in the state continued.[17]

From their relatively conservative platform, Wisconsin's bishops watched the liberal gains of the next few years with growing alarm: the Faribault and Stillwater plans, Catholic participation in the Parliament of Religions at the Columbian Exposition, the effort "to promote a close alliance between the spirit of the new democracy and the Church."[18] They were therefore relieved when in January 1899 Leo XIII issued the letter *Testem Benevolentiae,* which cautioned against modifying the discipline and teaching of the Church so as to make it more acceptable in a democracy. "Americanism," as the error was called, was not attributed to any American churchman. But the pope did indicate his alarm at the evil such practices could cause.[19]

Although Americans were unanimous in thanking the pontiff for the warning, they could not agree on its significance. The Irish liberals, embarrassed by the letter, emphasized that the pope did not say the forbidden doctrine had ever been taught in the United States.[20] The Germans, on the other hand, regarded the letter as putting an end to a serious threat. Wisconsin's prelates told the pope that the errors had indeed been present; whoever denied it, they asserted, was guilty of using mental reservation to mask the truth.[21] Only New York's archbishop, Michael Corrigan, agreed with the Wisconsinites. As a result, Ireland accused Katzer and Corrigan of being "two men who belied America." Another acrimonious clash might have ensued, but Gibbons intervened and the discussion ended.[22]

The papal letter largely resolved the controversy over the development of Catholicism in the United States. Ethnic individuality was to be permitted at the parish but not the diocesan level. The Church would be "American," but it would keep pace with the assimilation of its members and would not impose absolute standards of cultural acceptability. Within each province, the conciliar procedures of 1884 would be strictly followed in determining succession to vacancies. The contestants thus found common ground in accepting moderate assimilation for Catholic Americans, and both sides avoided the subject of immigrant adjustment within the Church.[23]

The bishops of Wisconsin were never quite able to reconcile themselves to the liberals' stress on loyalty and identification of Catholicism with the United States. Like Frederick Katzer, they continued to regard the Old Country as a mother and America as a bride.[24] The experiences of the 1890s had taught both groups that it was dangerous to tie the Church too strongly to either the Old or the New Country, and German Catholics thereafter preferred gradual Americanization of the Church and its leadership (a condition which other immigrant groups, such as the Poles, would be expected to accept). In the meantime, Wisconsin remained a stronghold of German Catholicism. Its leaders had defended the pluralistic ideal in a bitterly emotional battle. Memories of a difficult past, no less than new assimilationist goals, colored their approach to later Catholic immigrants.

To form judgments in the light of experience is a common tendency, and the Poles who were beginning to enter the Catholic life of the state were no less influenced by their past than were the Church authorities they encountered. Like the bishops who received them, the newcomers had been through a tumultuous period; but for the Poles the issue had been survival, not dominance. Catholic history in nineteenth-century Poland demonstrates the difficulty of the aphorism *Polonia semper fidelis*. Most of those who emigrated from German and Russian Poland after 1870 were aware of that reality. Like some of the German immigrants, Poles arrived with memories of religious persecution under Bismarck—but the Iron Chancellor's denationalization policies had been reserved for them alone. Like the Irish, Poles had encountered political suppression which strengthened the ties between religion and nationality. But they faced three enemies (Russia, Austria, and Germany), not one, in the struggle for liberation. These factors helped shape the Polish reaction to the persons and situations they encountered in America. Intellectual or peasant, each, in his own way, carried to the New World a remembrance of things past.

Romanticism walked in the company of skepticism as intellectuals pondered Poland's future in the mid-nineteenth century. Exiles after the

1831 uprising, gathering in Paris, fostered the idea of a Poland which would reemerge, messiahlike, to bring peace and justice to the world. The movement's religious dimension led Peter Semenenko and others to form a religious order, the Congregation of the Resurrection. Adopting the motto "Serve God, Poles, and God will save Poland," the group ministered to the exile community and later to Polish-Americans.[25] But some intellectuals, angered by Pope Gregory XVI's condemnation of the insurrection, urged Poles to break with Rome. "Remember, Poland," said Julius Słowacki, "that the pope is your cross; your ruin lies in Rome." Resurrectionists responded that love of God in the Catholic Church is the true source of Polish patriotism.[26] The disagreement became an important theme in Polish intellectual history and a major article of contention among Poles who migrated to America.

The intellectuals' battles at first had little effect on life at home. Scarcely aware of the ramifications of romantic nationalism, Poland's peasantry failed to support the new uprising in 1863. Discouraged by the third failure in three generations to prevent partition militarily, leaders turned to the organic work of improving the social and economic status of the uneducated classes.[27] Their task was formidable. Primarily agricultural, Poland at midcentury was an area of small villages which supported a traditional and backward way of life. Farming methods were primitive and the land was often parcelled out in minuscule plots. The illiteracy rate, ranging up to a high of 95 percent in Austrian Galicia, hampered efforts at enlightenment and fostered hostility toward change.[28]

Within this peasant society, Roman Catholicism was pervasive. Religion reinforced and stabilized peasant mores and attitudes, teaching respect for authority and meaning in the humblest life. Pressure to conform was strong; the few who failed to comply with religious discipline risked social ostracism.[29] The priest played a special role in this system. Viewed as a special representative of God, he was expected to be conscientious in fulfilling his responsibilities as the leader of community worship. His teaching, advice, reprimands, and praise were received with special attentiveness.[30] According to Jan Slomka, a turn-of-the-century mayor in Galicia, "The clergy were held in high esteem, being thought of as God's chosen, as people who already on this earth counted as saints. Everyone turned to them . . . with full confidence."[31] Because the priest was often the only person in the village who had received a formal education, his influence extended to the secular realm. This usually made him the most important individual in the village, both in personal status and in direct and indirect forms of power.

With the advent of public education, economic growth, and rapid population expansion after 1863, the peasants' ways began to change. Polish areas of Germany were the first to alter. There compulsory education, though not universally enforced, reduced illiteracy. By 1867 the rate for the province of Poznania had dropped to 13.8 percent and most other areas were even lower.[32] The ability to read gave villagers better understanding of the world beyond and access to its knowledge. Newspapers urged scientific farming and productivity slowly rose. The press began to waken among the peasants a sense of being Polish. In Germany, where the partitioner was neither Catholic nor Slavic and repressive measures were most severe, Polish distinctiveness was most threatened. But newspaper editors helped explain the broader meaning of official measures so that their implications for the national life of Poles could be appreciated in all the towns and regencies.[33] Common bonds were forged. Polish national consciousness on a massive scale had its first blossoming in the German Empire.

The point is important because the eastern marches of Germany were the land of origin of the majority of Wisconsin's Polish settlers. The federal census of 1900 indicated that 80 percent of the Polish community in the state traced their roots to Germany.[34] And since later immigrants from the Austrian and Russian partitions favored other American localities, the Poles of Wisconsin remained relatively homogeneous in their origins.[35] Some have argued that nationalism among the emigrating Polish peasants was weak and was actualized mostly after their arrival in the United States.[36] The point is valuable, but it should be remembered that the European experience helped prepare even passive newcomers for greater group awareness in America. In general, Poles from Germany had the earliest and most highly developed sense of Polishness.

This development started, inadvertently, with the desire to strengthen the internal unity of Germany. The least-German provinces of the Hohenzollern empire were Poznania (over 50% Polish) and West Prussia (30%), and significant Polish minorities inhabited Lower Silesia and Pomerania. Bismarck's goal was to create a homogeneous German-speaking population as quickly as possible. To accomplish this he introduced Germanization programs in the schools. At first the effort was little more than inculcation of knowledge of the German language.[37] Polish leaders tried to be accommodating. Mieczyslaus Ledóchowski, head of the Polish Catholics after he became archbishop of Poznan-Gniezno in 1865, attempted to win Bismarck's friendship by avoiding grounds for antagonism. He warned priests not to participate in politics and forbade the singing of the patriotic hymn, *Boże, coś Polskę*.[38] But after the Germans' victory over the French, conciliation was a forlorn hope.

Once unification was complete, the Iron Chancellor addressed himself to the presumed threat posed by Catholic forces and by the Polish population of the empire. Between 1872 and 1876, the Polish language was eliminated from schools and all public functions. Poles were denied positions in public service. The Catholic Church was subjected to state control and the teaching of religion in Polish (even privately) was strictly forbidden. Most Catholic religious orders were abolished, and the Old Catholics were encouraged to lure Germans and Poles away from Rome. Massive arrests followed Ledóchowski's advice to engage in passive resistance. The primate and other priests were imprisoned; others went underground.[39] While he was in prison in 1873, Ledóchowski was named a cardinal by Pius IX, and the following year was called to Rome. The primacy remained vacant for twelve years, as Bismarck and the Vatican refused to agree on a successor. Finally, Leo XIII agreed to the appointment of Julius Dinder, formerly of Königsberg, who was willing to collaborate with the government. A German thus became the first non-Pole to occupy the see traditionally associated with leadership of all Polish Catholics. This, together with the designation of George Kopp to the Archdiocese of Breslau, put most Polish Catholics in Germany under German prelates.[40] Such appointments were, perhaps, the best the pope could make in balancing the needs of Polish Catholics against the demands of the German government. But they aroused unforgettable bitterness in the minds of many Poles.

The continuing campaign to root out (*ausrotten*) Slavic life in Germany led Bismarck to change his policies in the 1880s, and he assaulted the Poles on the economic front. In 1886 he appropriated 100 million marks to promote German colonization of the Polish provinces, but the scheme achieved only limited success. In 1894, as ex-chancellor, Bismarck enthusiastically supported the *Ostmarkverein* (an organization to colonize and Germanize the Polish areas of Germany). The group's policy of economic and social pressure was soon dubbed Hakatism by the Poles, because of the initials of the three founders: Hansemann, Kennemann, and Tiedemann. In the first year it grew to 20,000 members and attracted important German support, but its tactics increased the determination to resist.[41]

Besides the religious and economic offensives, German governments accelerated the cultural effort to Germanize the children. Educators strove to inculcate loyalty to Berlin, and, to this end, schools were located in almost every village from an early date. Although a disproportionately high percentage of children in the Polish countryside did not complete elementary school, the illiteracy rate continued to drop—from about 14 percent in 1867 to three percent in 1911.[42] Since most schools were "religious," the policies of the *Kulturkampf* gave force to the idea that religion and nationality must be defended simultaneously. In the village of Fałkowice, for instance, children attended a bilingual school administered by the Polish pastor; he was fired in 1876 for refusing to teach the catechism in German, and the ensuing fight with the authorities lasted ten years. Such priest-patriots promoted the emergence of ethnic awareness, while counterproductive government policies assured that its content would be both Polish and Catholic.[43]

German prelates, on the other hand, cooperated more fully with the central government. In 1887 Julius Dinder directed that religion be taught in German in all the middle schools under his jurisdiction.[44] The reaction of many Poles was illustrated by a cartoon which showed the prelate, seated in full regalia upon the episcopal throne, crushing Polish prayers beneath his foot and holding a paper marked *Vater Unser*. Jesus stands in the background protecting a child who holds a copy of *Ojce Nasz* (the opening words of the Lord's Prayer in Polish).[45] Under the circumstances, Poles learned to resist high-level ecclesiastical authorities. Prayers and hymns, learned secretly in peasant huts and city dwellings, conveyed more than religious faith to adults and children.

The campaign against school, Church, language, and property intensified national feelings almost everywhere in German Poland. Łucja Borodziej has studied the evolution of national consciousness in terms of the efforts to Germanize Polish school children, and the result, she says, was creation of the Polish community as early as 1890:

> Society, attacked on all sides by German authority, identified the struggle for preservation of national distinctiveness with the defense of the Catholic Church. This identification . . . united within itself the anti-Prussian stand of the majority of the Poles, particularly the villagers.

In addition, Borodziej points out, growth of national sentiment even in such Polish borderlands as Pomerania, Masuria, and Silesia forced Berlin to alter its view that persons in those regions spoke only dialects and were not true Poles. Like the others, these Polish outlanders learned to connect the rights of Catholicism with national interests. In the process, Poles from north to south developed ties which "ripened into a national consciousness."[46]

Lech Trzeciakowski, another scholar of German Poland in the late nineteenth century, has interpreted the results of the *Kulturkampf* in similar but slightly more guarded terms. The determination to persecute Polish Catholic leaders, he wrote, was felt by the broad masses of Poles as an attack on themselves. The Germanization of schools and public life fell hardest on the poor and the peasants, but the result was resistance "from practically the entire Polish community in the Prussian partition." Poles of Poznania, West Prussia, and parts of Lower Silesia were strongest in their feelings; theirs was a "subjective" national awareness, which he described as "a readiness actively to defend national distinctiveness." The growth in ethnicity was strongest where religion differentiated Poles from Germans. In these areas "the specific Polish-Catholic type was called into being." Trzeciakowski credited other Poles with a more primitive national consciousness which rested on the awareness of external differences of language and custom. This was especially true in parts of Silesia, where there were German Catholics, and in Masuria, where some of the Poles were Protestants. In general, Trzeciakowski concludes, between 1872 and 1885 German policies produced an ever widening commitment within the Polish community to work for the preservation of national selfhood.[47]

National awareness developed more slowly in the other partitions. Illiteracy still stood at 60 percent in the Russian Partition in 1911, and the peasants made only slow progress in improving their agricultural production. Until the Revolt of 1905, they remained a relatively passive element within the Russian Empire, displaying only occasional hints that national feeling was growing. Even the suppression of Roman Catholic monasteries, decreed in 1864, affected American Poles more directly, since a number of Polish clerics worked in the United States after their communities were disbanded.[48] To the south, in Austrian-held Galicia, was the densest population of any Polish area outside Silesia, about 90 percent Polish in its western areas. The relative autonomy of Poles under Hapsburg rulers slowed the growth of national consciousness. Jan Slomka remembered draftees returning from the service and singing "We're all good Polaks, and also good Austriaks."[49] In Galicia it was not particularly difficult to be both. Seasonal migration to Germany promoted the diffusion of Polish ideas in the three partitions,[50] but the dissimilar factors at work in each area affected the rate at which national consciousness emerged.

The Poles who left Germany in the 1870s and 1880s, therefore, brought the most vivid memories of a struggle for faith and fatherland. Their experience differentiated them from Poles of other partitions who migrated later. In part, they coupled religion with nationality because German ecclesiastical leaders had tried to use the former to promote the latter, that is, Germanization. The meaning of these developments was more fully defined in some hearts and minds than in others, but few missed the point completely. For this reason, the arrival of Poles in Wisconsin set the stage for an unusual interaction with the German church leaders who preceded them.

2. The Model Community

To SURVIVE, IMMIGRANTS NEEDED places to live and employment to provide the necessities of life. To form ethnic groups, they needed a sense of common identity, institutional expressions of their distinctive qualities, and leaders to articulate the shared bonds. To achieve wide gains as one element of a pluralistic society, they also required broadly based, united leadership to channel the efforts and enthusiasm of individuals toward the same end. Poles in the United States experienced all three possibilities. Most survived the initial difficulties; most also participated in an ethnic community; few, however, reached a level of unified and sustained advancement within the larger social context. Small groups could do it for a time, but often a dissident group or a troublesome issue arose to divide them. Large communities rarely pulled together for long; their size engendered diversity and competition, setting newcomers at odds with each other. Then only larger causes, such as the need for Polish relief after 1914, could overcome the tendency.

Until 1896, Wisconsin's Poles were different. Widely applauded by their countrymen in other states, they were singled out as the example to be emulated. A visitor from Lwów caught the mood when he visited Milwaukee in 1892; he attributed the striking success of the city's 35,000 Poles in public life to deliberate cooperation between the intellectual leaders and the clergy. True enough—unity among the leaders was remarkable in those days, and abiding. A combination of factors made it possible. Similarity of origins made Wisconsin's Poles a relatively homogeneous group, with shared memories and common hopes. Also, their early arrival enabled them to claim economic and social places before all the patterns were determined. Such coincidences helped assure relatively stable and unusually successful community life in the early years.

Opportunities and promotional activities drew large numbers of immigrants to Wisconsin after the middle of the nineteenth century. Agriculture moved steadily west and north from Lake Michigan as forests yielded to the lumberjack's ax. Competitive up-bidding of land

18

prices was less severe here than in states farther west, but abundant harvests soon attested to the value of the land. Such related industries as lumber and flour mills, dairies, and tanneries offered employment to urban workers. Foundries and machine shops followed, especially in Milwaukee, where there were at least 200 iron and steel plants by 1920.[1] Recruiting by state and private agencies helped attract farmers and industrial workers. Wisconsin generally sponsored immigration agents from 1852 to 1915, and railroads, especially the Wisconsin Central, promoted their lands, partly to gain new customers along the routes. Most of the publicity was directed toward Germans and Scandinavians, but many Poles in eastern Germany were bilingual; thus the information was available to them and it corroborated the message in the letters from America: in Wisconsin one could get ahead.[2]

The number of Polish immigrants in Wisconsin is difficult to determine. Political circumstances in Europe distorted the statistics and the federal census bureau was unclear and inconsistent in its policies. The result was a rather consistent underestimation of the number of Polish Wisconsinites, from the 417 tabulated in 1860 to the 150,000 first- and second-generation Poles listed in 1920.[3] More accurate figures were supplied by the *Kuryer Polski* (Polish Courier), established in Milwaukee in 1888. Its editors kept a careful watch on the growth of the community, estimating 115,000 Polish-Americans in the first two generations in the state in 1896 and 225,000 in 1915. Milwaukee County, by *Kuryer* estimates, numbered 30,000 Polish-Americans in 1890, 58,000 in 1902, and 100,000 in 1915.[4] Those figures are close to the ones accepted by Bayrd Still in his history of Milwaukee,[5] and even if slightly exaggerated, are probably not far from the actual number.

The totals alone, however, do not tell the whole story of growth. The federal census of 1900 and the state census of 1905 enumerated Poles according to the partition in which they had been born. These figures indicate that Wisconsin's Poles were distinct from those in other states because of the preponderance of those whose origins were in the German Empire. According to the census of 1900, 80 percent of Wisconsin's Poles were from Germany, while 11 percent came from Russia and 9 percent from Austria or an undisclosed partition. Nationally, at that time, only 39 percent of the Poles traced their origins to Germany, compared with 40 percent from Russia and 15 percent from Austria.[6] In 1905 the census showed that 69.6 percent of Wisconsin's Polish newcomers had been born in Germany, and several years later investigators for the Dillingham Committee found that nearly 81 percent of their sample of Polish Milwaukeeans had German origins. By way of contrast, a similar sample in Chicago showed far greater balance, with Russian-born Poles having a plurality.[7]

The facts also indicate that the heavy immigration from the Russian and Austrian partitions after the turn of the century was not moving to Wisconsin in numbers large enough to displace German-born Poles from their numerical primacy. Rather, children of the earlier arrivals and some late-coming arrivals from Germany were swelling the size of Wisconsin's Polish community. By 1920, only about a third of the state's Poles were first generation. Those who came after 1900 tended to settle in places where economic opportunity developed later. Racine, Kenosha, and Superior received the largest share, but a few took up farming north and west of Green Bay in the last areas of the state to be logged. Thus despite the uncertain statistics, the profile of Wisconsin's Polish community is clear. Its members arrived relatively early in the migration of Poles from Europe; its origins were heavily based in the German Empire; and by 1920 it ranked second in foreign-born members among the state's ethnic groups.[8]

The first purely Polish settlement in the state was at Poland Corner, Portage County, about six miles east of Stevens Point. The availability of land at $1 to $2.50 per acre and the presence of a Polish priest, Jan Polak, in Stevens Point attracted the first Poles to the area in 1858.[9] The work of clearing stumps and scrub growth lasted for years, with the husband often spending the winter working as a lumberjack or on the railroad to earn money to pay the family's debts. When Albert Sanford studied the Portage County settlements in 1907, he spoke of the "persistent industry and capacity for drudgery" which had enabled Poles a half century earlier to wrest a living from their hilly, partially forested farms. Often their low standard of living and the capacity to live from agricultural products they could not sell enabled them to succeed where others (like the Norwegians at Alban) had failed.[10]

The willingness of many Poles to dispense with personal comfort in order to acquire and clear their land led some observers to judge that the quality of their lives was poor. The Dillingham Commission described Polish farms in this part of the state as "not homelike, inviting, nor indicative of thrift. Unpainted houses, dilapidated barns, poorly drained, ill-kept barnyards, sagging gates, and weed-ridden lawns and fence corners are the typical marks of Polish farmsteads."[11] Yet Sanford noted that the more prosperous Polish farmers enjoyed a standard of comfort comparable to that of other farmers in the area.[12] Clearly, the first priority was to acquire land; improvements were made later.

By 1905 the patterns of Polish settlement in central Wisconsin were clear. At least 15,000 Poles inhabited Portage and Marathon counties. The economic center was Stevens Point, which had about 5,000 Polish inhabitants. Market days were held there each Thursday and Saturday, and small businesses were in Polish hands, including the press. *Rolnik* (The Farmer) was founded as a weekly in 1892 and *Gwiazda Polarna* (The North Star) in 1908. *Rolnik* encouraged allegiance to the Democratic Party among Polish voters, and by the early 1890s Poles were regularly elected to city and county offices.

Churches formed the center of religious and social life. In 1863 the early settlers built the second Polish Roman Catholic church in the country at Poland Corner. About a dozen Polish parishes were founded in the two counties before 1900, their celebrations and activities providing respite from the wearisome toil on the land. Parish schools reflected the isolation of these settlements: instructions were frequently given only in Polish. Most children attended school to the time of First Communion, or about age twelve. Even in Stevens Point, where English was taught in the Polish school, only a few Polish children attended the high school in 1914.[13]

Except for a quiet community of four parishes in the Mississippi River boundary region of Trempealeau County,[14] the only other large Polish farm area in Wisconsin was northwest of Green Bay in Brown, Shawano, and Oconto counties. Settlement there was primarily associated with the Norwegian-born land agent, John J. Hof. Although his first sales were to immigrants from Scandinavia, Hof began to sell exclusively to Poles in 1877 and continued the policy until his death in 1910. Villages named Krakow, Sobieski, Pulaski, and Hofa Park (after Hof) were built in 1880. As in Portage County, the settlers had a difficult time clearing the stump-filled land, but Hof gave generous terms of payment and even supplemented public relief with his private funds when a forest fire ravaged the area in 1886.[15]

Acting on the theory that a Catholic church was important for Polish settlement, Hof set land aside for a church in each town and 100 acres in Pulaski for the Polish Franciscans, who established a monastery there in 1888. Consisting mainly of monks displaced by the suppression of monastic orders in Russia and Germany, the monastery opened a boarding school in 1901 and a printing press in 1907. *Miesięcznik Franciszkański* (The Franciscan Monthly) featured articles of religious interest and commentary on local events and the growing pains of the state's Polish community. An almanac was published after 1912.[16] Because of its proximity to Green Bay, Pulaski never became as important a commercial center as Stevens Point, but the friary and the influence of the monks in parish work and publications gave Pulaski a constant and important role in the religious development of the state's Poles.

In sheer numbers, the importance of Polish urban settlements in Wisconsin overshadowed the agricultural areas. In 1900, nearly half of the state's Poles lived in the greater Milwaukee area, and thousands more lived and worked in smaller industrial centers. Many others labored a number of years in the cities to accumulate funds for the purchase of a farm.

The first Polish settlers came to Milwaukee in the 1840s, but their number rose slowly at first. In 1850 there were about seventy-five Poles in the city, and their number had only doubled by the end of the Civil War. Most of them resided on Walker's Point, in the southern section of town. After the war, settlement grew more rapidly. The first parish was founded on the South Side in 1866 and on the North Side in 1871.[17] By that time, the heavy influx of Poles from the German Partition was evident. Early records indicate that Poles found jobs at the steel works, in the leather industry, and as common laborers in other developing industries. About 3,000 Kashubes, immigrants from the Baltic Coast north of Danzig, settled on Jones Island on Lake Michigan, where they engaged in their hereditary occupation, fishing. Small entrepreneurs in the city provided fellow Poles with food, clothing, and drink, mostly at corner stores. Few in the first generation were professionals. A survey in 1895 found only two doctors and two lawyers among 40,000.[18]

In Milwaukee, as elsewhere, parish life was important for Poles. "Whoever is familiar with the history of these churches," the *Kuryer* remarked in 1903, "will know at the same time the history of the development of Polish immigration in Milwaukee."[19] By 1900 there were nine Polish Catholic churches in the city and its suburbs; the number grew to fourteen by 1920. As in other parts of the state, great sacrifices were made to build churches, schools, rectories, and convents. The beautiful, often extravagant churches built by the Poles were an indication of the importance of the parish in their lives. The opportunity for personal recognition and the chance to sink neighborhood roots led Poles to identify as much with their parish as with the larger community. A newcomer would therefore think of himself as living in "St. Stan's" or "St. Casimir's," much as he would have associated himself with his village in the Old Country. The result was local pride and friendly competition among the congregations.

Accomplishments in the religious field were matched by political successes. Poles were regularly elected as city aldermen and county supervisors, beginning in 1878. Poles were sent from Milwaukee to the Wisconsin Assembly in 1887, and in 1892 the first Polish state senator in the nation was elected from Milwaukee. Roman Czerwinski was elected city comptroller in 1890, and the job generally became identified with Poles in subsequent years. At first mostly Democratic in their political leanings, Milwaukee's Poles later responded to appeals from Socialists and Republicans. In 1912, for instance, a South Sider was elected alderman on the Socialist ticket, and in 1918 the state's first Polish-American congressman was elected as a Republican.[20]

An active press charted the community's accomplishments. The first paper was the short-lived weekly *Przyjaciel Ludu* (Friend of the People), which appeared in 1880. *Zgoda* (Harmony), the national organ of the Polish National Alliance, was published in the city for a few years after 1883. Establishment of the *Kuryer Polski* in 1888 gave Milwaukee the first successful Polish daily in the United States. After several unsuccessful efforts to establish a Catholic counterpart, *Nowiny Polskie* (The Polish News) succeeded as a weekly in 1906 and became a daily in 1908. *Głos Polek* (The Voice of Polish Women) appeared in Milwaukee in 1910 as the national organ of the Polish Women's Alliance. About a dozen other daily, weekly, and monthly papers were issued in the city before the First World War, but they failed eventually because of financial mismanagement or lack of support.[21]

An effort unique to Milwaukee was the formation of the Kościuszko Guard in 1874. Approved as Company K of the Wisconsin National Guard, the group remained an object of interest and pride among Poles, particularly at the time of its mobilization during the Spanish-American War. Captains of the guard were prominent members of Milwaukee's Polish community, and the group was widely touted as "the only Polish company in America." In 1886 the Guard built its own armory in the Polish South Side. Thereafter, Kościuszko Hall was used frequently for dances, public meetings, and military drills.[22]

Other organizations reinforced the sense of Polish distinctiveness. Musical and theatrical companies specialized in performing the composers and playwrights of the homeland and the immigrant community. Local chapters of the Polish National Alliance and the Polish Roman Catholic Union kept the Poles in touch with the wider immigrant community. Parish and citywide observances each January and November kept alive the memory of the ill-fated uprisings of 1831 and 1863 and served to remind the Poles of their less fortunate compatriots in Europe. Such organizations and activities helped the Poles foster their understanding of the special quality of their cultural and historical traditions. Up to 1918 and even many years thereafter, they retained their preference for living in close proximity to their fellow countrymen and resisted extensive intermingling with other groups they encountered.[23]

Smaller numbers of Poles were attracted to other cities of the state. Early hosts of Polish-American life were Manitowoc and Green Bay. Manitowoc had a Polish parish by 1870 and an orphanage and home for the elderly by 1890. Green Bay elected a Polish alderman for the first time in 1894 and had a Polish superintendent of schools in 1910. After the turn of the century, Poles began to settle in Racine and Kenosha in the southeastern corner of the state and in Ashland and Superior in the far northwest.[24]

After settlement, the next question was community life—the quest for a common togetherness which would promote continuity while taking advantage of the new freedoms and opportunities of America. Transition was hardly ever the question for first-generation immigrants; adaptation was inevitable because the circumstances of American life differed greatly from those in Europe. Immigrants themselves differentiated between "greenhorns," who had just arrived, and those who had already come to terms with the new ways. The fundamental challenge, therefore, was to find stability between the Old World and the New and to choose guides to show the way. In Poland, the lines of authority and the norms of conduct had been clearly established; tradition and wealth largely determined the leaders and indicated standards of behavior. In America it was different; fluid circumstances, particularly in the early years, created uncertainty and a large group of contestants for leadership. When clashes resulted, they emphasized the importance of institutions and leaders as sources of stability in the adjustment process. Where harmony was characteristic, it was because leaders identified individual interest with the community good and exercised tact in maintaining their positions. Both possibilities were explored by Wisconsin's Poles in the years of settlement.

The first parish dispute among Polish-Americans in the United States took place at Poland Corner, where a Polish parish had been started in 1863 at a crossroads on the highway which led east from Stevens Point. Taverns soon opened on the corners across from the church and their noise frequently disturbed the services. Five successive pastors attempted without success to reach an accommodation with the saloon owners. From 1868 to 1870 the pastorate was vacant, but in the latter year Bishop Joseph Melcher of Green Bay assigned to the parish the newly ordained Joseph Dombrowski, who had recently arrived from Rome. After several months Dombrowski asked his parishioners to dismantle the church and rebuild it on a new location. The young pastor backed his request with a threat to resign if cooperation were denied. Opponents gathered and threw rocks as the work began, but the project was carried out and the church was newly situated so that no nonecclesiastical building could be constructed within a quarter mile.[25] It became the center of the new community of Polonia.

But the saloon faction did not give up. They filed charges against Dombrowski and Melcher because of the loss of business, but the suit failed. Then they resorted to violence, placing hollowed-out logs, filled with gunpowder, in Dombrowski's woodpile. Fortunately, the priest left the room immediately after he put one of the logs in his stove, and the explosion injured nobody. Finally, abandoning any hope for reconciliation, the dissidents constructed on the old location a new church which was called the Red Church because of the color of its roof. Jan Frydrychowicz, a former Catholic priest who had been suspended from the Polish-Czech mission at Malberry, Texas, became pastor of the Red Church, the first independent Polish church in the United States. The group was most active during the life of Frydrychowicz, who arrived on the scene in 1872 and died in 1874.[26]

Reconciliation was long in coming. Those who were discontented made several appeals to the Vatican and to Melcher's successors in Green Bay. The last appeal, addressed to Sebastian Messmer in 1892, warned that "the Heavenly Comforter calls out with a harsh voice that the [red] church is built for the service of God."[27] Messmer, like his predecessors, was willing to let the matter rest. The movement collapsed in 1894, but the return of the schismatics to the parish at Polonia carried a certain amount of strife into the congregation. Disagreements generally concerned financial administration, which was strained by several disastrous fires. Full peace was restored by Thomas Grenbowski, who served as pastor from 1891 to 1904.[28]

Paradoxically, the key to the crisis and its resolution was the leadership exercised by Joseph Dombrowski. One of the most remarkable immigrant priests to serve the Poles in America, he had resolved the intolerable situation at Poland Corner by building a parish which was too attractive for the dissidents to resist. Dombrowski's most important accomplishment at Polonia was persuading the Felician Sisters to send teaching nuns from Krakow to central Wisconsin. The five Felicians who arrived in November 1874 were the first Polish women religious to immigrate. Their educational effort thrived; not even the two fires of 1875 discouraged the Poles, who sent children from as far away as Milwaukee to study under the sisters.[29] Dombrowski also brought a printing press to Polonia to publish the textbooks he wrote. The primers and catechisms stressed the traditional Catholic and Polish identity. The school, church and press, as well as the sisters, gave assurance that traditions would be maintained. When poor health forced Dombrowski to retire from Polonia in 1882, it was clear that his methods had succeeded. Long before he left, only six families were left at Poland Corner to dispute his leadership.[30]

Parish disputes also emerged in other places. The first of two in Milwaukee broke out at St. Stanislaus Parish in 1875, when two prominent families clashed over the ordering of a new church clock and the parish organist. The disagreement led to fist fights and rock throwing. Archbishop Henni closed the church and eventually resolved the conflict by removing the pastor, John Rodowicz. His successor restored peace so quickly that the Milwaukee *Sentinel* commented: "There has not been an insurrection among the Polacks for two weeks. What can the matter be?"[31]

Ten years later the hapless Rodowicz became involved in another imbroglio, this time at St. Hedwig's Parish in Milwaukee, where he had been assigned after his removal from St. Stanislaus. Parishioners disagreed over the tenure of the organist-schoolmaster. The pastor's opponents claimed the organist was unable to teach English and his supporters accused the opposition of wanting the job for a relative of one of the trustees. A riot erupted on September 20, 1885, after the opposition faction refused to permit the organist to play for the Sunday services. On the following day, front-page headlines in the *Sentinel* proclaimed: "Poles up in Arms, A Catholic Priest Gets Into Hot Water. His House Stormed By An Angry Congregation. Bloody Fracas Resulting in Smashed Heads, Destruction of Furniture and Many Arrests." The story claimed that the interior of the rectory, which had been stormed by about 100 men, "looked as though an Iowa cyclone had just swept through it":

> On all sides the work of the rabble was visible. One whitewashed wall showed a picture in blood, which had also stained the carpet. In the corner were several handfuls of reddish brown beard, which the owner had forgotten to take along after somebody had plucked the hair out by the roots. Several cravats were in another corner. The contents of broken spitoons were scattered all over the carpet. A crucifix, broken in two, lay beneath a picture of the Madonna, which had escaped the ruthless hands. Archbishop Heiss, in a rich gilt frame, looked down calmly on the scene. A package of wafers for communion purposes lay crushed into bits where somebody's broad heel had stepped on them. An inverted inkstand and a wide circle around it were observable on the red cover of a table. The white sliding door between the parlor and the sitting room was torn from its fastening and leaned against the wall like a man on a spree against a lamp post. Most of the furniture with its solid purple plush, looked as if it had come out of a second-hand store. The front door was broken in and was split in several places.

Rodowicz was not hurt in the encounter, but the deep split continued to divide the congregation. Archbishop Heiss closed the church until December. Peace was restored through the mediation of Hyacinth Gulski, pastor of St. Hyacinth Parish, who already was preeminent in his leadership of Milwaukee's Polish Catholics. Once again the desire for restoration of harmony led to the removal of Rodowicz, who eventually found his way to Baltimore. His successor at St. Hedwig's restored calm and served a sixteen-year pastorate.[32]

Other church controversies erupted at Thorp in 1891, at Manitowoc in 1893, at Stevens Point in 1894, and at Green Bay in the mid-1890s, when Rene Vilatte, an ex-Episcopal priest consecrated a bishop by the Old Catholic bishop in Ceylon, attempted unsuccessfully to form a schismatic church among the Poles. Except in the case of Vilatte, the difficulties fell into a similar pattern: dissidents challenged the pastor for control in the parish and peace was restored by appointment of a new pastor. In Thorp, as at St. Hedwig's, the difficulty was over the organist. In Manitowoc and Stevens Point, as at Polonia, the problem came from saloonkeepers, accustomed to exercise influence in the immigrant community.[33] Where lines of authority and influence were tenuous, disruption was always possible.

The violence of the parish disputes, no less than the sacrifices people were willing to make in constructing churches and schools, indicated the importance which Poles attached to the parish as the center of their lives. In the beginning, little individual attention and recognition were possible outside the parish or combination of parishes which formed the local community; therefore, the relationship between individuals and the priest could become emotional. The tendency was reinforced by the fact that donating money and services to the church fostered a proprietary attitude among parish members. Under the circumstances, patronage and other issues led to rivalry and clashes. The larger community was sufficiently affected by these incidents to express concern and search for solutions.

Although some blamed the difficulties on the "hot blood" of the Poles,[34] a Silesian priest who had visited America offered a more reflective answer. In an article cited by the *Kuryer* on June 16, 1894, he took priests to task for a lack of charity, tact, and patience. He criticized lay people who thought that financial support entitled them to control the parish. And he condemned clerical rivalry as a third difficulty: "It has happened that one priest has kicked a hole under the second in order to put himself in the place of the first." This analysis grasped the fundamental problem: leadership was difficult to establish and maintain. Secular and religious leaders needed each other to survive, however, and those who maintained equilibrium between individual ambition and the good of the whole received in return the support and cooperation they needed. Dombrowski clearly understood the potential and demands of his office and was able to preside over a lively community. Others, like Rodowicz, could never quite keep the balance.

In Milwaukee, the cornerstone of clerical participation in leadership of the community was Hyacinth Gulski, a native of West Prussia. Gulski came to the United States in 1875, after two years in hiding from the German police when his monastery was closed during the *Kultur-kampf.* In 1876 he assumed the first of his three Milwaukee pastorates. Widely praised as an orator, Gulski was in great demand to address various public and religious gatherings. An indication of Gulski's popularity came in the summer of 1890, when he found it necessary to write a public letter to the *Kuryer* to scotch rumors that he was traveling to Europe to secure appointment as auxiliary bishop in Milwaukee. In 1891, Frederick Katzer appointed him diocesan consultor. The first Wisconsin Pole to be chosen for that office, Gulski served as a special adviser to the archbishop and was on the board which nominated successors to the see when it was vacant. In making the appointment, Katzer gave official recognition to an office which Gulski had been exercising unofficially, at least since he had represented Heiss in the disorders at St. Hedwig's in 1886. Later in the same year, at an organizational meeting of the short-lived Society of Polish Priests in the United States, the Milwaukee pastor was chosen president by the sixty-nine participants, including twelve Wisconsin priests who attended in person or sent proxies.[35]

Significant as he was in the emerging leadership of Wisconsin's Polish community, Gulski was surpassed in prestige and reputation by Michael Kruszka, who began a thirty-three-year journalistic career in Milwaukee in 1885. The son of a prosperous farmer in Poznania, Kruszka had received a high school education. During the *Kulturkampf,* he had witnessed the repeated arrests of his older brother, Rev. Simon Kruszka, and had written articles for a number of Polish papers, attacking German policies. Arrested in 1877 for working to elect a Polish candidate to the Reichstag, he was charged with being a "dangerous agitator against the . . . German Empire," but was released because he was under eighteen. Three years later he left for the United States.[36]

After working for a while in New Jersey and learning English, Kruszka came to Milwaukee in 1883. Two years later he bought a small printing press and began to publish the weekly *Tygodnik Anonsowy* (Advertising Weekly), a small (6 by 9 inch) and amateurish paper which probably offered little competition to the two other Polish weeklies that were published in the city at that time. After three months, however, Kruszka formed a partnership to publish a new paper, *Krytyka* (The Critique). The editors and publishers were young (Kruszka, at 25, was the oldest) and the paper reflected their youth in the lively battles it fought with other Polish publications.[37] Adopting a strongly pro-labor editorial position, *Krytyka* became a source of controversy because of its position on the labor riots of May 1886.

In Milwaukee, the disorders in support of the eight-hour workday started on May 1 with the support of the Knights of Labor, who claimed a local membership of 10,000. In response to the rioting, the First Regiment of the Wisconsin National Guard, which included the Kościuszko Guard, was mobilized. On May 5, a crowd of 1,500 threw rocks at the militia. In retaliation, a volley was fired into the crowd, killing eight demonstrators, five of whom were Poles. The riots immediately subsided but ill feeling remained.[38]

The impact of *Krytyka* on the dispute is difficult to determine because the copies have been lost. Later, however, the *Kuryer* claimed that *Krytyka*, while supporting labor's demands, had urged the workers not to strike or engage in violence. Kruszka's support of labor candidates in the fall elections of 1886 brought him into conflict with the Polish priests, nevertheless, because the clerics feared socialistic tendencies in the press. *Krytyka*'s eventual demise, however, had nothing to do with clerical opposition. In the spring of 1888, the effort to found a daily, *Dziennik Polski* (The Polish Daily News), collapsed because of financial mismanagement, bringing down *Krytyka* in the process.

Undaunted, Kruszka borrowed $125 and began to publish the highly successful *Kuryer Polski* on June 23, 1888. Four years later, he started the agricultural weekly *Gazeta Wisconsinska* (The Wisconsin Gazette), and in 1894 he began to issue the news weekly *Tygodniowy Kuryer Polski* (The Weekly Polish Courier). By 1893 the company was operating on an annual income of $14,000, and in 1896 the offices and presses were moved downtown, close to the large German and English dailies.[39] Building upon the lessons he had learned from *Krytyka*, Kruszka avoided controversy and stressed education, better wages and conditions for workers, allegiance to Roman Catholicism, and maintenance of the Polish language and customs. In a signed editorial which appeared in the inaugural issue, the publisher pledged that the new paper would be politically independent and would defend the Polish interest in all cases.

At first, that amounted to a pledge of allegiance to Roman Catholicism. In that spirit, the *Kuryer* supported the Polish Roman Catholic Union above the Polish National Alliance: "Poland has never been anything else, and nobody has ever thought of it as anything else but Catholic. . . . Therefore, if a Polish organization wants to be truly Polish, it must be Catholic." Another article pledged that because most of the readers were Catholic, "we may not give them any material which would undermine the faith inherited from their ancestors." And when in

1890 the state legislature passed the Bennett Law to restrict parochial and foreign-language schools, the paper supported the strong protests of the state's Catholic bishops.[40]

Kruszka's ideological and pragmatic support of Catholicism gained a personal dimension when, in October 1890, he was nominated to the Wisconsin Assembly as the Democratic candidate from the Twelfth District, which included the Polish areas of Milwaukee's South Side. During the campaign, the *Kuryer* repeatedly stressed the opposition of the priests to the Bennett Law, and Kruszka appeared at a public meeting at which he shared the platform with several Polish pastors.[41] The election on November 4 produced a Democratic landslide in the city and the state. Roman Czerwinski led the Democratic ticket in Milwaukee in his election as comptroller, and Kruszka's plurality of 2,140 was the largest margin of victory in any of the state's 100 assembly districts. Kruszka's support of his own candidacy in the *Kuryer* undoubtedly increased his margin of victory, but the issues of the campaign and the reaction they evoked were the most important factors.

When the postelection edition of the *Kuryer* gloated that "the Poles have stood like a wall in defense of their schools," it was getting at the heart of the matter.[42] Under attack from outside forces, the Poles worked together to assure that they, as Poles and Catholics, could continue to build their own institutions and preserve their own values. The right of the state's Polish community to determine its own development had been threatened by the Bennett Law, and the instinct for self-preservation had prompted every constituency within that community to rally to the defense.

Kruszka thus emerged from the campaign considerably stronger than he had entered. His election added to his personal prestige, and through the paper he was able to publicize his activities in Madison. Prominent secular and religious members of Milwaukee's Polish community who visited the capital were introduced to the governor and other officials by Kruszka, who included news of these visits in his reports. His most important effort during the 1891 session was a bill to require the municipal business of the city of Milwaukee to be printed officially in Polish. Since a similar concession had already been granted the Germans, the measure was a test of pride and recognition. After the bill was enacted, Kruszka pointed out that the Poles of the state now stood on an equal footing with their Anglo-American and German-American neighbors. Beginning in April 1891, the *Kuryer* masthead carried the notation "Official City Paper" in English and Polish. The company earned a profit of about 20 percent for carrying municipal notices.[43]

Once again, Kruszka had succeeded in identifying the prestige and advancement of the larger community with his own interests.

Because of his wide popularity, Kruszka was nominated in 1892 to the newly created Eighth Senatorial District by Milwaukee's Democratic Caucus. His victory in November made him the first Polish state senator in the United States, and wide publicity was given to his victory in the Polish-American press. Recognizing the priority of national over partisan affiliation, a group of Polish Republicans sent a telegram from Boston just before the election to express their hopes for Kruszka's victory. Many congratulatory telegrams followed the election, including one from Father Edward Kozlowski of Manistee, Michigan, who would become the first Polish auxiliary bishop in Milwaukee twenty years later.[44] Kruszka's two terms in the state senate were progressive but undistinguished. His accomplishments involved bills to introduce the secret ballot, to make Labor Day a state holiday, and to equip city streetcars with vestibules.[45] Nevertheless, his six years in Madison gave him undisputed claim to leadership in the state's Polish community.

Interestingly, the most serious challenge to Kruszka's preeminence came from a coeditor of *Kuryer,* Casimir Neuman. The two quarreled in 1893 over whether to support the international exhibition to be held at Lwów under the sponsorship of the Galician government. Dismissed by Kruszka, Neuman began to publish his views in a new weekly, *Słowo* (The Word), which appeared between 1893 and 1895. Although copies of *Słowo* have been lost, it is clear that a brief press war, complete with personal attacks, broke out in the fall of 1893. Polish editors in Buffalo, Toledo, Chicago, and Manitowoc, representing some of the most important journals of the day, publicly supported Kruszka, often using the *Kuryer'*s arguments. Even the scholarly periodical *Przegląd Emigracyjny* (The Emigration Review), published in Lwów, blamed Neuman for jeopardizing the unity and accomplishment of Wisconsin's Poles.[46] In the face of so much opposition, the only surprise was that Neuman held out as long as he did.

The immediate result of Neuman's departure from the *Kuryer* was the opportunity it gave Michael Kruszka to appoint his brother Joseph to the vacancy on the editorial staff. Two years younger than Michael, Joseph had been a postal official in German Poland until he emigrated in 1893. As a coeditor of the *Kuryer,* his special responsibility was preparation of the two weekly editions.[47] Quiet and content to work in the shadow of his famous older brother, Joseph remained in the employ of Michael for many years.

Only a few months after Joseph's arrival, Wenceslaus Kruszka, a younger half-brother of Michael and Joseph, arrived unexpectedly in Milwaukee. Born in 1868, Wenceslaus had entered the Society of Jesus in Galicia in 1883. A dispute with another Jesuit led to his dismissal from the group in 1891, but he was readmitted for two more years before being terminated again in 1893 because a problem with his eyes was thought to disqualify him from a life of study and ministry. He came to the United States and finished theological studies in Milwaukee, where he was ordained in 1895. Like Michael in temperament and disposition, Wenceslaus was active in seminary affairs, where he gave patriotic addresses and served as president of the society of Polish seminarians.

The *Kuryer* used photoengraving for the first time to print a picture of the young priest on the day of his ordination.[48] Soon the young Kruszka published a book, *Rzym* (Rome), a travelogue describing the city where he had stayed for several months in 1891. The *Kuryer* backed the book with an impressive advertising campaign and by reprinting enthusiastic reviews from Polish papers all over the country. The energetic Wenceslaus Kruszka increased the visibility and importance of the family in the Polish communities of the city and state. But at the start the young priest owed much of his success to the opportunities and publicity afforded by his older brother.

At the time Wenceslaus Kruszka was beginning his priestly career, Hyacinth Gulski led the Polish Catholics and shared with Michael Kruszka the responsibility for directing and articulating the goals and activities of an increasingly confident community. Veterans of the *Kulturkampf,* they appeared to have a lot in common in the New World as well. Neither could imagine a conflict in the identification of Poles in America with Roman Catholicism and patriotic binationalism. Gulski's view, supported by Kruszka, was that faithfulness to God through the institutional Church was the surest guarantee for the restoration of the Polish state and the success of the Polish-American community. A *Kuryer* editorial of September 18, 1891, extolled Gulski's accomplishments in helping make Milwaukee the intellectual, political, and spiritual capital of Poles in America. But Kruszka also relied on Gulski. *Wiarus* (The Old Faithful) of Winona once described him as "senator, by the grace of Gulski," in a statement which only partially exaggerated the influence the Church had brought to bear on Kruszka's behalf.[49]

Clerical and secular cooperation was evident in the early interest in a Polish bishop. The topic was discussed sporadically in the *Kuryer* during its first decade. Although expressing editorial disappointment at the rejection of the Cahensly proposals, the *Kuryer* reprinted (with approval) an 1893 article from a Poznanian paper that urged appointment of suffragan bishops of Polish descent in American cities with large numbers of Poles. In places like Milwaukee and Chicago, where

Hyacinth Gulski and Vincent Barzynski already filled the office of suffragan *de facto,* the writer argued, they ought to be accorded full honor.[50] The *Kuryer*'s approval of the article indicated sentiment for suffragans as a way of recognizing Polish Catholics while respecting the decisions of the pope. The appointment of Mieczyslaus Ledóchowski to head the Propaganda in 1892 buoyed hopes for Polish appointments,[51] as did Cardinal Gibbons' visit to the city in 1891. Professing surprise at the accomplishments of Polish-Americans when he toured the South Side, the cardinal hinted at future recognition:

> I have seen many colonies in America, even many Polish settlements, but I have never seen anything like this. Recognition is granted to your industry, harmony, unity, and adherence to the faith of your fathers; and if, up to this time, you have not been sufficiently recognized, it was probably because we didn't know. The Apostolic Capital will hear about this and you will be blessed.[52]

The *Kuryer* cited these comments as an additional motive for Poles to follow the leadership that had brought the community to its current status. Readers were urged to be true to their Church, which, through the actions of the state's bishops, seemed generally responsive and protective toward them.

The growing confidence of the Milwaukee community led to a split in the Polish Roman Catholic Union. Rivalry between Milwaukee and Chicago for control of the organization flared into the open at the 1892 convention, when the two groups battled over the decentralization of the group's Chicago offices, the editorship of its newspaper, and various elective offices.[53] Three years later, with the growing influence of Chicago Poles assured, some of the Milwaukeeans withdrew and formed a rival group, the Polish Association of America. Its organizational meeting was held in October 1895, when representatives of about 4,000 Polish Milwaukeeans formed a fraternal society similar to the one they were abandoning. By the time of the first convention in January 1896, the new association included sixteen groups, of which thirteen were located in Milwaukee. Father Gulski blessed the association at the first convention, and the delegates chose as first president Ignatius Czerwinski, a friend and neighbor of Michael Kruszka. Czerwinski told the delegates that the goal of the PAA would be to join together in the name of faith and patriotism, "for who can love his fatherland . . . which is 4,000 miles away if he cannot love his brother Pole who is near and can be seen?"[54] The *Kuryer* gave extensive coverage to the new organization during its first months, approving the determination of a community which now felt confident enough to stand on its own.

The confidence and unity of Milwaukee's Poles were never more apparent than in the exhibit they prepared for the Lwów Exposition of 1894. Twelve photographs, expanded to 4 feet by 5, were sent to Lwów to show the six Polish-American churches of the city, as well as portraits of the Polish pastors, the various church societies, and the Kościuszko Guard. Also included were the first yearbook of the *Kuryer Polski* and copies of the *Kuryer* for the first three months of 1894. Evaluating all this evidence of the progress of the city's Poles, the *Kuryer* warned that the exhibit could unintentionally create a false impression by showing Polish citizens standing in front of magnificent churches in their Sunday best. It would be easy for visitors at the exhibit, the paper concluded, to assume that wealth was easy to acquire in America, rather than requiring twice as much work as in the Old Country.[55]

The assessment was at least partially correct. True enough, the neatly dressed people in the pictures had worked hard to attain a standard of living substantially better than they had known in Poland, but the pictures told another story by implication. The inclusion of the carefully selected items, touching upon the various phases of Polish life in the city, suggested that Poles and their leaders, religious and secular, were living in a spirit of cooperation and mutual respect. The attitude which accorded a place to the achievements of Hyacinth Gulski and Michael Kruszka had permitted the Poles of Milwaukee and Wisconsin to work together for forty years for advancement of the entire community. The goal of working for faith and fatherland was a shared one, understood in essentially the same optimistic terms on all sides.

Divisive issues, to be sure, had arisen. Riots in local parishes, the National Guard shootings, political rivalries, personality conflicts—all had raised the specter of disunion and open conflict. But in each case the controversy was settled without a permanent rift. The combined disapproval of Polish leaders and the group as a whole overrode each threat to the established leadership. The cycle of action and reaction had been kept in check by leaders who were pleased with the success they enjoyed and too insecure to risk confrontation and isolation.

The most important component in the unity was clearly the mutual support which Michael Kruszka and the religious leaders gave one another. A shrewd businessman, Kruszka established in Wisconsin— by no means the largest Polish settlement in the nation—the first successful Polish daily. Several years later, with clerical support, he was elected to the Wisconsin Assembly and later to the state senate, becoming the first Polish immigrant to achieve that honor. Understanding the orientation of a group which was almost uniformly Roman Catholic, he reciprocated by supporting the priests of the state in their ideas and projects. For this reason, Kruszka's *Kuryer* consistently opposed parish disruptions, supported the Polish Roman Catholic Union, expressed confidence in the state's clerical leadership, and endorsed the movement to establish the Polish Association of America. Under these circumstances, it was difficult to overcome the alliance between Kruszka and the Church. When Neuman attempted to establish a newspaper on the basis of opposition to both elements, he failed, because there were too few outside the circle influenced by the older leaders to form an independent base of support.

As long as Michael Kruszka and Hyacinth Gulski maintained their tacit alliance, harmony was bound to continue. But, paradoxically, Kruszka's success in the early 1890s carried with it the possibility that the period of cooperation would eventually end, for it weakened his dependence upon the Church for his success. Furthermore, the arrival of Joseph and Wenceslaus Kruszka in 1893 provided him with a trustworthy helper in the management of the papers and a vociferous supporter within the ranks of the Church. Although the leadership alliance within the Polish community was still intact at the beginning of 1896, the growing influence of the Kruszka family was a potential threat to the spirit of cooperation that had been so carefully fostered.

3. The Emergence of Factions

FOR CENTURIES, WISE INDIVIDUALS have proclaimed that everything has its due season. An alliance is no exception. When the circumstances which prompted its formation begin to change, partners must find new bases for cooperation or allow their agreement to lapse. The point was clearly evident among Wisconsin's Poles as the turn of the century approached. Almost all the initial priorities had by then been achieved. Settled in locations where the patterns of life were familiar and established in the political, economic, and religious spheres, the state's Poles were no longer greenhorns. Their communities were beginning to mature, and such progress inevitably brought changes. As individuals and leaders became more confident about the future, they became more independent in exploring alternative and sometimes conflicting courses. Disagreements resulted. Although unity was still earnestly proclaimed, it became less essential as the leaders gained enough security to risk alienating some of the support which had previously been deemed essential. Having discovered and exploited the opportunities offered by America, they began to explore its freedom. Therefore, the onset of contention did not betoken the group's weakness but its buoyant vitality.

The first hint that the affairs of Wisconsin's Polish community were taking a new direction came in January 1896, when the Polish Educational Society was founded in Milwaukee with the help of the Polish National Alliance. The first officers included Thaddeus Wild, captain of the Kościuszko Guard, and Casimir Owocki, a coeditor of the *Kuryer*. Joseph Kruszka helped draw up the association's goals, the chief of which was "betterment of school and other educational facilities for children of Polish descent." To that end, plans were laid to found a Polish library and to petition for the introduction of Polish language instruction at the University of Wisconsin. But it quickly became evident that the major effort would be to secure the introduction of Polish instruction in the curriculum of Milwaukee's public schools. In April the members of the association petitioned the school board for this concession, "subject to the conditions and restrictions as obtain with

36

regard to the German language." They also asked for further Polish literature and history courses in one of the high schools. The petition was backed by a statistical study which indicated that there were about 8,000 Polish-American children of school age in the city at that time.[1]

Controversy resulted as the city's Polish clergy took action to block the request. Aware in advance of the plans of PES, the priests presented a counterpetition from the five largest Polish parishes at the April meeting. It urged the school directors to disregard the plea of the PES because the Polish parochial schools were meeting the instructional needs of Polish-Americans so well that it would be pointless to burden Milwaukeeans with the cost of additional language teachers and materials in the public schools. The document alleged that members of the PES were using the situation to secure personal political advancement. Alderman Frank Niezorawski, who introduced the petition for the priests, claimed that, if necessary, he could get a list of signatures three miles long to support the statement.

School commissioner Edwin Slupecki, a member of PES, responded that his group's resolution had been advanced by the city's Polish intellectuals on behalf of all Poles. Their goal, he claimed, was to encourage parents to keep their children in school longer, with public schools supplementing the parochial education the children were already receiving. By late May, Kruszka's *Kuryer* was backing the PES proposals by pointing out that there were already about 500 Polish children in the city's public schools and that the number was rising despite pressures to the contrary. It was a matter of conscience for parents to decide which school their children ought to attend, the editorials argued. Since they were enrolling their children in public schools, it was necessary to offer Polish in order to preserve these children for the Polish nation.[2]

The debate, therefore, was drawn on two levels. The surface issue was the extent to which the community should recognize the public schools as an acceptable option for Polish children. For Catholics who were obedient to the decrees of the Third Baltimore Council, the answer would ordinarily have been negative; but the PES and Michael Kruszka were beginning to argue that Polish children who attended public schools were still Polish, even if their nominally Catholic parents were flaunting the conciliar decrees by sending them there. Such children were entitled to Polish instruction, in the eyes of PES members. The pastors, fearful perhaps that the addition of Polish to the public school curriculum would enhance the attractiveness of those schools as alternatives to the parochial system, argued that their schools were already meeting the needs of the community. Beneath the surface, however, the issue was leadership. The fundamental question was not so much the

relative excellence of public and parochial schools as who was to define
the means of accomplishing the common goals. Nobody quarreled
about the necessity of preparing the children adequately for life, but
increasingly the question was What sort of life? Those who envisioned a
re-created Polish village, with the parish as the central institution and
the pastor as leader, answered in one way. Those who chose other
models proposed alternative solutions. Under the circumstances, the
pastors reacted swiftly to preserve an older model which was being
challenged by some of the secular leaders.

Having no newspaper of their own, Milwaukee's Polish priests
denounced the PES bill from their pulpits on Sunday, May 31. The
sermons varied in vehemence, but one of the most extreme was
delivered by John Szukalski of Sts. Cyril and Methodius Parish. He
characterized Michael Kruszka as a fool and unbeliever who consorted
with the devil. He denounced the *Kuryer* as a "horrible, atheistic, and
lying paper," which had printed slanderous material in its campaign on
the educational issue. Those who did not wish to send their children to
church schools, Szukalski argued, were obliged to build their own
Polish schools instead of imposing an extra burden on the taxpayers. At
St. Josaphat's, Wilhelm Grutza called his opponents criminals and
anarchists, and a third pastor characterized them as dogs, fools, rogues,
and devils. Each sermon ended with a plea for parishioners to sign a
protest, and several thousand complied.[3]

Members of the Educational Society reacted with predictable ire,
claiming that the priests had "denounced . . . their own nationality,
land, and mother which gave them birth."[4] A delegation consisting of
Michael Kruszka, Ignatius Czerwinski, and three others visited Msgr.
Augustine Zeininger, who was administering the archdiocese in the
absence of Archbishop Katzer. They told Zeininger that they were not
opposing parish schools but merely seeking additional opportunities for
their people. They asked him whether Katzer had ordered the sermons
against the PES to be preached, as one pastor had implied. Zeininger
denied that he or Katzer had applied pressure in the matter and expressed
his regrets about the emotional nature of the sermons. He promised an
investigation and offered his aid in effecting a resolution.[5]

The friendly tone of the meeting and Zeininger's denial of chancery involvement emphasized that the dispute was an internal struggle
for leadership. Under the circumstances, members of PES felt justified
in accelerating their attack. The campaign lasted through June and
involved harsh condemnations, mostly in the *Kuryer*, of the parochial
schools and the Polish priests. The high school that Father Grutza
conducted at St. Josaphat's Parish was frequently singled out: it was
attracting only forty-five students, and deserved to be called a high

school only because it was located on a hill. The paper also pointed out that the Baltimore decrees on parochial education were not binding when Catholic schools were of obviously inferior quality. The local Catholic schools, the PES now claimed, were inferior; therefore priests who made school attendance obligatory, without improving the teaching and the facilities, were hypocrites.[6]

With the Polish community thus publicly divided in an unprecedented manner, the school board's mediating role became more important. About 100 Polish Milwaukeeans attended the meeting of the Textbook Committee, which was to make the recommendation. After hearing from supporters (including Michael Kruszka) and opponents, the perplexed committee members voted an indefinite postponement. But a vociferous minority, headed by Slupecki, prepared a strong dissent for the full board at its meeting in July.[7] The minority report argued that introducing Polish instruction would demonstrate to Polish Milwaukeeans that public administrators wished them well and that Poles had nothing to fear from the public schools. Swayed by these arguments, the board voted to compromise by agreeing to consider the appointment of a Polish teacher as soon as 250 Polish children were enrolled in any public grammar school.[8]

Members of PES called the decision a great victory. The *Kuryer* claimed it would now be a duty for parents to send enough children to public schools to ensure that their number would climb to at least 250, but results were slow in coming. Polish parents continued to show an overwhelming preference for parish schools. As late as 1900, children in church-related schools in the Fourteenth Ward outnumbered public school children by 3,053 to 716. Nearly half the school-age children in the city who were not attending school (578) lived in the same ward. It was not until 1908, long after the school board lowered the minimum number to 100, that the first Polish teacher was hired.[9] Evidently, the publicity given to education left a large number of Poles unconvinced of the necessity of school training, or they were less able than others to afford it. It remained the norm to attend a parochial school until the time of First Communion. But the dispute had raised some important questions for the first time, and in the process it altered the community permanently.

A few months after the final school board meeting on the Polish issue, Michael Kruszka lost his senate seat. This time his opponents were not priests but a Republican legislature, which deprived him of most of his Polish constituents in a redistricting plan.[10] Out of office for the first time in six years, the publisher grew more critical of the Democratic party. His disenchantment at first focused on the failure of Milwaukee's Democratic mayor, David Rose, to favor the Poles with patronage appointments, but by 1898 the influence of war and economic prosperity had attracted Kruszka to the Republicans. The switch was reflected in new editorial policies, which earned Kruszka the enmity of some of his old friends, including Ignatius Czerwinski. The change at first had only a slight effect (Poles remained overwhelmingly Democratic in the 1898 elections);[11] but it showed that the rift within the leadership was becoming permanent.

Opposition to Kruszka's policies crystallized in efforts to establish an opposition paper in Milwaukee. *Katolik,* the first challenger, appeared for the first time in January 1897. Supported by a group of laymen and priests, including Hyacinth Gulski, the new journal was issued three times per week. *Katolik* was most closely associated with Wilhelm Grutza in presenting a Catholic interpretation of issues and avoiding unnecessary antagonisms. Except for a brief exchange of insults between Grutza and Kruszka late in 1897, the paper generally refrained from taking strong stances on local issues. In fact, it drew more criticism from Winona's *Wiarus,* which was more seriously concerned with rivals in the field of Polish Catholic journalism. Thus *Katolik* remained a relatively unambitious effort to voice a Catholic position in Milwaukee until it expired at the time of Grutza's death, in 1901.[12]

Part of the reason for the obscurity which surrounded *Katolik* was the emergence in March 1899 of a new paper, *Dziennik Milwaucki* (The Milwaukee Daily News). Supported by lay persons and priests who had been alienated by Kruszka's independence, the paper was a reasonable success until financial difficulties led to its collapse in 1905.[13] The *Dziennik* attacked Kruszka and his papers aggressively in the early years, reflecting a bitterness only possible among friends who have turned antagonists. Thus when the new paper accused Kruszka of earning excessive profits on his contract for printing municipal notices, an outraged Kruszka asserted that his opponents had profited from the *Kuryer's* help in the past. The strongest criticism to appear in the *Kuryer* was directed against Czerwinski in five "Open Letters to Ignatius Czerwinski," published in July 1899, under the signature "A Stockholder of the *Dziennik* and Kościuszko Hall." The charges included dishonesty and misrepresentation in real estate transactions, as well as financial mismanagement in the operation of the *Dziennik.* Czerwinski sued Kruszka for damages and mounted his own attacks.[14]

Michael Kruszka reacted to pressures from the new Catholic daily in a number of ways. He engaged in an almost endless argument about the circulation figures of the two papers, mostly for the benefit of the advertisers. He formed a legal corporation, the Kuryer Publishing Company, to oversee operations and stress the permanence of his enterprise. The value of the new corporation was set at $20,000. Kruszka and his brother Joseph held the offices of president and vice president.[15] Finally, Kruszka began to distance himself from strict Catholics by drawing distinctions between religion and nationality. No enlightened individual, one editorial claimed, could believe that Catholicism and Polishness are inseparable. After all, German bishops in Poznania were using the Church to cooperate with government officials in denationalizing the Poles. The chief value of Roman Catholicism, Kruszka argued, was the unity it provided in the absence of a Polish state.[16] This was to adopt a utilitarian view of the Church as a sort of national resource which would keep Poles together while they waited for an opportunity to unify around a restored Polish state. Thus, by the turn of the century, Kruszka had formulated a new and independent stance on the Church.

At this point, another problem arose to divide Milwaukee's Poles: the issue of St. Josaphat's Church. Wilhelm Grutza, founder and pastor of the parish, conceived the idea of building a monumental church in 1895, when Wenceslaus Kruszka, then a curate in the parish, was working on his book *Rzym*. Moved by young Kruszka's description of St. Peter's Basilica, Grutza decided to build a basilica in Milwaukee. Plans were drawn up to erect a building in the shape of a Latin cross, with a transept and central dome. The dimensions of the structure were to be 128 feet by 212 feet, and the dome, which would rise to 250 feet, was to be the fifth largest in the world at the time of its completion. The church was to seat 2,500 people, with standing room for another 1,500. Cararra marble was to be used for the high altar and the pulpit. The first estimate of costs was $100,000.[17]

Undaunted by the magnitude of the project, Grutza attempted to minimize costs in well-intentioned but ineffective ways. To save money, he bought the stones from the old post office building in Chicago for $35,000 and brought them to Milwaukee on 500 railway flatcars. Though Grutza saved money on the used stones, the expense of preparing them for the basilica made them more expensive than new material would have been. By the end of the year, estimates for the cost of the church were doubled, giving rise to doubts from some observers about whether the parish could afford such an expensive edifice. Michael Kruszka articulated the fears of some parishioners when he pointed out that the cost had risen to about $200 for each of the 1,000 families in the parish—about nine months' wages for the average worker.[18] Undercurrents of scandal also plagued the project. In 1899 the Polish pastor in Princeton, Wisconsin, accused Grutza of fraudulent misrepresentation in selling shares of a California mining company. The Original Quartz Hill Gold Mine, the Princeton pastor charged, had failed to pay a single dividend in the five years since Grutza had sold shares.[19] The charge shook confidence in Grutza's financial competence, but many continued to contribute to the project generously.

The cornerstone was laid in 1897 and the structure was ready for consecration on July 30, 1901. The ceremony attracted the papal delegate, Cardinal Sebastiano Martinelli, all the bishops of the Milwaukee Province, about 50 priests, and about 8,000 lay people. The *Kuryer* issued a special edition on the preceding day, calling the church one of the most magnificent buildings to have been built by Poles in America. At the same time, the editors warned that the building was too expensive for the parishioners and expressed the hope that the entire Polish community would band together to bear the costs. The extent of those costs became clear within a few months. Grutza died suddenly in August and his successor announced that the parish debts amounted to $382,000. Wenceslaus Kruszka estimated that the total cost of the church and furnishings was about $500,000.[20]

The enormity of the debt led to debate about who was responsible. "Every stone cries out to the Lord," wrote Wenceslaus Kruszka about the injustice of accumulating such a debt in the name of working-class Poles. He blamed Archbishop Katzer for permitting Grutza to carry his enthusiasm so far. The point had some merit: Grutza was an impractical man who started large projects without the resources to carry them out. With little help or support from the other Polish priests of the state, he had built and maintained a Polish high school, bought one paper (*Katolik*) and started another (*Źródło* [The Spring]), and built an enormous church. The school and papers expired when he died and the church was left with a crushing debt. As the obligations against the parish mounted, people asked openly whether Katzer should not have restrained the irrepressible Grutza. The most charitable opinion of the deceased pastor was probably Wenceslaus Kruszka's, who wrote that it was better for him to have been a builder than a destroyer.[21]

By 1900 the judgments of Wenceslaus Kruszka were becoming a force to be reckoned with in the state's Polish community. Assigned to be the founding pastor of the small Polish parish in Ripon in 1896, Kruszka had ample spare time for writing. By 1900 he had produced two more books. *Neapol, Wesuwiusz, i Pompeji* (Naples, Vesuvius, and Pompeii) appeared in Milwaukee in 1898 as a learned travelogue on the Neapolitan areas of Italy. It bore an elaborate dedication to Cardinal Ledóchowski. The second book, an English-language pamphlet titled *The Unbeliever before the Tribunal of Reason,* was an attempt to refute atheism by the use of reason.

Kruszka gained still more time for writing when, in 1900, Frederick Katzer removed the mission churches at Springvale and Eldorado from his jurisdiction. Kruszka protested the apparent demotion, which halved the number of his parishioners. He even threatened to resign his pastorate. But the archbishop, exasperated by an exchange of letters which lasted for two months, told Kruszka to find a better place if he could. He directed that no more letters be sent to him on the matter and expressed his dissatisfaction with Kruszka's attitude:

> Every individual makes mistakes, even a bishop. But I made a very large mistake when I accepted you into the diocese. Maybe if I had asked the Jesuits about your character, I would not have made this mistake.

Somewhat abashed, Kruszka complained in his memoirs that his acquaintances were beginning to call him—mockingly—the "irremovable rector" in Ripon.[22]

Blocked in his hopes for ecclesiastical preferment, he turned to another means of gaining recognition: preparation of a history of Poles in the United States. The idea of writing a history occurred to Kruszka in 1899, when he constructed a monument in Springvale at the grave of the state's first Polish priest. Dismayed by the fact that this man and his accomplishments had already been forgotten, Kruszka began to collect materials about the early efforts of the Polish immigrants so that they would not be lost to history. In addition to the standard sources, he relied upon reminiscences solicited by direct inquiry and through advertisements in the *Kuryer*. The information he requested centered on the founding of a parish and school in each locality, but he accepted whatever data people were willing to offer. Later, he used his travels, particularly in the East and in Rome, to gain additional information.[23]

After several years of work he had a trial draft, to be used to obtain additions and corrections. Serialized in the *Kuryer* between August 1901 and December 1904, the book started with a general explanation of the meaning of Polish-Americanism and a brief consideration of Polish efforts in colonial and early nineteenth-century America. The most extensive section, which dealt with the post–Civil War immigration, described the organizations, institutions, and newspapers formed by the newcomers. Then each Polish settlement was described individually, generally with emphasis on the Midwestern areas with which Kruszka was familiar and which generally were older. The work eventually appeared in thirteen volumes between 1905 and 1908, because that method enabled prospective readers to buy only volumes that dealt with the localities in which they were interested.

The most controversial section of the serialized version was Kruszka's concept of the Polish-American identity. Rejecting the narrow definition that a Pole is a person born in Poland, he argued that individuals who are born in America could claim to be Polish because, whatever the external circumstances, they remain Poles internally. Common descent determined nationality: "Wherever a Pole settles, a piece of Poland is born. Descent determines a nation, and not land." Thus affection for the Old Country made the American-born Pole a fellow countryman to Poles in Europe, while other Americans were his fellow citizens. Kruszka's ideas allowed the newcomers to adapt to American life, even to the point of abandoning the Polish language, as long as the inner feelings of Polish identity and a sense of obligation to Poland remained. For this reason he rejected the notion of a "Fourth Partition" of Poland in the United States. That approach would be too resistant to the new circumstances of American life. To remain Polish, it was most essential to maintain respect for the accomplishments of forebears. It was in the hope of conveying to later generations the saga of the founding of Polish life in America that he wrote the history.[24]

Kruszka's characterization of Polish-Americanism immediately drew criticism from the Resurrectionist-sponsored *Dziennik Chicagoski* (The Chicago Daily News). Denying that it is possible to differentiate between external and internal manifestations of national allegiance, the Chicago editors insisted that language and nationality must be more closely tied. It was doubtful, they wrote, that much of the "national idea" was present if an individual would not learn the language. The paper also expressed criticism of Kruszka's partly unfavorable view of Vincent Barzynski, the godfather and organizer of the Resurrectionist missions in Chicago. Closer to home, *Dziennik Milwaucki's* editors, displeased with Kruszka's description of St. Josaphat's Parish, encouraged indignation meetings. Such criticism led Kruszka to explain that he was writing a history and not a panegyric.[25] More importantly, he was beginning to form a somewhat independent vision of Polish-American life. Rejecting the inflexible tie between religion and language which the Resurrectionists advanced and the pragmatic view of Catholicism which his brother advocated, he wrestled with a third way of maintaining the triple allegiance to the Church, the Old Country, and the adopted land.

He developed his understanding further in 1900, when Bishops Frederick Eis of Marquette and Sebastian Messmer of Green Bay ordered that sermons be given in English at least twice monthly at each church in their dioceses. Immediately a storm of protest arose, as Polish-Americans misinterpreted the extensiveness and intent of the orders. The *Kuryer* called them a direct attack on Poles; the Polish Roman Catholic Union sent an official complaint to Cardinal Martinelli.[26] Wenceslaus Kruszka, however, disagreed; he explained that the chief thrust of the regulation was to alter situations in which priests preached sermons in French to uncomprehending congregations. Bishop Eis made a similar point when he clarified his intent, which was not to attack the use of Polish or any other language (where appropriate) but to ensure that English-speaking, younger-generation Catholics would hear sermons in a language they could understand.[27] Under the circumstances, the protests died away. Wenceslaus Kruszka's moderation in this episode again set him apart from his countrymen; he kept his perspective by assigning priority to the life of faith rather than defense of a particular language.

Kruszka's defense of Messmer and Eis may have been related to his approval of their actions in response to *Testem Benevolentiae*. Like Wisconsin's bishops, Kruszka accepted the fact that there was a heterodox dimension to the teachings of Hecker. He wrote an article in mid-1900 to explain that the pope's intent in issuing the warning had been to prevent modification of the faith and not to deny the relationship between faith and national custom. Faith, the Ripon pastor explained, should be considered one sun, which shines on many nations. Thus the support the Polish language had received from the Catholic Church in America was not jeopardized by the letter. Under the conditions which then obtained, the unity of the faith was being preserved through the use of Polish.[28]

Ruminations on the papal letter of 1899 and the episcopal decrees of 1900 led Kruszka to involvement in the movement for a Polish bishop in America. His first effort came during the summer of 1901, when he responded to an article in *Dziennik Chicagoski* which maintained that Polish bishops were needed to found a "Poland in America." In a letter to the *Kuryer*, Kruszka rejected that argument, stressing instead the essential office of bishop as teacher and pastor. The fulfillment of those roles made it essential that a bishop be able to communicate with the people in their own language. Drawing his justification from the writings of St. Paul, Kruszka argued that bishops since apostolic times have known or learned the languages of their flock, rather than the people learning the language of their bishop. For this reason he suggested that bishops be capable of ministering in the several vernacular languages of their diocese; otherwise, they were bound to refuse an office which they could not properly fulfill.[29] Thus Kruszka placed the significance of a Polish bishop on a different basis from the older arguments about a separate Polish presence within America or American Catholicism. His emphasis referred to the nature of the episcopal office; he sought the communication of Christian beliefs.

Kruszka carried his ideas to their logical conclusion in an English-language article, "Polyglot Bishops for Polyglot Dioceses," which was published in the New York *Freeman's Journal,* after it was rejected by the *American Ecclesiastical Review* because of its "aggressive and polemic purpose." The article, which filled seven columns when it was reprinted, praised the concept of unity in diversity which characterized the Catholic Church. Because the American Church represented a microcosm of the universal Church, he reasoned, the languages of the various immigrant nationalities ought to be the ordinary means of conveying the faith. To use only English would be destructive of that faith, and to expect the people to accommodate themselves to the language of the local bishops would be to argue that the diocese exists to serve the convenience of the bishop. Therefore, "if the diocese is polyglot, the bishop must be polyglot, too."

Citing the Pentecostal gift of "diverse tongues" as proof of divine sanction for preaching in the vernacular, Kruszka added a new and controversial argument:

> I do affirm with certainty, gained both a priori and a posteriori from experience among non-English speaking Catholics, that nowadays in the United States, whosoever (a candidate) dares to assume the duties of bishop in a polyglot diocese, without being a polyglot himself, takes duties upon himself which he knows he is unable to perform, and therefore commits a mortal sin. He should either learn "to speak with divers tongues" (for he cannot expect a miracle from God), or he should refuse to assume the responsible duties of a bishop in such a diocese.

The article concluded with a review of the growing importance of Slavic elements in the American Church. Their needs, Kruszka said, had not been recognized. Instead, certain American prelates had vowed that there would never be bishops of the Polish nationality in the United States. Kruszka pleaded with his readers not to take Poland's historic loyalty to the Holy See for granted, and not to imagine that, in asking for bishops, the Poles were looking for privileges which were not accorded to others: "We Poles in America do not ask for any special privilege, we only ask for just and EQUAL treatment in the ecclesiastical hierarchy."[30]

The article evoked a mixed response, with the statement on sin receiving the strongest criticism. The rector of the Milwaukee seminary told Kruszka that the assertion was too strong, and Bishop James Trobec of St. Cloud came to an understanding with Kruszka about the limits of that argument in missionary situations. The harshest reaction appeared in Cleveland's *Catholic Universe,* which argued for an American *and* Catholic Church. Kruszka's response was that the Cleveland editors were most interested in an Irish Church. Yet the article had its supporters.

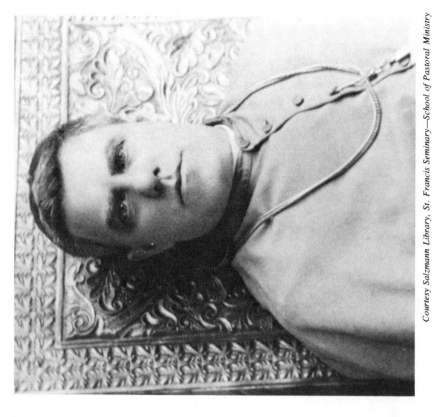

Frederick Katzer, archbishop of Milwaukee, 1890–1903.

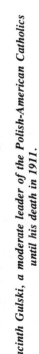

Rev. Hyacinth Gulski, a moderate leader of the Polish-American Catholics
until his death in 1911.

St. Josaphat's Basilica in Milwaukee, symbol of generosity and mismanagement.

Children in St. Josaphat's Parish School in 1901. The quality of parochial education had been disputed since 1896.

Kruszka claimed later to have read a draft to a number of Polish priests in Wisconsin, including a diocesan consultor in Green Bay. All had approved and encouraged him to publish it.[31]

Resistance to what appeared to him to be the moral necessity of providing bishops for the immigrant nationalities led Kruszka closer to the idea of separate dioceses. By 1902, according to his memoirs, he already regarded Cahensly's plan as "a completely healthy and normal movement in the development of the Catholic Church in America." He attributed its failure to the "almighty Irish episcopacy," which had destroyed the idea and then claimed Rome had done so.[32] Whatever the role of the Irish in suppressing the proposals of the Lucerne Memorial, there was logic in Kruszka's deduction, for unless a bishop were a gifted linguist, he could not know the languages of all the Catholics in many American dioceses during the immigrant era. In effect, each bishop was limited in serving those people with whom he could not directly communicate. In a way, then, the United States already had national dioceses, but only for English-speaking and German-speaking Catholics.

Articulate portrayals of the Polish cause gained widespread attention for Kruszka at the second Polish-American Congress, which convened at Buffalo in September 1901. Convoked by Rev. John Pitass with the support of Bishop James Quigley, the convention attracted 150 laymen and 75 priests, representing Polish organizations all over the country. The question of a Polish bishop was considered, along with education and other matters. The rapid growth of independent Polish churches during the previous decade lent urgency to the meeting. The appointment of Polish Roman Catholic bishops, it was assumed, would prevent further defections and also facilitate solving the other problems which were on the agenda. Therefore the delegates resolved to appeal to the American hierarchy for Polish auxiliaries. If that effort failed, they resolved to petition the pope in a delegation consisting of Pitass and Kruszka.[33] The two delegates were placed under the direction of the Executive Committee, which was assigned the task of promoting action on the various plans approved at the meeting.

The Executive Committee's first action, in accordance with the wish of the delegates, was an appeal to the American archbishops at their annual meeting in November. The petition stressed the success of schismatic Polish movements, which were already claiming 50,000 adherents and disrupting the religious life of Poles. The request attributed the appeal of these dissidents to the nonrecognition of Poles by Catholic authorities in America. As a result, loyal Polish priests and lay persons were made to appear to be "ignoble slaves of the [Irish and German] hierarchy." "The schismatics have the popular side of the

affair: they have so called Polish bishops, whereas they accuse the
Polish Roman Catholic clergy of treason to their nation, when holding
allegiance to Irish and German bishops, as they say." The congress
asked not for national bishops but for Polish auxiliaries in areas in which
they could be effectively employed.[34] In this way, the credibility of
Polish priests who had been faithful to their bishops could be restored
and the danger of further losses of Polish Roman Catholics prevented.
Kruszka's arguments from the nature of the episcopal office were not
used. Instead, practical arguments appealed to the prelates' interest in
averting further losses among Polish Catholics.

The Executive Committee received a reply from Archbishop John
J. Keane of Dubuque, secretary of the archbishops' meeting, stating that
the memorial had been considered and its importance recognized.
However, "as the Archbishops have no authority in the selection of
Assistant Bishops,—a matter which belongs exclusively to such Diocese or Province as it may concern,—it was not in their power to take
any action in regard to it."[35] Carefully following this advice, the
committee turned to Frederick Katzer, widely known to be the American prelate most sympathetic to the Polish cause. The committee
members visited Katzer in person shortly after receiving Keane's reply,
and Katzer promised to help.[36]

He did his best to fulfill his promise. In January 1902 he wrote to
Cardinal Ledóchowski to request a Polish auxiliary for Milwaukee.
Ledóchowski, however, refused. His reply praised the desire of the
Milwaukee archbishop to contribute to the tranquillity of the Poles. But
for unspecified reasons, the request for a Polish bishop was denied:
"After maturely considering the matter . . . this sacred congregation,
for the gravest reasons, does not think it opportune to come to a
nomination of this kind." Ledóchowski concluded with the hope that
the movement for a Polish auxiliary would soon die down because of the
cooperation of the Polish priests in presenting "an example of the
observance of ecclesiastical discipline."[37]

Undeterred, Katzer left for Rome with Hyacinth Gulski several
weeks after receiving the letter. He rejected the request of Kruszka and
Pitass to accompany him because he was reluctant to have too much
attention focused on the connection between himself and the Polish-
American Congress. He felt he could present a stronger case in Rome
for the Poles if he appeared to be acting out of his own convictions and
not in response to outside pressure. Gulski's public position was that
Polish bishops were not necessary to solve the difficulties of Poles in the
United States, but it is possible that he adopted this position to make
himself more acceptable for the post of auxiliary bishop. He could not
have been unaware that his name was often mentioned as a possibility

for the position. Attaching special importance to the invitation to accompany Katzer to Rome, the *Kuryer* confidently predicted that he would return to Milwaukee as Bishop Gulski.[38]

Despite the high hopes, Katzer's efforts were unsuccessful. In part the failure was due to Ledóchowski's terminal illness while Katzer was in Rome. Upon his return to Milwaukee, Katzer admitted that although he had journeyed to Europe primarily in the interest of his health, he had waited several weeks in Rome in hope of receiving an interview with Ledóchowski on the Polish matter. Although the cardinal's death had temporarily halted the process, Katzer expressed confidence that the new head of Propaganda, Cardinal Girolamo Gotti, would eventually resolve the matter.[39]

Only after it became clear that Katzer had been unsuccessful in his efforts on its behalf did the Executive Committee consent to the departure of Kruszka and Pitass for Rome. Executive Committee members acknowledged Katzer's strenuous efforts in their behalf, but admitted that his intervention "has not led to the desired result." To explain his forthcoming mission, Kruszka wrote an article which was carried by the *Freeman's Journal,* Milwaukee's *Catholic Citizen, Dziennik Chicagoski*, and other papers. He reiterated that the effort for a Polish bishop arose from a sense of just care for Polish Catholics and from the desire to prevent further losses to the independents. Forced Americanization in the Church, he wrote, was a more nationalistic policy than allowing members of each Catholic immigrant group to care for their own. Kruszka also disclosed that support for Polish auxiliaries was growing, and he added the names of James Quigley, newly appointed archbishop of Chicago, and Bishop John Spalding of Peoria to Katzer's on the list of prelates sympathetic to Poles. These men received Kruszka's thanks, while the other bishops were urged to consider that they were "bearing the national standard higher than the Catholic standard."[40] As a delegate of the Polish-American Congress, he scrupulously subordinated his private views on the matter of national dioceses and polyglot bishops.

Kruszka's departure for Rome was delayed until June 1903, while he waited for Jan Pitass to put his affairs in order. Although Pitass eventually decided to remain at home, he helped the mission in a number of ways. Following the resolution of the Buffalo meeting to include a layman in the delegation, he secured the participation of Rowland B. Mahany, a Republican politician who had served as ambassador to Ecuador under Benjamin Harrison and as congressman from Buffalo, and who was then collector of the port of Buffalo. Disturbed by the report of Katzer and Gulski that Vatican officials were afraid of opposition in Washington to the appointment of non-English-speaking prelates, the delegates reasoned that the choice of a man who was acquainted with Theodore Roosevelt would be helpful. In addition, Pitass secured letters from Roosevelt to Leo XIII and from Cardinal Gibbons to the Propaganda, both warmly supporting the Polish cause. A third letter, from Secretary of State John Hay to the American ambassador in Rome, requested the ambassador to aid the Polish delegates.[41] The delay gave Kruszka the opportunity to solicit funds for the mission, and he collected over $500, nearly half of which was a gift from the PRCU. Some priests contributed, but others scoffed and said that Kruszka could scarcely succeed where the archbishop of Milwaukee had failed.[42] They underestimated his tenacity and resourcefulness.

Kruszka's efforts for the Polish-American Congress were not the only indication of restiveness among Wisconsin's Poles in the early years of the twentieth century. In 1900 six Polish women withdrew from the Franciscan convent in Milwaukee, claiming that their German-American superiors discriminated against Polish members. With Bishop Messmer's approval, a new congregation, known popularly as "Józefinki" or the "Polish School Sisters of St. Joseph," was organized at Stevens Point. Vatican approval soon followed, and by 1903 the group numbered eighty sisters and candidates, who were teaching nearly 4,300 children in Wisconsin, Illinois, and Michigan.[43] Such desire for self-expression did not, however, indicate support for the independent movement. Neither the schismatic Chicago bishop, Anthony Kozlowski, nor Buffalo's Stefan Kaminski had much success in attracting the state's Poles. Even the *Kuryer* ridiculed the independents, and Kozlowski's brief success with a group of dissidents in South Milwaukee ended with resubmission to the authority of Katzer.[44]

The efforts demonstrated, however, that all aspects of Polish life were henceforth open to question. With the ecclesiastical and secular leadership no longer automatically united, the connection between faith and nationality became a matter for debate. The result was that even agreement on specific issues was becoming tenuous because the parties based their accord on fundamentally different assumptions.

Shortly before his brother departed for Rome, Michael Kruszka printed an editorial to remind his readers that, as Poles, they shared "one blood, one faith, one Mother, and one heart."[45] In light of the events of the previous seven years, the sentiments were optimistic. Wisconsin's Poles, to be sure, could still agree on the words but they were beginning to disagree about their meaning. Wenceslaus Kruszka had been right; his countrymen were indeed learning to live a Polish life under non-Polish conditions, but they were learning to do so in different ways. The meaning of Polish-Americanism was still crucial but it was no longer so narrow. It had grown broad enough to permit leaders openly to challenge one another without being excluded from the community. Schools, the press, the need for a bishop, the forays of the independents, and other issues forced leaders to reconsider the relationship of religion to nationality in the American context. As the centripetal forces of the early years became more diffuse, agreement weakened. Division was the unexpected cost of success.

4. The Promise

WHEN WENCESLAUS KRUSZKA SET out on the road to Rome, he was undertaking a labor of love. It was not a complete surprise, therefore, that his energetic application eventually won a sympathetic response from the pope. With a jubilant heart he returned to Ripon, proclaiming that the Polish matter would soon be resolved. But in his enthusiasm the young pastor failed to allow for the opposition his efforts engendered. Most of the bishops continued to resist his cause and, gradually, many of Kruszka's contemporaries within the Polish-American community began to oppose his tactics. As before, there were arguments on both sides, but for the first time Kruszka was adopting such an aggressive stance that individuals *had* to react. In the process, he was becoming part of the issue. Because he had spoken personally with the pope, he was convinced that his foes were opposing the Vatican; therefore, he began to test the limits of dissent against the bishops. And the bishops, frightened by the vehemence of the demands that were voiced in Ripon and printed in the *Kuryer,* imposed more stringent limits and scrambled for allies among the Polish Catholics. As the disagreement grew more acrimonious, the lines of division became more pronounced and inflexible.

When he arrived in Rome on June 24, 1903, Wenceslaus Kruszka was thirty-five years old and had already achieved prominence because of his writings and outspoken advocacy of Polish bishops. With high hopes, he prepared a document, *Supplices Preces* (Prayerful Supplications), which presented arguments for appointing Polish bishops in the United States. About fifty pages long, the memorial included the mandates of Kruszka and Mahany from the Executive Committee of the congress, the request for bishops, and Kruszka's statistics on the number of Polish-Americans. As a helper and patron, the delegates enlisted the aid of Msgr. Joseph Antonucci, a secretary of the Congregation for Studies, who had been a friend of the deceased Milwaukee pastor, Aegidius Tarasiewicz. Under Antonucci's guidance, the delegates began to meet with the sixteen cardinals who comprised the Propaganda. Cardinal Gotti, the congregation's head, called their cause "just and important" and promised to consider the matter at the next meeting of the Propaganda. Most of the other cardinals were equally sympathetic, according to Kruszka, but Cardinal Agliardi warned the delegates that the American bishops were opposed to the scheme. He advised them to seek support from Polish bishops in Europe in order to apply counterpressure.[1]

In the meantime, Leo XIII became ill, and died on July 20, temporarily suspending the advance of the cause through the Vatican. When the election of Pius X was announced early in August, Kruszka, Mahany, and Antonucci took advantage of the new alignments by visiting Cardinal Svampa, a close personal friend of the new pontiff.[2] On September 11, about five weeks after his election, Pius X received the delegates in a private audience. He told them he was acquainted with their cause and had read the petition completely. He also noted that consideration of the matter was under way in the Propaganda and promised to do what he could to help. Satisfied and encouraged, Kruszka and Mahany left for Poland to seek support among its prelates.

In the midst of a successful series of meetings with Polish bishops and dignitaries, Kruszka received news of a countercampaign in the Vatican against the petition. Cutting short the Polish visit, he reached Rome in mid-October. There he learned that an unknown American source had sent to the Propaganda clippings from the American press which were hostile to the Polish cause. They included public statements of Cardinal Gibbons and others who opposed the selection of bishops on purely nationalistic grounds and accused Kruszka of endangering standard procedures for the selection of bishops by his direct appeal to Rome.[3] Much of the confusion in America resulted from Kruszka's request in *Supplices Preces* for Polish bishops either as local ordinaries and auxiliaries, to work within the existing diocesan structures, or as national bishops with exclusive jurisdiction over Polish-Americans. For this reason, Casimir Sztuczko wrote to Kruszka for the Executive Committee, requesting him to make a clear statement that the group was not asking for national dioceses but only for Polish representatives in the American hierarchy. But Kruszka was not able to do this. He claimed that the existence of national parishes made the basis of the Church in the United States national and that territorial dioceses, consequently, were an anomaly. Despite this disagreement, the Executive Committee and the Society of Polish Priests continued to send Kruszka financial support, and the Polish-American press continued to follow the mission with considerable interest.[4]

Nevertheless, Kruszka was alarmed by the American opposition. On October 27 he wrote to all the American bishops, asking their assistance for his crusade. Specifically, he wanted them to send supporting letters to the Vatican and to nominate worthy Poles for appointment. The response was disappointing. Few bothered to reply, and only one, Bishop John Lancaster Spalding of Peoria, answered that he had written to the Propaganda as Kruszka requested. The most realistic assessment came from Bishop James Trobec of St. Cloud, who warned Kruszka early in October: "There are grave difficulties in the way as long as the present mode of electing bishops for the United States obtains." He professed to be sympathetic to the Polish cause, but counseled that it would be better to have special delegates or vicars general in each diocese to deal with Polish affairs.[5]

Under the circumstances, there was little Kruszka could do but continue his visits to church dignitaries. Propaganda delayed through the fall and winter of 1903–4, and Cardinal Gotti explained that the cause was the opposition of the American bishops.[6] To sustain the pressure, the delegate prepared a new petition in February to call attention to "the most wretched state of affairs . . . growing worse daily" among Polish-American Catholics. He claimed that 50,000 had already joined the schismatic Polish churches in America and asked that the pope forestall further losses by requesting that Polish candidates be included on the *terna* whenever an American see with a substantial number of Poles fell vacant and that U.S. bishops appoint Polish auxiliaries and vicars general.[7]

On April 15, Kruszka was summoned to a second papal audience. He told the pope he had already waited ten months for a decision and asked what to tell the Poles in America. In reply, Pius X stated: "It will be decided as soon as possible. Tell the Poles in America that the decision will be made as soon as possible, and it will be made according to your wishes." With that, Kruszka thanked the pontiff and left. Outside, he recited the *Te Deum* with a friend and then wired to the United States that Rome had given a favorable decision. Elated by the pope's promise, Kruszka speculated on the meaning of the decision:

> Roma locuta est, causa finita est. Rome has spoken, the matter is closed. With this verbal declaration of the Head of the Church my mission to Rome ended, and ended favorably. My task, as a delegate, was to knock at the gates of the Vatican and receive a favorable answer in the matter of equality for the Polish clergy in America. I attained this goal. The pope, after a long delay and after much consideration, finally clearly and unequivocally made a declaration for our cause. And the pope's words are not wind. Let the doubting Thomases say, "We will not believe until we see a Polish bishop in America!" I believe in the word of the pope, and I believe strongly, and the faith is not to be shaken, that the pope's

words: "the decision will be made as soon as possible and according to your wishes," would be fulfilled soon, that we would shortly have Polish bishops in America, just as we have wished.

Filled with gratitude to God and convinced that April 15 was "a day of triumph and victory" for Polish-Americans, Kruszka embarked for America.[8]

After arriving at New York early in May, he traveled first to Buffalo, where he discussed the mission with John Pitass and preached at Pitass's parish, recounting the story of his efforts and administering the papal blessing. On May 10 he arrived in Milwaukee, where he was welcomed warmly by his brother and received confirmation of his appointment to Ripon from the newly installed archbishop, Sebastian Messmer. When he returned to Ripon the following day, the small depot was filled to overflowing. People escorted their pastor to his rectory with shouts of "Hurrah!" and "Long may he live!" Soon he was besieged with requests to tell his story and administer the papal blessing.[9]

The first reactions to Kruszka's report were predictably mixed. Casimir Sztuczko, reporting for the Executive Committee, accused the Irish and German Catholics in America of working for their own national interests under the guise of Americanism. For that reason, he predicted, the matter would take some time to resolve. Francis Hodur, head of the Polish National Catholic Church in Scranton, issued a circular accusing Rome of using delay to destroy the Poles in America. "Between the Polish nation and the Roman-Irish Church in America," he wrote, "there can be no understanding." He called for a synod of his church to defend Polish interests in America by more appropriate means.[10] And Archbishop Messmer also warned against undue enthusiasm; he refused to share Kruszka's excitement, expressing his belief that the Poles in America did not particularly desire bishops of their own nationality. He attributed the agitation to Polish priests.[11]

A more patronizing evaluation came from Msgr. Kelly, writing from Rome under the signature "Vox Urbis" to English-language Catholic journals in the United States. Kelly interpreted the pope's remarks to Kruszka as a kindly reassurance that the pontiff had the interest of all Catholics at heart, including American Poles. But he doubted that the pope had completely endorsed the petitioners' point of view, and held it unreasonable to insist upon nationality as the basis for episcopal appointments. Nevertheless, he praised the competence with which Kruszka had carried out his mission:

> Father Kruszka has performed a very difficult mission with great skill and perseverance and he deserves the thanks of his country-

men for his efforts to make the Roman authorities see their side of the question.[12]

Such reactions from outside the Polish community ought to have alerted Kruszka to the fact that he could not expect immediate results from his mission. But he continued to watch the Vatican for encouraging signs and to insist upon vindication for a position he regarded as morally right.

That attitude was shared to a large extent by the members of the Third Polish-American Congress, which met in Pittsburgh in September 1904. Eleven Wisconsin parishes sent delegates to the meeting, including important congregations in Pulaski, Stevens Point, Berlin, and the Milwaukee parishes of Hyacinth Gulski and Jan Szukalski. The delegates received Kruszka's report enthusiastically but they refused to accept most of his proposals for follow-through or to reimburse him for additional expenses until they received word of the appointment of a Polish bishop. In the meantime, they delegated Kruszka to continue to work with the campaign and to send a telegram of thanks to the pope.[13]

Evidence that the pope was responding to the Polish memorials followed quickly. Late in 1904, Kruszka learned that Francis Symon, archbishop of Płock, would come to America "to visit and examine every Polish-American parish" for the purpose of making a report to the Vatican. Both Antonucci and Symon's secretary, Dom Sisto Fiori, corresponded with Kruszka about the visit.[14] Evidently, the pope wished Symon's visit to have an official nature, but Gotti opposed him because he feared the hostility of American bishops to a mission which might appear to interfere with their jurisdictional authority. Several efforts were then made to learn whether American bishops would receive Symon graciously if he came with the status of a papal delegate. When the opposition became clear, the pope and his advisers decided that Symon would go to America unofficially, but that he would report to the pope and the Propaganda upon his return.

The announcement of Symon's impending arrival in the spring of 1905 engendered a lively dispute in the Catholic and Polish-American press about the visit. Wenceslaus Kruszka wrote that Symon ought to be accorded a welcome befitting the first Polish bishop to set foot on American soil, and the *Kuryer* printed a picture of Symon with the caption "Papal Delegate in the Polish Matter." But William J. D. Croke, Roman correspondent for Milwaukee's *Catholic Citizen* and other Catholic papers, denied that Symon was coming in an official capacity, adding that the cause for Polish bishops "has been greatly prejudiced, not to say practically spoiled, by excessive zeal" on the part of those who were trying to goad the Vatican into hasty action. "There is nothing in the affair," he concluded, "but gracious concession and paternal indulgence for the Poles and the Polish descendants."[15]

Francis Symon, archbishop of Plock, who visited Polish-American settlements on behalf of the Pope in 1905.

Rev. Boleslaus Goral, guiding force of the Nowiny Polskie during the Church War.

Michael Kruszka, founder and publisher of the Kuryer Polskie from 1888 to his death in 1918.

Rev. Wenceslaus Kruszka as he looked about the time of his visit to the Pope, 1903–4.

Symon obviously disagreed. Shortly after his arrival on May 18, he told a group in Buffalo that he had come "with the knowledge, desire, and blessing of the Holy Father," and admitted that the chief purpose of his visit was to study the relationship of Poles in the Catholic Church in the United States to the other nationalities. He also counseled patience and warned against expecting national dioceses. Symon presented the documents relating to his visit to the papal delegate in Washington.[16] He was warmly received by Cardinal Gibbons and by President Roosevelt, who said: "If the official relationship between church and state did not forbid it, I would tell the pope that it would be good for the Polish people to have its clergy represented in the ecclesiastical hierarchy in America."[17]

Symon arrived in Milwaukee on June 17 to participate in the dedication of a statue of Thaddeus Kościuszko on the following day. The festivities attracted about 50,000, including Archbishop Messmer, Mayor David Rose, and Hyacinth Gulski, who gave the main speech. But the high point of the afternoon was Symon's address. He urged the audience to follow Kościuszko in fighting for freedom in every circumstance and told them that, to be good Poles, they must also be good Americans. An effective orator, he concluded with the words: "*Niech żyje Polska . . . niech żyje Ameryka!*" (Long live Poland! Long live America!) The crowd repeated the phrases after him and then, amid prolonged applause, began to chant: "*Niech żyje . . . Symon!*"[18] The archbishop remained in the city about a week, visiting all the Polish parishes, then departed the state. He returned to Wisconsin in mid-July, toured many of the smaller settlements, and came back to Milwaukee to participate in the installation of Augustine Schinner as bishop of the newly erected diocese of Superior.

The Polish archbishop did not go to Ripon on either visit, an omission that cannot be explained simply as antagonism toward Kruszka's stance on the bishop issue, since he told a *Kuryer* interviewer that Kruszka was "an industrious and patriotic priest" who had made a good impression in Rome. Furthermore, Fiori kept assuring Kruszka of Symon's desire for a visit.[19] So the decision to avoid Ripon may have been tactical. With a mission as suspect and, presumably, unwelcome in many places as Symon's, the archbishop probably decided to avoid giving grounds for further controversy by keeping his distance from the person whose actions had been responsible for his tour. Kruszka has had his say, the omission implied; it is time to hear from the others.

Symon departed at the end of September, having handled a difficult mission reasonably well. He left a sense of optimism among Polish-Americans and a willingness to be patient a while longer with the slow workings of the Vatican. In his reports for the pope and the Propaganda, Symon praised the progress of the Poles in the New World and affirmed that Polish-American priests were "locked out" of the hierarchical structure.[20] Fiori continued to write optimistic letters to Kruszka about the Polish matter. Kruszka had one of them published in the *Kuryer* to indicate the friendly disposition of Rome toward his countrymen and the constant nature of his own participation in the campaign.[21]

A somewhat different interpretation of the visit was provided by Croke, who wrote in late December that Symon's visit had changed things very little:

> At the Propaganda I can say for certain, since Archbishop Symon's return, nothing has been done in the matter, nothing will be done . . . and nothing can be done in the matter, except, kindly, to counsel the American hierarchy to favor, within the bounds of their own wisdom, all the aspirations of the Poles.

Privately, Croke, who had met Kruszka in Rome, wrote that it would be wise to continue to utilize the services of Msgr. Antonucci, "a warm friend, who has influence and will spend it to the best of his power." He also told Kruszka that he thought the American Poles would ultimately be sustained, but he never lost sight of the fact that the initiative would have to come from the United States.[22]

The likelihood that such an impulse would come from Wisconsin was affected decisively by the enduring popularity of the *Kuryer Polski*. By the time of Symon's visits to the state, Michael Kruszka was in the process of bringing to a victorious conclusion a bitter newspaper war with the editors of the *Dziennik Milwaucki*. The dispute had begun in 1903, when the newer daily had won the contract for municipal printing away from the *Kuryer*. Kruszka had then filed suit, alleging that the *Dziennik*'s circulation was below the legal minimum (5% of the registered voters in Milwaukee, or 2,987 at that time) for the contract to be let. He also charged that Ignatius Czerwinski and other Polish Democrats who held mortgages on the *Dziennik* were using their municipal influence for personal profit. In the trial, the *Dziennik* failed to prove it had the required circulation; as a result, Kruszka recovered his costs and the contract. The publishers of the *Dziennik* tried desperately to raise circulation during the remainder of 1903 and throughout 1904, chiefly by lowering prices, but they failed to attain 2,987.[23]

After the trial, the papers battled for two more years. In the spring elections of 1904, when Archbishop Messmer forbade the use of parish halls for political rallies, the *Dziennik* protested. But the *Kuryer* applauded the prelate, defending him (for perhaps the last time) as the supreme head of church property. In 1905 the controversy was about the proper person to present the new Kościuszko statue to the mayor; the *Dziennik* favored the head of the statue committee, a prominent Democrat, but the *Kuryer* pointed out that he had been convicted of misconduct in office, and successfully campaigned for Father Gulski instead.[24] Under the circumstances, it is hardly surprising that the *Dziennik* went into bankruptcy on September 21, 1905, leaving the *Kuryer* an open field.

The situation was unusual in that the political alignment of the two papers had little apparent effect on their popularity. Despite the *Kuryer*'s support for Republican candidates, most of Milwaukee's Poles remained Democratic and Socialist in the spring and fall elections of 1904.[25] The *Kuryer*'s popularity is best explained in terms of Michael Kruszka's abilities as publisher and editor. His paper was meeting a demand. In 1906 he continued his expansion program by leasing the location of the old Milwaukee *Herald* and buying $25,000 of its equipment. Hyacinth Gulski spoke at the public inspection of the new plant, calling the *Kuryer* "the best and largest Polish daily in the United States" and praising Michael Kruszka effusively. The paper's annual report for 1906 showed a circulation of 19,000.[26]

The reappearance of peace among the Poles of Wisconsin after the demise of the *Dziennik* was more apparent than real, as events were to demonstrate. The question of the best means of obtaining Polish bishops continued to divide the community, and the Kruszka brothers seized upon the issue so forcefully that they could not be ignored. Wenceslaus was the catalyst in the renewal of factional bitterness. As months passed without the appointment of a Polish bishop, he became increasingly hostile to the American bishops who, in his view, were standing in the way. "It is necessary faithfully to fulfill one's obligations and to try to claim one's rights," he wrote. "The first without the second means to submit to slavery, and the second without the first means to rise in rebellion."[27]

Kruszka could not accept Messmer's belief that his approach was wrong. Nevertheless, Messmer kept claiming that campaigns like Kruszka's made him wary of honoring the Poles' requests. In January 1905 he wrote to Gibbons about the dangers of appointing a Polish bishop simply on the basis of nationality:

> The longer I think it over the more it seems to me a dangerous experiment at this stage to give the Polish people a bishop, for the very reason that he will be considered the bishop *for all the Poles* of the U.S. I know it. Whenever a bishop would have any difficulty with a Polish parish, *their bishop* would be appealed to. The Polish are not yet American enough & keep aloof too much from the rest of us.[28]

Milwaukee's archbishop made similar points to Kruszka. He wrote him privately on October 31, 1905: "I always blamed the priests for this agitation and I still believe that the Polish people would never have taken it up, if they had not been led first by the clergy."[29]

Kruszka's response was a growing determination to oppose the archbishop by whatever means he could. He called Messmer's opinion that the priests were responsible for the agitation "historically inaccurate and morally unjust." The letter constituted proof that the Polish priests had deceived themselves in supporting Messmer for the Milwaukee see after Katzer's death. He had made himself their enemy.

> This thesis [about the origins of the discontent among the Poles] gave me authentic and clear proof that Archbishop Messmer was always an enemy of the Poles, for he was an enemy of their most vital cause in America. Having such authentic proof, I had to regard Messmer as clandestine and therefore that much more a dangerous enemy for the Poles, and to proceed on that assumption in my life.

Kruszka lamented the fact that Messmer's letter had been labeled private and that his confreres would therefore be ignorant of Messmer's lack of sympathy.[30] Thus the Ripon pastor held Messmer responsible even for the growing sense of estrangement between himself and some of his fellow Polish priests.

But Messmer's attitude does not totally explain why Kruszka turned against the archbishop so decisively during the first two years after his return from Rome. Part of his motivation was his frustration at being kept in Ripon long after he was entitled to a parish in Milwaukee under the seniority system for pastoral appointments. In February 1905, he complained to Messmer that he had been sidetracked six times in his hope for a pastorate in Milwaukee. Not only was the situation a personal disappointment, he stated, it was also causing schismatic Polish newspapers to speak of his persecution at the hands of American bishops. A year later, Kruszka wrote again, asking to be transferred immediately after celebrating the tenth jubilee of the parish he founded in Ripon. He asserted that there was too little work in Ripon for a young priest and referred to his time there as "10 years' imprisonment." The result was that he had taken to "scribbling . . . a necessary evil," and he was tired of it. Ripon would be good for a retired priest, he concluded, but he, Kruszka, needed a more challenging assignment:

> I am now in my full manhood. If I cannot exert my energies in pastoral work, I must necessarily exert them in other directions— perhaps less pleasing to your Lordship. . . . You cannot kill . . . the energies in me,—all you can do, you *can direct them*—and I

will gladly accept Your direction, for you are my divinely appointed director.[31]

The appeal was in vain; Kruszka remained in Ripon.

A good part of the reason for the archbishop's refusal to promote Kruszka rested on allegations, made shortly after Kruszka's return from Rome, that the young priest had broken his vow of celibacy. The charge was made by the pastor of St. Casimir's Parish in Milwaukee, Anthony Lex. Kruszka discussed the matter in a letter to Messmer of August 24, 1904, quoting Lex's statement that Kruszka had "stayed overnight at the home of a family in . . . St. Casimir's parish and committed there adultery." Kruszka emphatically denied that he had stayed overnight in the parish or that he had engaged in any misbehavior. He asked the archbishop to intervene: "Let Fr. Lex either prove his assertion or stop that talking and recant the calumny!"

But the archbishop sided with Lex. He refused Kruszka's February 1905 request for transfer "for reasons I do not care to state here." But he referred to the allegations, telling Kruszka he was "in conscience bound" to assist the woman in question. "I need not say more than that I know all & so do others." Kruszka returned the letter, noting at the bottom that he was "in conscience bound" to return the insulting letter. However, he agreed to send money to the woman over a period of time "just on account of her being unable to work . . . and not for other reasons." Again terming the accusations a calumny and a lie, Kruszka claimed he could prove his innocence by producing letters she had written to him while he was in Rome and "before she went insane." By now, he claimed, his adversaries "have *driven her mad . . . by extorting from her a false testimony.*"[32]

The three letters do not supply enough evidence to make a judgment about the truth of the charges against Kruszka. All that is certain is that he denied any wrongdoing and agreed to help support the woman in question. It is also clear that Messmer's acceptance of the story contributed to Kruszka's state of outraged innocence and unjust persecution. Much of that frustration came out in his writings during the next few years.

Although he engaged in a public debate on the Polish matter with the rector of the cathedral in the *Sentinel* during the summer of 1905,[33] Kruszka began a more systematic effort late in the fall. On December 6 he wrote the first of a series of biweekly columns for the *Kuryer*, "Sprawy Narodowe i Kościelne" (National and Church Affairs), that hammered away at Messmer and others he believed to be enemies of the Poles. His excuse for the articles was his refusal to allow the campaign for bishops to be buried. Later, he regarded their importance so highly that he devoted several hundred pages of his memoirs to reprinting the entire set. On their impact, he stated:

> Through writing articles to Polish newspapers, I first forced American bishops to read Polish newspapers—in translation, of course; and again, I forced them to publish a new paper . . . in defense of their episcopalism.[34]

He defined episcopalism as the stance of American bishops in placing their own interests ahead of the good of the whole Church, while his approach, papalism, relied on the authority of the pope, who had been rendered impotent in his efforts to help Polish-Americans.

The articles contained little that was new. Kruszka continued to condemn Irish-American bishops for their insensitivity to the needs of Poles and to advocate national dioceses as the best solution for the situation. He denied that Poles must become more fully Americanized to merit ecclesiastical promotion: to give up their language would be to abandon "a priceless gift of the same Creator who gives the holy faith." He also attacked the German-American prelates, finding parallels between the *Kulturkampf* and the status of Poles in America. Forced Americanization at the hands of a German bishop, Kruszka claimed, was no different than forced Germanization at the hands of the kaiser and his episcopal allies. In other columns, Messmer and Archbishop Henry Moeller of Cincinnati were styled "Teutonic Knights," who persecuted Poles under the guise of religion in the manner of the fourteenth and fifteenth centuries. The references were potentially explosive. The *Kulturkampf* was a vivid memory for many of his readers, and *Krzyżacy* (The Knights of the Cross), Henryk Sienkiewicz's ardently pro-Polish novel about the Teutonic Knights, had appeared in 1900. Kruszka used such rhetoric repeatedly. "As long as the world is whole," he wrote in 1907, quoting a familiar proverb, "a German will not be brother to a Pole."[35]

Michael Kruszka's efforts to pressure the bishops paralleled those of his brother. Addressing a group at Milwaukee's commemoration of the November Insurrection in 1904, he told his listeners that, to remain Polish, they must take active steps to safeguard their identity. The first step, he argued, was to obtain Polish bishops. He was careful, however, to assert that the ideas were his own and that he had not spoken out at the request of priests. He further differentiated his thoughts from those of his brother in an editorial of March 1905, insisting he was far less willing than Wenceslaus to be patient with the Church: "If the American bishops don't want to listen to the pope, why must we?"[36]

The paper's policy was to embarrass the archbishop in whatever ways it could. On October 12, 1906, it covered a meeting at St.

Josaphat's Parish at which Messmer disclosed that the debt had risen to $400,000 and that the parish was unable to meet the interest payments. He pleaded for patience, asking the parishioners to disregard the advice of those who urged them to apply at the rectory for the money they had loaned. Eleven days later, the editors suggested that Wenceslaus Kruszka could have solved the financial crisis, had he been the pastor.

Messmer and his supporters tried valiantly to win a following for their idea that patience and trust were the best plan for Poles to follow. At a Catholic Day observance in October 1906, the archbishop told the 5,000 participants that the gathering was proof that Catholics of all nationalities could be brought together:

> I insisted that there should be no speaking in foreign tongues, but to have all in the language of this great nation we so dearly love. It is of the highest importance that the Catholics of Milwaukee should be thus brought together. . . . I am especially glad to have the Polish Catholics take part in this meeting.

In response, Father Bronislaus Celichowski, pastor of St. Hedwig's, gave an address titled "The Loyalty of the Polish People to the Holy See." He thanked Messmer for his "good graces and hard labor for the benefit of the Polish people," but he pleaded for Polish bishops as the solution to the problem of the independent churches.[37] Shortly afterward, Wenceslaus Kruszka belittled the meeting in his column.[38]

A more threatening response came two weeks later, when a public meeting at Kościuszko Hall petitioned Messmer on the bishop question. The 800 participants represented forty-two societies from all seven Polish parishes in the city. Their leader was Martin Cyborowski, a composer and officer of the *Kuryer*, who was becoming active in the campaign for equality. Cyborowski cited the meeting itself as proof that the movement had the support of the Polish people and not just the priests. The petition professed loyalty to the pope, archbishop, and clergy. It denied that the campaign for bishops was the "personal caprice" of the clergy, and it stated that "to have Polish bishops, is the most ardent wish of us all."[39] The annual convention of the Polish Association of America, meeting that year in Milwaukee, passed a similar resolution.[40]

During 1906 the growing momentum of the campaign caused persons on both sides to suggest caution. In January Michael Kruszka wrote his brother confidentially that his articles were being translated at the Chancery Office with a view to bringing charges against him. He advised his brother to desist for a while, although he admitted that the column had a strong following. In response, Wenceslaus wrote to the archdiocesan chancellor for an opinion of the series; his answer approved the right of the Poles to a bishop but deplored the tactics of the Kruszkas.[41] In February, Father Jan Pociecha, a pastor of the Green Bay Diocese, persuaded the officers of the Association of Polish Secular Priests to issue a letter of condemnation against the Kruszka brothers for fomenting anarchy and rebellion.[42] But Wenceslaus Kruszka persisted in his writings. Not even letters from his brother, Father Simon Kruszka in Poland, and from Archbishop Symon could persuade him to stop.[43]

On April 7 his article argued that subservience in religious matters is more dangerous than independence. By then, Messmer was ready to act. Pressured by Jan Pociecha on behalf of a group of priests in the Green Bay Diocese, he wrote Kruszka a private letter to urge him to abandon the articles:

> I take this opportunity . . . to ask you in all earnestness and in fatherly kindness to stop your writing on the Polish Bishop question and in general on the Polish religious question. Your writings breathe the spirit of religious anarchy and revolt and must be doing an immense harm among the Polish people, as I am assured by many good and zealous Polish priests. So for the love of our Holy Father and our Holy Church I beg you to let the matter rest. Trust to the Holy Spirit in God's Church and trust—at least a little—to the Catholic spirit of the American Hierarchy.[44]

Kruszka replied that if what he wrote was bad, it was only because he was testifying to evil. He also argued that the outlet he provided for general discontent was responsible for arresting the progress of the independent movement.[45]

Kruszka's relationship with Messmer grew still more strained with publication of *The Polish History in America*. Volumes began to appear in early 1905, under Messmer's *imprimatur*. There was no problem until the appearance of volume IX, a study of the activities of the Resurrectionists in Chicago. Profiting from spare time during his stay in Rome, Kruszka had received permission to read letters in the Resurrectionist archives concerning their activities in the United States.[46] These letters, which had not appeared in the serialized version in the *Kuryer*, dealt mostly with problems of authority and gave the impression of great dissension within the religious congregation. Messmer became involved when Kruszka noticed that, in the letter granting the *imprimatur* for the ninth volume, Messmer stated that he was "gladly" giving his consent for publication. Kruszka attached special significance to the word, adding on the last page of the book: "Notabene: His Excellency Archbishop S. G. Messmer has granted an unusual imprimatur to this volume. It reads thus: 'The Imprimatur of Vol. IX is hereby GLADLY given.' '" When the volume appeared in the fall of 1906, Father Francis Gordon sent a protest to Messmer on behalf of the Resurrectionists in Chicago. He claimed that Kruszka had abused the confidence of the order and was guilty of "public criminal detraction" by attaching "malicious" annotations to the letters and publishing secret materials.

The archbishop issued a public apology to Gordon and his congregation. He explained that he had been unaware of the contents of the volume when granting the *imprimatur* and he expressed regret for unsuspectingly offending a group which he admired. He also criticized Kruszka's part in the episode. "If Rev. Kruszka tries to give the term 'gladly' used by me the meaning of endorsing anything at all in the volume, I must condemn such an endeavor as a most dishonest and contemptible trick." Messmer asked Gordon to give wide publicity to his letter, and it was published in *Dziennik Chicagoski* on December 10, with Gordon's original complaint.[47] Kruszka protested his innocence in this public embarrassment of Messmer,[48] but in the context of hard feelings it was easy for the archbishop to conclude that the attempt had been deliberate.

By the time of the Resurrectionist muddle, plans were well underway to attempt to counter the influence of the Kruszkas in another way. In December 1906, Messmer and his supporters among the Polish clergy of the archdiocese founded a new weekly paper in Milwaukee, *Nowiny Polskie* (The Polish News). The editor of the new paper was Rev. Boleslaus Goral, a professor of languages at the diocesan seminary. Something of a linguist and philologist, Goral had been teaching at the seminary since his ordination in 1899 and had gained some writing experience by collaborating in preparation of the *Catholic Encyclopedia* and by publishing *Orędownik Językowy* (The Language Messenger), a magazine devoted to Polish grammar. Not surprisingly, he was also an old antagonist of Wenceslaus Kruszka.[49]

Twenty-two priests wrote a letter, published in the *Nowiny* of June 19, 1907, stating they had formed the corporation voluntarily and that Messmer owned stock principally because he had been asked for support. However, the evidence shows that Messmer was heavily involved in the paper's origins. Wenceslaus Kruszka reported that Messmer had asked every pastor to buy ten shares (at $50 each) and every assistant pastor to buy four shares to help provide capital.[50] Three weeks after the first issue, Goral wrote to Messmer about the discouraging status of the paper: subscriptions had not yet reached 1,000; cooperation from other priests was "not always encouraging"; money was short; and most of the responsibility for advancing the project lay with Goral. In seeking a solution, he cited Messmer's previous activities for the paper: "Your Grace knows well that without you, the local priests would never have come to an agreement."[51]

Goral therefore directed a series of requests to the archbishop, reminding him "how much personal attention you are giving this matter" and appealing to his interest in having a "real Catholic paper" in Milwaukee. Unless the archbishop came to the aid of the shaky enterprise, Goral insisted, it would fail, and so he asked Messmer to communicate with the other bishops of the state to ask for their influence in requesting all Polish priests to buy shares. He also asked the prelate to instruct the pastors to announce from their pulpits that the paper had the "full and warm approval" of the archbishop. Goral also suggested that Messmer instruct the priests to recommend the paper personally; otherwise, he believed, many would simply read the episcopal letter without comment. Finally, he asked Messmer to write a letter of support, for translation into Polish and eventual publication in the *Nowiny*.

The archbishop complied with all three requests. He sent a circular letter to the Polish priests of the archdiocese, telling them that the support of the clergy was "absolutely necessary" for the paper's success and asking them to encourage subscriptions from the pulpit.[52] He addressed a letter to Goral, congratulating him on publishing a paper "to protect and promote the religious interests of the Polish Catholics . . . especially in our State of Wisconsin and [to] furnish reliable discussion and correct views on the religious, moral, and social questions." He especially recommended the *Nowiny* as an alternative to other papers which, pretending to be Catholic, were undermining the faith as "wolves in sheepsclothing":

> Nor can we admit to our Catholic houses any newspapers that will injure or weaken the strong and hearty Catholic faith and loyalty by spreading upon their columns every scandal occurring here and there among the children of the Church, priests or laymen, or by perverting the true teaching of the Church regarding her authority and her laws, or by sowing the seeds of suspicion, dissatisfaction, and disobedience regarding the lawfully appointed Bishops through continual haughty criticising of the Hierarchy and its ordinances.

The letter, which appeared in the *Nowiny* on February 27, 1907, disclosed that the bishops of the province endorsed and supported the paper. Messmer concluded with praise for Goral's "noble and arduous undertaking." On June 5, when the paper carried a picture of Pius X and his apostolic blessing for the directors, workers, and subscribers of the *Nowiny*, the circle of hierarchical endorsement was complete.

Although they had the full force of Church authority on their side, the *Nowiny*'s writers were at first moderate in their relationship with the *Kuryer*. The inaugural issue pledged that the paper was not interested in condemning those who were more nationally minded, but it defended Messmer against charges of being a German (he was actually German-Swiss) and it published letters from individuals who were dissatisfied with Wenceslaus Kruszka's column.[53] Later, when the editors had gained more confidence, they began to attack the *Kuryer* and the Kruszkas with gusto. Despite Goral's early fears, the *Nowiny* attracted enough subscribers to convert to a daily in April 1908. By then nobody could deny that it had become a permanent opposition paper to the *Kuryer*.

Wenceslaus Kruszka reacted to the new paper with predictable ire. He refused the archbishop's request to support a paper he regarded as having been formed to make polemical attacks on his brother. He accused its backers of trying to carry forward the campaign for Polish bishops by ingratiating themselves with German and Irish church leaders. And he dubbed the new publication "Nowiny Niemiecki" (The German News), sponsored by "Hakatists who wish to devour the whole Polish nationality." For him, it was further proof that the Catholic bishops of the state were "Teutonic Knights" trying to preserve their domain from the encroachments of Poles. "Away with your hypocritical faith of the Teutonic Knights!" he wrote angrily. "Long live the Catholic and Polish faith!"[54] The *Kuryer* followed his lead by referring to the *Nowiny* as "the local organ of the German bishops, printed in Polish," and claimed that Jan Pitass had expressed a similar opinion.[55]

Such protests drew the bishops' attention ever more to Wenceslaus Kruszka's columns. Ultimately, his public defiance of Wisconsin's hierarchical authorities led them to means sterner than warnings in their attempt to preserve their authority and the loyalty of Poles. The first bishop to act was Green Bay's Joseph Fox, who forbade Kruszka to preach the eulogy at the funeral of the Polish pastor in Antigo on March 23, 1907. Four days later, Fox circulated a letter revoking Kruszka's faculties and preaching rights in the diocese.[56]

Kruszka's angry response, in his column of April 4, termed Fox an oppressor who was worse than the pagans for refusing to honor the last wishes of the dead. At the same time he wrote to Messmer, reminding him "that it is the 12th year that I am oppressed" by being left in Ripon without transfer to a larger pastorate. "You oppressed me so long and you may oppress me even longer," he wrote, "but don't wonder then, I have a bitter feeling of 'no confidence' in you." He concluded the letter with the same aphorism he used in the *Kuryer* article against Fox:

"Every oppressor is guilty not only of the wrong he does but of the evil to which he inclines the heart of the oppressed."[57]

Almost immediately, Kruszka received a Latin dispatch from Messmer (dated March 30), forbidding him "under strict command" to write any more articles for the *Kuryer*. The stated reason was Messmer's desire to prevent further danger to the Catholic faith and additional scandal among faithful Polish Catholics. The letter was appended to the April 4 article, together with Kruszka's pledge that he would obey, although he felt himself innocent:

> "True, my conscience does not reproach me at all, but that does not prove that I am acquitted: the Lord alone is my judge." (1 Cor. 4:4)

> Be well, Countrymen! May God keep you in His care!

To Messmer, Kruszka addressed a short, almost jaunty letter:

> You suspended my pen for the "Kuryer Polski"; and I need not tell you, that, no matter whether the pen is guilty or not, I hang it up on the wall—although by this your precept I suffer a heavy financial loss. This will be the best proof, that it was and is a Catholic pen.[58]

The *Kuryer* retained Kruszka's column for a while as a format for letters of protest and sympathetic editorials from other papers. The *Nowiny* was silent about the affair, except to print a letter speculating that disobedience would lead to Kruszka's excommunication.[59] But there was little likelihood that he would refuse to comply. From the start, he had made it clear that he preferred to press his cause within the structures of the Church. He had summarily rejected overtures from independent bishops in Scranton and Chicago, and urged that the dissidents return to Rome. At the time of Symon's visit he had released a public letter to the independents, urging them to make their submission to the pope through the mediation of the Polish visitor.[60] The stilling of Kruszka's pen (and even his voice in some parts of the state) considerably limited his options for publicizing the cause, but he continued to cling to the papal promise and his belief that American bishops were the real villains. That was enough to justify his loyalty to the Church and his opposition to the bishops.

On April 10, less than a week after Wenceslaus Kruszka's final column, Michael Kruszka and his wife invited the city's prominent Poles, clerical and lay, to the celebration of their Silver Wedding. Unlike the opening of the *Kuryer*'s new plant one year earlier, however, the only priest to attend this celebration was Wenceslaus Kruszka.[61] In the course of 1906, the other Polish clerics had abandoned whatever pretense of friendship they might have shared with Michael Kruszka. With varying degrees of enthusiasm, they had formed a newspaper to oppose the *Kuryer*'s policies and cooperate more closely with the bishops. Now they had to take care to emphasize their differences because feelings of self-righteousness and moral superiority were making the barriers too high to transcend. Ironically, the goals on both sides were virtually identical: a greater voice for Polish-Americans in the life of their Church.

Thus the pope's promise, originally a source of hope and almost unanimous joy, had become a stumbling block. For Wenceslaus Kruszka, it was the force that activated an entire crusade, a principle against which he could judge the pastoral effectiveness and good faith of the American bishops. For Michael Kruszka, it was a justification for insisting on national recognition in the most forceful manner. And for the *Nowiny* priests, driven by fears of ecclesiastical disunion into the arms of bishops who were still on record against the forced appointment of Polish-Americans, it was a sign of hope, to be protected rather than proclaimed. Few of them disagreed on the desirability of Polish bishops, but Wenceslaus Kruszka's confrontational stance was forcing them to take open positions. Neither his "exile" in Ripon nor his silencing had driven him from the Church. And as long as he remained a loyal son of Rome, Kruszka could not let his fellow Catholics forget about his conversation with the pope.

5. From Resistance to Revolt

SEBASTIAN MESSMER'S DECISION to intervene in the campaign for Polish bishops led to a more acrimonious phase in the dispute. To maintain his authority, the archbishop attempted to attract support among Polish Catholics by assaulting the ideological positions and popular following of the Kruszka brothers. In the process, he relied rather heavily on Boleslaus Goral and the *Nowiny Polskie*. For better or worse, Messmer became identified with the editor's policies and his argument that the archbishop could be trusted to protect both religion and nationality. Even after Wenceslaus Kruszka was silenced and the *Nowiny* was launched, however, the Kruszkas retained their influence and resourcefulness. Less afraid of conflict than their opponents, they continued to press for change while yielding to the increasingly emotional nature of the arguments. After several years had passed in this way, it was no longer the controversy but its nature which posed the greatest challenge to the archbishop's attainment of his goals.

By late spring of 1907 straws indicating the growth of animosity were in the wind. The *Nowiny* was in full attack on the Kruszka family, criticizing Michael for not sending his daughter to a Catholic school and for destroying the unity of the Church. Priests and teaching sisters attacked his *Kuryer* from the pulpit and in the classroom. Wenceslaus, too, was denounced: he opposed the authority of the Church; he had violated the regulations of the Green Bay Diocese; he was a "good-for-nothing" and "strictly bound in conscience to remedy the evil and the scandal sowed." Other articles claimed that he was being punished for his activities by his prolonged assignment to Ripon and that his expulsion from the Jesuits was an indication that he lacked a vocation to the priesthood.[1]

Michael Kruszka responded to the attacks in a twenty-three-page personal letter to Messmer on June 13. The archbishop, he wrote, was responsible for influencing and publicly supporting a paper which had been formed for a dubious purpose: "to slander your personal enemies, real or imaginary, and—their families!" He criticized the choice of Goral as editor, claiming the priest's classmates had considered him "foolishly arrogant, of shallow mind, and servile to his superiors." Finally, Kruszka held that the papal blessing for the paper had been obtained under false pretenses, "for no one would knowingly bless such products of human depravity and degeneration." He also defended his brother as a loyal Catholic priest whose only mistake had been to draw attention to himself by his mission to Rome. The *Nowiny's* attacks on Father Kruszka, Michael wrote, were part of a plot to goad him into disobeying the prohibition so that there would be grounds for excommunication.

Kruszka next considered nationalism and schism within the Church. Citing the traditional loyalty of European Poles to Catholicism, even in the face of "Pole-baiting" by German bishops, he argued that the American Poles who had joined independent churches had been forced to do so by the circumstances:

> They were driven from [Roman Catholicism] by the grossest injustice, by the trampling upon their human rights by some anti-Polish bishops with the help of some depraved Polish priests. Had we here truly Polish bishops, men with knowledge of Polish customs and character, men *just and true Apostles of Christ,* nothing of the kind would have ever happened. And *if the Roman Catholic Church loses the three million Polish Catholics of this country, it will be because they will be driven from the Church by some anti-Polish bishops,* whose motto seems to be, "If we cannot keep the Poles for ourselves, if they should have bishops of their own, then let them rather leave the Church. What *we* cannot have, the *Church* shall not have either."

The real reason for the failure to admit the necessity of Polish bishops, he concluded, was fear that American bishops would lose political influence and income as a result. Even the schools, Kruszka claimed, had been mobilized to force support for the *Nowiny* by ostracizing and even punishing students who defended the *Kuryer*. In the process, the need for real education and upgrading the inferior teaching staffs was ignored.

Near the letter's end, Kruszka defended himself against the charge of pugnacity. He said he respected religion and that his primary concern as a publisher was truth, but he would engage in combat when it was forced upon him.

> . . . as much as I dislike "war," when that is *forced on me,* especially in a scandalous way, I do not shrink from it. I fight to the best of my ability, not forgetting the motto that "in war everything is fair", especially in a defensive war. The present warlike state of

affairs *has been forced upon me by your organ,* and therefore I cannot be blamed for it, but those who started it.

The publisher warned Messmer that his authority among the people was being weakened and he urged him to be more fair minded in the future, to prevent further erosion of his reputation. The desire of the Poles, he concluded, was that their nationality be respected.

Kruszka backed his words with deeds in November and December by printing letters critical of Messmer and a series of articles titled "Why Is Father Kruszka Persecuted?" He also visited Archbishop Diomede Falconio, the papal delegate, in January 1908. The delegate refused to endorse the idea of separate bishops for Poles, but claimed that once the Polish priests settled their disagreements a Polish bishop would be selected. Kruszka described the meeting as cordial and printed a full report.[2]

Wenceslaus Kruszka was also taking steps to defend himself against the *Nowiny*. At the end of May 1907 he asked Messmer's permission to answer the accusations by writing to the *Kuryer*. Instead of that, the archbishop recommended an ecclesiastical trial and asked for a specification of charges. After receiving the response, Messmer temporized on a date for hearings. Kruszka protested that the attacks were continuing and that their content publicly contradicted Messmer's private assurances to him. Finally, failing to gain satisfaction in Milwaukee, Kruszka wrote to Falconio in June to ask for $10,000 damages and assignment to a Milwaukee parish as proof that the Ripon assignment was not a form of punishment, as the *Nowiny* claimed. The delegate wrote to Messmer, but it was October 4 before the preliminary hearings started.[3] In four meetings, held over more than two months, Kruszka and Goral presented their cases to Rev. Richard Smith and Rev. Joseph LaBoule, professors at the seminary. According to the minutes, most of the discussion concerned the correct translation of questionable passages from the *Nowiny*. But in the end, there was little question that the articles had impugned Kruszka's reputation.[4]

As months passed without submission of a report, Kruszka impatiently and repeatedly petitioned Messmer for a decision. The matter, he claimed, was all the more urgent because the articles were continuing and were damaging church authority and the *Nowiny*'s reputation as a Catholic paper. In March 1908, Messmer explained to Kruszka that the delay was caused by LaBoule's failure to submit an evaluation.[5] Smith's report, however, was a clear vindication for Kruszka. Goral, he wrote, had to be presumed guilty of either slander or detraction "until [he] shall show . . . that said charges are truths and facts about the plaintiff which the defendant had a right to publish in a Catholic paper in the interests of the Church." In Smith's opinion, there was sufficient matter to proceed with a canonical trial, but he urged that Kruszka be persuaded to accept a compromise because such a trial would be detrimental to Catholic interests.[6]

The chances for compromise, however, were slight. Although Wenceslaus Kruszka had severed his formal connection with the *Kuryer*, Boleslaus Goral continued to hold him responsible for its policies. For that reason, he wrote to Kruszka in January 1908 to urge him to withdraw the complaint. He warned that his patience was at an end, particularly because of the *Kuryer*'s attacks on him and he threatened to print more extreme articles, if necessary.

> Withdraw publicly and privately those vile insinuations; withdraw your complaint before the Delegate and the Archbishop—in a word, try by every means conscientiously to correct the wrong done against me, and I will offer you the hand of agreement and give up all further steps. If, however, this does not happen in the shortest possible time, I will not be responsible for whatever I have to do on my part—and in my own defense![7]

If Goral believed he could intimidate Kruszka with such a letter, he was naive. More interesting was the fact that, like Michael Kruszka, he saw no more in his actions than legitimate self-defense.

Partly in his own defense and partly to relieve some of Wenceslaus Kruszka's bitterness over the continuing attacks in the *Nowiny* and the slow progress of his canonical complaint, Messmer undertook several conciliatory gestures in 1908. In March he promised Father Kruszka a larger parish as soon as an appropriate opening occurred. And in April he confided that his coming trip to Rome would be used partly to support the effort for a Polish bishop:

> I can answer you—*privately and not for the public*—that I shall do all I can in Rome to hasten the appointment of a Polish bishop, be it in Chicago, Buffalo, or Milwaukee. Now this I tell *to you* to let you see that it is not I that fights the Poles, as the "Kuryer" always insinuates.[8]

While in Rome, Messmer discussed Kruszka and his campaign with Joseph Antonucci, who later assured Kruszka that Messmer bore him a fatherly love and wished for reconciliation. He advised his friend in Ripon to be more understanding of the archbishop, to abandon further concern for the *Kuryer*, and to trust in Messmer as a friend of the Poles.[9]

When he returned in the fall, Messmer announced the appointment of Boleslaus Goral as pastor of St. Vincent's Parish in Milwaukee. The transfer was a result of Goral's urgent complaint that his health was beginning to suffer under the strain of editing a newspaper and teaching in the seminary.[10] He had requested a new assignment in March but Messmer, evidently, had not informed Kruszka about Goral's priority for assignment to a Milwaukee parish. Not surprisingly, the announcement led to a strong protest in the October 15 *Kuryer*, suggesting that St. Vincent's would now be forced to use its funds to bolster the financially troubled *Nowiny*.

Messmer's response, equally forceful, was printed in the *Nowiny* two days later. He called Goral "one of our most exemplary and educated Polish priests" and accused the *Kuryer* of trying to poison the hearts and minds of the parishioners against their new pastor. The *Kuryer*, he concluded, was totally unreliable in reporting church affairs and was "working continually against the true spiritual and religious interests of Polish Catholics."

Wenceslaus Kruszka, still angered by the "outrageous injustice" by which he was forbidden to answer the constant attacks from *Nowiny* and frustrated by Messmer's failure to expedite his case against Goral, also took to the public forum. He told a *Sentinel* reporter in an interview published on October 23 that Goral had libeled him and that Messmer refused to stop it. Kruszka characterized the archbishop's statement on Goral as "a disgrace to the Polish priesthood." Bernard Traudt, vicar general of the archdiocese, responded in Messmer's absence. The following day he told the *Sentinel* that Wenceslaus Kruszka's actions "deserve of drastic punishment":

> In my opinion the archbishop has been too kind—too considerate. He has long overlooked rebellious actions. A man less kindly by nature would have snapped the neck of that opposition long ago.

Traudt also discussed Kruszka's suit against *Nowiny*, reporting that the ecclesiastical council had found it inadvisable to allow Kruszka to proceed. At that point, Traudt said, Kruszka "had the temerity" to write to the apostolic delegate. The root of Kruszka's anger, he concluded, was jealousy of Goral.

When Messmer returned to Milwaukee, he refused to follow the vicar general's suggestion to discipline the younger Kruszka, probably because of the letter Wenceslaus Kruszka sent him (pointing out that Traudt's statement suggested that a decision had been made without informing either the plaintiff or the apostolic delegate). When it turned out that Traudt's information had been incorrect, Kruszka resumed his efforts to obtain a decision.[11]

At about the same time, the archbishop began to distance himself publicly from the *Nowiny*. The policy was evident when Bernard Traudt, in a *Sentinel* interview on October 22, called Michael Kruszka's allegation that Messmer had financial interest in *Nowiny* "a damnable lie." Two days later, the *Kuryer* carried an unprecedented English-language front page, featuring a letter from Kruszka to Messmer as the "controlling publisher of . . . *Nowiny*." The archbishop soon issued a denial that he had ever been an officer, director, or stockholder of *Nowiny*. His shares, he stated, had been assigned to a third party, and his only intervention had been to exhort the editors to print the truth and avoid personalities.[12]

But Goral saw the matter in a somewhat different light. In a long report on the status of the paper at the time of its conversion to a daily in March 1908, he had written the archbishop: "You have made me the possessor of 10 shares. . . . I regard it not as a donation, but only as a fund 'placed in my trust' in order to remove every possible clue from the Kruszkas [sic] penetrating eye." The letter also revealed the tendency of Goral, hard pressed by the *Kuryer*, to turn to Messmer for support and encouragement "as a son writes openly and with full confidence to his good and kind Father."[13] Nevertheless, by the end of 1908 it was becoming clear that Messmer was no longer eager to have his name identified with the *Nowiny*. He could not fully control the material which was being printed, and the paper's continuing criticism of Wenceslaus Kruszka put him in a difficult position.

The younger Kruszka pressed his case against Goral through 1908. In November he visited Falconio on the matter but found the delegate hostile. He urged Kruszka to withdraw the complaint and suggested that his activities were partly responsible for the continued growth of the independent movement. But Kruszka replied that the *Nowiny* was the real aggressor and that the schism could have been stopped earlier by appointment of a Polish bishop. Falconio maintained later that his only concern in the interview had been to warn against further scandals, but Kruszka found in it another occasion for protesting his own innocence:

> I prayed and pray God to die rather than to lose the grace of true faith. By the grace of God I avoided and will avoid sinful scandals. But I cannot be held responsible either for the past or for future pharisaical scandals, nor for such scandals which are the necessary outcome of an unjust treatment.[14]

Thus Wenceslaus Kruszka, too, had come to the point of denying responsibility for the situation, while claiming the right of self-defense.

The impasse over Kruszka's suit against Goral was finally resolved by the appointment of a Polish bishop, after Archbishop James Quigley of Chicago requested a Polish auxiliary for Chicago in 1907. At Quigley's direction, the new bishop, Paul P. Rhode, was chosen by the Polish priests of the archdiocese from their own ranks. His consecration, on July 29, 1908, was celebrated by Polish Catholics all over the country. The Polish press of Wisconsin, including Milwaukee's two papers and the new Franciscan magazine, *Miesięcznik Franciszkański* (The Franciscan Monthly) of Pulaski, shared in the joy. The *Kuryer* presented Rhode with a congratulatory address on parchment and the *Nowiny* pointed proudly to the fact that the bishop was a stockholder.[15]

The peculiar circumstances of Rhode's nomination and the reception given him by the other prelates made clear that Rhode's responsibilities extended beyond Chicago, to caring for and mediating among Polish Catholics in the entire United States. That was the view of Rhode's Polish contemporaries, including Wenceslaus Kruszka and Edward Kozlowski (later auxiliary bishop in Milwaukee), and it has been the view of several generations of historians. Rhode himself acted as one whose responsibilities had special application to an entire ethnic group. He received the return to Roman allegiance of independent parishes and priests in Cleveland, Duluth, St. Louis, and Bayonne (N.J.) shortly after his consecration, and in August 1908 he visited the Polish settlements in Portage County to administer confirmation and dedicate a school.[16] *Rolnik* wrote on August 14 of his appearance in Stevens Point: "The first bishop-countryman on this foreign soil brought the emotions of the . . . people to a zenith."

Wenceslaus Kruszka took advantage of Rhode's appointment to ask for his help in the campaign for a better assignment. Rhode urged patience and tact, but he contacted Messmer. In December 1908 he asked Kruszka to drop his unresolved suit against the *Nowiny* and Goral; the charges, he said, discredited both sides, irritated Church authorities, and did damage to the general good of Poles. He promised that withdrawal of the charges would work to Kruszka's benefit. Although Kruszka resented the request as evidence that Rhode was attempting to ingratiate himself with the American bishops by sacrificing the interest of Poles, he complied. He wrote to Rhode, Messmer, Goral, and Falconio on the last day of 1908 to withdraw the charges, insisting that he was acting only in response to Rhode's request and warning that he would enter a new complaint if the personal attacks of the *Nowiny* continued. All but Goral replied with thanks and praise for Kruszka's decision. Messmer even wrote that he would ask Goral to make Kruszka a salaried contributor to the *Nowiny*, though nothing ever came of it.[17]

Nevertheless, the *Nowiny*'s attacks on Wenceslaus Kruszka continued, and after a few months he renewed his complaint. Once again, he asked Messmer and Falconio for justice.[18] Although Kruszka didn't know it, Falconio was more sympathetic by then. He wrote to Messmer that some of the paper's passages about Kruszka were "indeed objectionable.'' Responsibility for stopping the attacks, Falconio wrote, rested squarely with Messmer:

> It is indeed a source of deep regret and concern, that a Catholic Newspaper, and one which is under Your Grace's protection, should speak so uncharitable [sic] and so bitterly of anyone, much less against a priest. The results cannot but be most serious. . . .
> It is imperative that something be done to put an end to these scandals, for I fear that if a speedy termination is not put to the trouble, a much more painful and scandalous condition of affairs will result. I beg Your Grace to do your utmost to restore peace and harmony among the Polish people, and to end this disastrous war and threatened schism.

Falconio's impatience was understandable: Wenceslaus Kruszka's persistent appeals and the danger of more serious division made the situation urgent. And the delegate had reason to doubt Messmer's desire to expedite a solution. He had written to the archbishop three times in 1907 and 1908 to counsel speed in resolving Kruszka's first complaint, and he wrote in April 1909 that his letter of March had received no reply.[19]

Ultimately, Messmer responded by granting Kruszka's desire for a Milwaukee pastorate. In September 1909 he offered him St. Adalbert's Parish, noting that the assignment was given through the intervention of Bishop Rhode. In moving to Milwaukee, Messmer suggested, Kruszka would have the opportunity to exercise a moderating influence on the *Kuryer*; but the hope was unrealistic. Kruszka had resigned as a director of the company in 1907 at the archbishop's request and, in June 1909, had written Messmer that he had little influence over the *Kuryer*'s policy: "I can assure Your Excellency, that if I had any authority over the Kuryer, the whole Kuryer's spirit and tendency would be changed *in one day*."[20]

In fact, Wenceslaus had already tried to persuade his brother to change the editorial direction of the paper. In February 1909 he had disagreed strongly with Michael over an issue of parish finance in Milwaukee. In rejecting his brother's allegation that he was advocating disobedience to canon law, Michael urged Wenceslaus not to abandon the rights of the people or open himself to ridicule from the archbishop. Church politics, the publisher maintained, was concerned with "favoritism, intrigue, cunning in giving little and obtaining much." The issue at hand, therefore, was purely a matter of strength and force. Wenceslaus viewed that statement as an indication of his brother's growing bitterness and his own lack of influence at the *Kuryer*.[21] He felt caught between the hammer and the anvil. On one hand, his brother ignored his advice and chided him for attempting to change the *Kuryer*; on the other hand, the archbishop believed Wenceslaus had influence and wrongly refused to use it.

Among the other points of conflict which emerged while Kruszka's complaint was pending, few aroused greater debate than the catechism issue. According to an instruction in the *Handbook for Catholic Parishioners of the Milwaukee Archdiocese* (issued in 1907), religious instructions were to be bilingual, using catechisms with English and foreign-language texts on facing pages so the children could read them in whatever language they understood better. Those who opposed the method, the *Handbook* stated, showed "a lamentable ignorance of the needs of the Catholic Church in this country or a sinful and blind national fanaticism." The instruction provoked an immediate reaction from many Polish Catholics who regarded it as another instance of forced Americanization through the Church.

Wenceslaus Kruszka saw the situation as additional proof of the necessity of Polish bishops in America. He wrote to Messmer that the double catechism was against all didactic principles for the Poles because, unlike the relationship between German and English, there is no affinity between Polish and English. Children would be tempted, he argued, to "waste more time comparing the *languages* than in learning the *thing*." He was not opposed to teaching English, Kruszka concluded, but simply to using so important a subject as religion to accomplish that purpose.[22]

Kruszka gained support from Casimir Sztuczko, who wrote for the Executive Committee of the Polish American Congress that the new rule was a "moral slap" at Poles because it implied they were ignoramuses and sinners when they taught religious subjects in Polish. The *Kuryer* concurred, finding in the measure another instance of the archbishop's "Hakatism."[23]

This sense of outrage prompted Messmer to address a letter to Hyacinth Gulski which was published in *Nowiny* on September 28. There were practical reasons, the archbishop insisted, for teaching religion in English when the students could understand it. "A few self-conscious agitators" among them, unfortunately, some priests, were trying to mislead simple people by encouraging them to believe the bishops were their enemies, "at the risk of leading the Polish people away from Catholic unity into schism and rebellion. . . . [under] the trumpet of a false patriotism which would plant the flag of Polish nationalism even higher than the standard of the Catholic faith." It had not been his intention, Messmer wrote, to attack Polish repute and nationality; his sole concern was the good of the Catholic religion in the

United States. Under the circumstances, it was difficult for many Polish Catholics to understand the distinction.

A second issue which regularly entered the debate was the quality of the parish schools. Michael Kruszka had been concerned about the matter since the early 1890s, but his efforts to apply pressure had consistently engendered opposition from the pastors, who regarded the schools as their prerogative. Kruszka was correct in finding the condition of many parochial schools lamentable, but it would be incorrect to single out Polish schools in this regard; even the public schools were not necessarily preparing the children of immigrants for the sort of upward economic and social mobility which Kruszka envisioned. After the appearance of the *Nowiny*, Kruszka's ideological concern was reinforced by his business sense: he started to protest that the *Nowiny* was promoted in parochial classrooms. But the *Nowiny*'s writers sprang quickly to the schools' defense, arguing as early as 1907 that Kruszka's criticism of the schools did not result in their improvement.[24]

Another critical disagreement involved the St. Josaphat debt. By 1908, estimates ranged as high as $700,000, and Messmer was forced to journey to Rome in the hope of finding a religious order to assume responsibility for the parish and its financial obligations. His reasoning was that a religious order would have greater potential for raising the funds because of its simpler way of life and the additional income it could earn by giving parish missions and devotional exercises around the country. At the end of the year he announced that the Conventual Franciscans, with American headquarters in Buffalo, would take the parish and assume $400,000 of the debt. Father Hyacinth Fudzinski, the new pastor, was the American provincial of the order and had a reputation for financial acumen. Fudzinski, in accepting the appointment, noted that his group was not in any sense "buying" the basilica but merely assuming a huge obligation which would be difficult to discharge.[25]

Fudzinski's first action after coming to Milwaukee was to call a meeting of the parishioners for January 13, 1910. The session, widely covered in the press, met at the height of a terrible blizzard, and Fudzinski acknowledged that the weather matched the mood of those in attendance. He placed the debt at $600,000 on church properties valued at $350,000; furthermore, the total annual income of the parish amounted to barely half the interest. The Franciscans' share of the debt, he stated, included $200,000 in private notes held by the parishioners. He pledged all the resources and efforts of his order to relieve the situation, but requested sacrifice by the parish members as well. Specifically, he asked them to accept repayment of 75 percent on their

notes, without interest. There were few alternatives: full repayment
could not begin for at least twenty-five years, and suing the parish would
waste money in litigation. Furthermore, this contribution of $50,000
would decrease the interest rate on the debt. Generously, the parishioners voted to accept the offer.

To expedite payment of the archdiocesan share of the debt,
Messmer set up an assessment committee to apportion the amount over
all the parishes in five annual installments. He stated his reasons for the
collection in a circular letter in September 1909.[26] It was useless to
assess blame, he wrote, because the responsible parties were dead. His
real concern was for the parishioners themselves—"innocent victims of
years of maladministration." He praised the Conventual Franciscans
for their help in avoiding a terrible scandal and in helping to preserve the
financial reputation of the Catholic Church. Above all, he was careful to
consider the pride of the Poles; he particularly praised their generosity
and loyalty to the Church, and urged others in the archdiocese to follow
their example.

> Nationality must make no difference. The very contrary; for are
> not the Polish Catholics best known among us . . . by their
> generous liberality towards the Church. The very greatness of the
> disaster . . . is a loud attestation of Polish Catholic generosity.
> And if we look at the Polish Nation in the history of the Catholic
> Church, what other nation surpasses her in the hard battles fought
> for the defense and the protection of the Catholic religion . . . .

The message concluded with an appeal for brotherly love and understanding in remedying an unfortunate situation.

Reactions to the message followed predictable channels. The
Nowiny praised the arrangement as the best which could be expected,
but the *Kuryer* condemned the leaders of the past, who "sucked the last
drop of blood, and when it [was] gone, discard[ed] it to look for other
plentiful delights." The real losers, it concluded, were the Poles.[27]
Wenceslaus Kruszka concurred. He was especially angry because he
had always been willing to accept the Josaphat pastorate. Instead, he
claimed, Messmer had chosen young and inexperienced men.

Wenceslaus also noted widespread anger among the Poles. Although he may have exaggerated the point, there were grounds for
discontent. According to the Third Baltimore Council, money could be
borrowed at interest by priests and parishes only with the bishop's
consent. Whatever their efforts to retire the debt before 1908, therefore,
Katzer and Messmer bore the ultimate responsibility for allowing the
problem to develop. That the archbishop did not undertake full repayment seemed to Kruszka an example of his failure to meet his respon-

sibilities toward the Poles. At St. Adalbert's, Kruszka backed his trustees in their refusal to pay the Josaphat assessment and in introducing full financial disclosure as a regular parish policy.[28]

Kruszka had developed his ideas on episcopal responsibility in May 1909, when by request he wrote two articles for the Chicago publication, *Polonia*. (Although the second article was refused for publication, he included it in his memoirs.)[29] Essentially, he argued the principle that love is the necessary content of the form supplied by faith. There is, he claimed, only one way to evaluate the dedication of church leaders to that principle: Christ's statement, "By their fruits you shall know them" (Mt 7:16). In Kruszka's judgment, the fruit of many American churchmen did not indicate love of God and neighbor in the context of faith:

> Such a priest who wastes the money of poor people, or who slanders people or insults other associates; a bishop who allows all this—can they be successors of the Apostles?

Based on these assumptions, his conclusion was inescapable: leaders who did not practice love as an essential complement of faith were theoretical but not practical successors of the original disciples. In that context, loyalty to bishops assumed a more tenuous character.

In addition to his infrequent writings, Kruszka used his pulpit and the public forum to carry his crusade forward and to attack his opponents. In a sermon of September 1910 he responded to the *Nowiny*'s criticism by calling it a "lying, calumnous, Teutonic, cowardly paper." Several months later, he preached against socialism and clericalism as opposite evils. When Messmer summoned him to a hearing on the sermon, Kruszka acquitted himself by professing to condemn the clergy only when they went astray, as in the situation at St. Josaphat's.[30] In July 1910 he voiced his opinions at Milwaukee's commemoration of the 500th anniversary of the Battle of Grunwald. Addressing a crowd of 40,000, Kruszka linked the circumstances of Poles in Wisconsin to the persecution of Poles by Teutonic Knights who professed to act in the name of Christianity. Thus he placed responsibility for the present plight of Poles on the doorstep of the Germans:

> Look around you. Who is here the chief administrator of our public institutions, of our churches and schools? A German. Who educates our priests? A German. Who educates our teachers and organists? A German. Who educates our teaching nuns? A German. Who supplies the pews, altars, chalices, vestments and other decorations for our churches? A German. In a word, in our public life we are still paying rent . . . to the Germans.

The time had come to stand alone, for Poles to follow the pope in matters of religion but to be independent in developing commercial enterprises, seminaries, dioceses, and other forms of self-expression. Strong determination, not politeness and forbearance, was to be the means. "Neither hospitality nor pleas nor gifts will please the Teutonic serpent," he concluded, quoting from Adam Mickiewicz, the national poet. Other speakers, even outspoken supporters of the *Nowiny*, argued similarly in extolling the victory of Poland over the Germans. But the greatest impact, by far, was made by Wenceslaus Kruszka, who again became the object of rumors that action would be taken against him.[31]

The *Kuryer* adopted a parallel line, particularly after it announced, on December 8, 1910, that Bethman-Hollweg's government had forbidden its circulation in the German Empire on the grounds of "inciting dangerous political agitation." Michael Kruszka told an interviewer that he suspected the prohibition had been inspired by persons in the United States. Editorially, he stressed full control by Poles over all aspects of their religious life, including property ownership. Wisconsin's bishops, one article suggested, were most interested in relieving Poles of their money; so the obvious answer was to withhold contributions. Thus the "Don't Pay" campaign, which the *Kuryer* had been advocating for several years, achieved new prominence. It was to be the means by which the bishops would be forced to recognize the rights of Poles.[32]

Refusal of payment, as Michael Kruszka shortly learned, can work in both directions. At its annual convention in September 1910, the Polish Association of America approved the recommendation of its chaplain, Boleslaus Goral, to transfer its official printing from the *Kuryer* to the *Nowiny*. The *Nowiny* insisted that the action amounted to a repudiation of Kruszka's paper, but Kruszka responded with charges of corrupt administration. He supported dissident members in a complaint to state insurance officials which eventually forced the officers to pay for their printing from the treasury instead of levying an additional assessment on the members.[33] The Catholic press also continued its efforts to encourage loyalty—and contributions—to the Church. As early as 1909, the *Nowiny* printed reports from Polish parishioners that the Don't Pay campaign was unsuccessful. Other editorials and letters stressed the Old Country idea that priests are the true and natural leaders of Poles. The best solution to the problem of the bad press, writers repeated, was to cooperate with Catholic organizations and priests. Francis Manel adopted a similar stance in his publications in Pulaski. The correct solution to the plague of "godless papers," he wrote, was not to pay for them, by canceling subscriptions.[34]

In this way the struggle continued, with evidence of success and failure on both sides. Indications of the *Kuryer*'s influence began to appear with regularity in the annual parish reports submitted to the Chancery Office of the Green Bay Diocese. At the end of 1907, for instance, the pastor at Krakow complained that the paper was having an adverse effect on his congregation, and in 1908 the pastor in Oshkosh reported that the *Kuryer* was the bane of his parish and that he had forbidden children to read it under pain of being refused absolution. By 1911, the pastor at Krakow complained that about half of the 108 families in his congregation were not paying their parish assessments because of the paper's influence.

Early in 1911, having constantly searched for ways to advance his cause and press his opponents, Michael Kruszka appealed publicly to *Kuryer* readers all over the country for information on the financial management of Polish parishes. The replies spurred the editors to send a twenty-four-item questionnaire to 10,000 Polish families all over the country in July and a similar query to the Poles of Milwaukee County in September. The questions probed all facets of parish life, including the level at which financial decisions were made, the popularity of the pastor, and the priests' stance on the *Kuryer*. As the responses began to come in, they were printed under a heading which left little doubt about the editors' expectations: "Our Motto: We Demand Polish Bishops for the Poles! We Demand That Polish Parish Property Be Assigned to the Polish Parishioners. We Demand That the Parishioners Themselves Control Parish Finances." Surprisingly, however, the respondents expressed general satisfaction with parish life and the parochial schools.[35]

Questionnaires, it turned out, were only the first step. In mid-August, the Milwaukee press reported that a group of laymen was being organized under the leadership of Martin Cyborowski to demand the appointment of Polish bishops.[36] The organization's true derivation became clear on September 23, when Michael Kruszka announced in the *Kuryer* the formation of the American Federation of Polish Catholic Laymen to work for Polish bishops and financial self-government in the parishes. To achieve these aims, Kruszka asserted, the Poles needed strong organization, even in the face of the "losses and persecution" which might attend the efforts. Organization was to begin with the parishes, which would be grouped in city and state organizations under the direction of a national steering committee. The first national convention would pass resolutions of support for the goals, set up a plan for Polish dioceses within the United States, and elect delegates to agitate the matter in Rome. Membership was to be open to Roman Catholics and to independents who signed pledges to return to Roman allegiance after the principal ends of the federation had been achieved.

The organization grew quickly. Eight hundred attended a meeting in September, and by early November officers claimed ninety-three groups in thirteen Polish parishes in the Milwaukee area. Michael Kruszka promoted the expansion by his willingness to adapt. When it became clear that the secularization of parish properties and finances was an unpopular issue, he published a personal letter to explain that he was dropping it as a federation goal. The issue was political, he said, and difficult to understand; it would be best advanced in cooperation with Catholics of other nationalities through state legislatures.

The citywide meeting of mid-December endorsed the remaining goals, relating to bishops and schools, and issued a plea for all Poles, clerical and lay, to join the effort. Kruszka also promoted the federation in the *Kuryer*, guaranteeing publicity in the four-state area—Wisconsin, Michigan, Minnesota, Illinois—where it circulated most widely. Papers in Buffalo, Detroit, and Chicago also offered support. Although Wenceslaus Kruszka publicly endorsed the federation, other priests were critical. Their objections, however, were not always effective: the *Kuryer* reported that 250 attended an organizational meeting at Boleslaus Goral's parish early in October, despite his opposition.[37]

Goral had several misgivings about the new group. The *Free Press* of August 18 carried his statement that national dioceses would destroy the unity of the Church. Furthermore, he argued, the Church had always enjoyed the right to make its own policies, whatever the consequences. "History bears lucid testimony to the fact that the Catholic church will rather suffer desertions than allow herself to be dictated to in matters regarding grave points of church policy." Goral admitted that the Polish priests and people in America would like more bishops, but he refused to sanction the means the federation proposed. Unless the effort were conducted in a manner indicating filial support for the Church, he predicted, it would fail:

> . . . influential Poles and Polish priests will not, cannot, identify themselves with the present movement. Let proper means and ways be resorted to and every true Polish Catholic will heartily cooperate. I repeat, let responsible persons take hold of the movement, let true Catholic means and ways be adopted and we all will join, because we all long for the day to see more Polish bishops in the American hierarchy.

Although he didn't mention Michael Kruszka by name, Goral attacked his right to pose as a Catholic leader, stating it was well known that he "has not been for many years a practical member of the Roman Catholic Church." Even the more moderate Hyacinth Gulski asserted that the matter of Polish bishops properly resided in Rome. Influenced by these arguments, a number of groups withdrew their initial approval of the federation's plan of action.[38]

It was an ironic coincidence that, at the very time the federation was being launched, word came that Joseph M. Koudelka, of Czech descent, had been appointed first auxiliary bishop in Milwaukee. Koudelka had been auxiliary bishop since 1908 in Cleveland, where he had exercised special jurisdiction over the Slavic people of the diocese. The *Nowiny* greeted the announcement with a noticeable lack of enthusiasm, giving only a short biographical statement on the new appointee, who was able to speak eight languages, including Polish. The *Kuryer* expressed unhappiness with the choice, calling it an insult to choose a Czech as bishop in a diocese in which Poles held a numerical preponderance over other Slavic immigrants. It was, the paper claimed, another instance of Messmer's "Machiavellian politics."[39]

The most surprising reaction by far was the petition which twenty-five Polish priests of the archdiocese addressed to Messmer about a month after the announcement. Although the petitioners did not mention the new auxiliary by name, they argued that his appointment was inadequate to stop the "virulent ferment" which boded great evil among the Poles. The cause of the unfortunate circumstances, they asserted, was the lack of a Polish bishop. While they were careful to dissociate themselves from the *Kuryer*'s efforts to increase lay participation in ecclesiastical policymaking and property ownership, they supported the campaign for Polish equality in the hierarchy. The endorsement had the ring of authenticity because they admitted that personal interest was involved: "The current report that wrangling among the Polish Clergy makes the appointment of a Polish bishop impossible is a slur on the Polish Clergy." For that reason, they indicated their willingness to set aside personal differences and accept any Polish priest as bishop. Finally, they pleaded for such an appointment as the best means to restore peace:

> We are in Conscience Convinced that the appointment of a Polish bishop for the Archdiocese will pacify the present pernicious agitation and tend to restore normal conditions; *therefore* we the Polish Clergy of the Archdiocese entreat Your Grace, in the name of religion, humbly but emphatically, to procure the appointment of a Polish Bishop.

Among the signers of the petition were Hyacinth Gulski, Boleslaus Goral, and Wenceslaus Kruszka.[40] It was a remarkable expression of solidarity for the times, an accurate indication of the priests' conviction that Koudelka's appointment was an inadequate gesture and a slur on them. Implicit also was an acknowledgement that, unaided by positive actions on Messmer's part, they could not resist Michael Kruszka's efforts to build a popular movement through the federation.

Wenceslaus Kruszka's stand against Koudelka was even stronger. The crux of the issue for him was that the appointment contradicted the pope's promise: "I do not believe that the pope would so disregard our wishes and his own promise as to appoint a Bohemian over us." Kruszka's protests to the English-language press drew a strong warning from Joseph Rainer, the archdiocesan vicar general, who told Kruszka he was risking schism for an unreasonable goal and asked him to use his influence among the Poles to restore tranquillity. But Kruszka replied that the only way to secure peace was to insist that the papal promise be fulfilled:

> This is the rock on which we stand. And still more, when not long ago the Polish people were incensed to the highest degree at the appointment of Bishop Koudelka, it was enough to remind them of the pope's words to quiet them. Neither you nor I can deny what the pope himself promised the Poles. And you can be certain that the Poles will not be content until they receive Polish bishops.[41]

Early in November, Kruszka wrote to Messmer to complain about Rainer's charges that he was not using his influence wisely. "I have striven for peace," he protested, "but I have also striven for justice." A broad, popular movement, such as the campaign for bishops, he argued, cannot be stopped but only channeled—which he had attempted to do. But, he claimed, with obvious exaggeration, the pope had promised Polish bishops in twelve dioceses, and Kruszka preferred death to seeing the promise deferred any longer.[42] Kruszka repeated substantially the same sentiments at a public meeting of Poles in Kenosha on December 10. People had asked him, he told his listeners, whether, in view of Koudelka's appointment, the pope had really promised Polish bishops. The answer was that the pope had indeed made a promise, and that it would be fulfilled.

> I believe firmly and unhesitatingly in this word of the Supreme Pontiff that it will be realized very soon, so soon, that you can rest assured that no other foreign bishop will enter officially my church, because the Archbishop himself will secure very soon a Polish Bishop in accordance with the Pope's promise and wishes,—if not, he will kill me and pass over my corpse on the way to my church. Such is my firm belief, such is my unshaken faith in the Supreme Pontiff's word. Any layman, priest, or bishop

who can take away this my faith in the Pope's word can just as well take my life.[43]

Easily interpreted as a direct assault on diocesan authority, the speech increased the pressure on Messmer to respond in an equally forceful way.

The Church's power was being mobilized to turn back the challenge to the hierarchy. In June 1911, Bishop Rhode preached a vigorous sermon in Milwaukee against the "bad press," and in August, Bishop E. A. Garvey of Altoona imposed the ban on the *Kuryer* and fourteen other papers. An anonymous writer told the *Kuryer* that her confessor had asked in the confessional whether she read the *Kuryer* and then had urged her to give it up. And in June the pastor of a parish in Waukesha complained to Messmer that he was yielding too much to the "more or less foreign dynasty within the arch-diocese."[44]

One of the last elements that was holding the situation together was removed on Christmas Eve, 1911, when Hyacinth Gulski died. Although he had been less active in the last years of his life, Gulski was the Pole who enjoyed almost universal respect. He had cooperated with Messmer and Goral in the organization of *Nowiny* but had remained inconspicuous in the journalistic war which ensued. Michael and Wenceslaus Kruszka accepted his titular leadership as one who stood above the factions. As a diocesan consultor, his influence was moderate, but nobody could question his devotion to the Polish cause. He had signed the petition at the time of Koudelka's appointment, and may even have helped to bring Kruszka and Goral together in agreeing upon a common gesture. He had been the most potent rallying point for union.

Shortly after Gulski's death, when he appointed Boleslaus Goral diocesan consultor, Messmer signalled that a more aggressive phase of the confrontation with the Kruszkas was about to begin. He could have chosen a more moderate individual if he had been interested in peace; instead, the archbishop deliberately dismissed whatever hope of reconciliation there might have been with Michael Kruszka and his newspapers. In the future, Messmer would receive stronger advice on methods of dealing with the publisher than he had ever received from Gulski, for Goral was more ambitious and subservient. He had already spent almost five years in a bitter, personal, and highly emotional public debate which Gulski had largely avoided. Goral had relied on Messmer to rescue him from failure at several points in the early days of the *Nowiny*, and Messmer had sheltered him, at least indirectly, from the wrath of Wenceslaus Kruszka and the impatience of the papal delegate at the time of the formal complaint. Although he had shown independence in signing the 1911 petition, Goral's thoughts were close to Messmer's. He was the archbishop's man.

Michael Kruszka, on the other hand, exhibited growing independence from the Church in pressing for goals which remained remarkably consistent over the years: better schools, tighter controls over the financial administration of parishes, and equality for Polish priests in the American hierarchy. Initially, he had advocated these reforms in a spirit not irreconcilable with the positions of the Church. But the appearance of the *Nowiny,* its semiofficial relationship to the archbishop as a Catholic journal, the forcefulness of its attacks on his family and his positions, and the failure of his personal appeals to Messmer and Falconio ultimately drove him to the strong and often unfortunate vehemence which characterized his journalism. Finally, he turned to the drastic measure of establishing the federation, an organization which professed to be both Catholic and opposed to the policies of the American bishops. The early indications of the federation's success and the worried reports from Polish pastors indicated that his efforts to effect a disenchantment of Poles with the structures and leaders of their Church were meeting with success. Controversial though they were, his methods produced results. Both Koudelka's appointment and the priests' petition of 1911 demonstrated how far his opponents were willing to go to meet his challenge.

Wenceslaus Kruszka, for his part, maintained his loyalty to the Church—and his obstreperous insistence that the pope's promise be respected. But the reactions to his efforts increased his disappointment and frustration. Messmer, after all, had left him in Ripon for a humiliating length of time and had been unwilling or unable to stop the *Nowiny*'s personal attacks. The irony was even more bitter when Paul Rhode, whose appointment was the first result of Kruszka's efforts, pressured him to drop the complaint against Goral. Despite the restrictions and opposition, the younger Kruszka remained in the public arena, highly visible and articulate. For the most part, his role in the campaign for Polish bishops continued to display energetic improvisation and application. The popularity of his arguments was acknowledged even at the Chancery Office, the starting point of so many letters that urged him to use his influence to promote loyalty and unity among the Poles. But his impassioned declaration that he would receive no non-Polish bishop at his church in an official capacity, qualified though it was in terms of the papal promise, amounted to a near repudiation of the authority of Messmer and Koudelka. Although he was determined to give the archbishop no grounds for more drastic measures against him, he was straining the limits of acceptability.

It was hard to make sense of the tangled pattern of events and emotions which characterized Wisconsin's Polish community in the years before 1912. The Kruszka brothers and Boleslaus Goral denied responsibility for it at an early date. Doubtless, all three were sincere; but their protestations did not touch the heart of the matter. Responsibility was not so much at stake as accountability. Not fully understanding the situation, each man believed his justification for his actions lay with a different authority. Wenceslaus Kruszka's primary allegiance was directed to the pope; his brother's was to the Polish nation; and Goral's was to Messmer and the American hierarchy. This difference accounted for the righteous indignation and extended the dispute to the bishops, who insisted all the while upon the traditional teaching that all Catholics are answerable, in some sense, to them.

Under these circumstances, Messmer's role was crucial. He, too, had several times implied that the responsibility for the troubles was not his. But he had more power than the others to alter the circumstances of the debate by exercising his episcopal prerogatives. Toward the Poles, his fundamental principle was concerned less with national recognition than with preservation of authority as the essential instrument of church unity. Accordingly, his main efforts were calculated to bolster his standing with the Poles, mostly by working through Goral and, later, Rhode and Koudelka. But his attitude toward the Kruszkas (and their resistance) assured that many of his gestures would be regarded as inadequate and counterproductive. By 1911, the press was out of control on both sides, and even the most loyal Polish priests had asked him to be more responsive to their wounded dignity and the feelings of their increasingly agitated people. Elsewhere, resistance to his policies had already become revolt. Inextricably involved in the dispute, Messmer had no choice but to reconsider his responsibility and find more effective ways to intervene.

6. The Archbishop's Counteroffensive

THERE WAS ONLY ONE discernible advantage in the circumstances of Wisconsin's Poles at the start of 1912: the situation had become so intolerable that it could not endure for long. The Poles were now publicly committed to insist upon the appointment of Polish-American bishops, but in seeking the best means to this end they had stumbled into a dilemma. If they chose one set of options, they risked schism, and if they chose the other, they weakened the campaign for recognition within the Church. The individual who had the greatest influence on the alternatives was the archbishop, whose own concerns were so intimately connected with their choice. He pondered the possibilities with the benefit of experience. The years had taught him that he could not win an open debate with his opponents; neither could he satisfy the Poles with promises of good will and halfhearted compromises. To maintain his authority, he would have to intervene more forcefully, but in ways which safely accommodated both sides in the Polish dilemma. The decision was in his hands.

At first there was little indication that 1912 would be different from the years which had just passed. The newspaper wars continued, with only minor variations interrupting the repetitiousness of the arguments. The *Kuryer* still insisted that the people were the true owners of the parishes and that the bishops were obliged to serve them. To that end, Michael Kruszka announced on January 6 the formation of a Central Committee of the federation to work for the transferral of parish titles to lay trustees. Later that month, a group of parishioners in Milwaukee staged a walkout during an anti-*Kuryer* sermon, and Messmer excommunicated the leader of the group. Paul Rhode attempted to mobilize support against Michael Kruszka by collecting the signatures of ninety-eight Polish priests on a letter condemning *Dziennik Narodowy* (The National Daily News), a Chicago paper which Kruszka had owned since 1909. In Pulaski, Francis Manel kept up his journalistic participation in the newspaper war; and the *Nowiny* continued to attack the Kruszkas as godless men who were testing everybody's patience in agitating for Polish bishops.[1]

The *Nowiny* was correct in describing the universal end to patience. Sebastian Messmer proved it when he summoned Wenceslaus Kruszka to a meeting, January 11, to sign the statement: "I, the undersigned . . . will admit Bishop Koudelka to my church if the archbishop sends him to me." The confrontation was the result of Kruszka's address in Kenosha the previous month, and Messmer had convoked the diocesan consultors to witness Kruszka's reaction. Wenceslaus asked whether the other Polish priests were required to sign; when he learned that they were not, he refused to comply. The archbishop threatened to suspend him, but Kruszka said he wanted to appeal to the interim apostolic delegate, Bonaventure Cerretti, who told him Messmer had the right to send Koudelka to St. Adalbert's. But Kruszka was unyielding. The people, he insisted, would be so incensed by such disregard for the word of the pope that the result of such a visit would be violence.

After about two weeks, Messmer again summoned Kruszka to the Chancery Office "to give you another opportunity to repair the scandal given by your public address in Kenosha, . . . and to justify yourself with the Church." For his second appearance, Kruszka had prepared a document which included his version of the speech and an explanation of his intent:

> I am identified with the Pope's promise to procure several Polish Bishops in this country, and if the truth of this promise is successfully denied, I am practically dead in all social matters. This is the meaning I intended to convey in my address at Kenosha, and I believe that those of the audience who intelligently and without bias listened to the address, must have understood me in no other way.

He explained that the real problem was not his address but its misinterpretation by the cub reporter who covered for the *Kuryer*. He attributed the harshness of his remarks to his desire to answer the attacks of the *Nowiny*, adding that he would gladly publish a correction. Unmoved by the explanation, Messmer insisted on Kruszka's signature and refused a counterproposal that he first send Koudelka and then suspend Kruszka if he refused to receive him. The archbishop wanted assurances but Kruszka held firm, repeating that signing the statement would imply that he desired to receive non-Polish bishops. One of the consultors asked Kruszka whether the pope might not change his mind, but Kruszka replied that there was no evidence for this. With that the hearing ended. As Messmer escorted Kruszka to the door, he said: "It would be better if you broke openly with the Church." Kruszka replied: "Perhaps, Your Excellency, you see the need for breaking with the Church. I don't see the necessity at all."[2]

About ten days later, Kruszka's loyalty to the Church received a

more severe jolt when he was expelled from a convention of Polish
priests. The meeting was the result of requests from (among others) the
Polish Roman Catholic Union that Paul Rhode organize the Polish
priests. In his letter of invitation, the bishop noted that the more than 700
Polish priests in the United States faced common problems, including
the maintenance of Roman Catholicism among their people, the challenge of the "corrupt" press, and the problems of parish schools. He
appointed committees to work on these issues and prepare reports for the
full meeting in Detroit, February 7–9.[3] As the Detroit meeting began to
take shape, Wenceslaus Kruszka protested by telegram to the Arrangements Committee that it had invited only reporters from the *Nowiny* and
the *Dziennik Chicagoski* to cover the convention. "It follows," he
concluded, "that this will not be a meeting of all the priests, but only
. . . a meeting of the *Nowiny* and Resurrectionist clique. Am I right?"[4]
This set the stage for the confrontation.

Tension was in the air as soon as Kruszka arrived in Detroit.
Entering a hotel restaurant, he was greeted by a colleague with "*Ave,
Rex Judaeorum!*" Although bystanders claimed the remark had been a
joke, Kruszka regarded it as a portent that he was about to be
"crucified." Other signs also pointed to trouble. The *Nowiny* reported
that many priests were avoiding Kruszka's company at meals and at the
opening Mass. He himself became the first order of business when his
telegram was read—inappropriately, he claimed—to the entire general
session, after the greetings from the pope and other absent dignitaries.
Angry protest resulted, but Kruszka defended the right of the secular
press to be represented, claiming he was identified with no paper but
wished only to protect everybody against the pharisaism of the Arrangements Committee. The statement was received with shouts of
"Shame!" and "Throw Kruszka out!" Then a delegate asked him
whether he could—literally—stand as a morally righteous man, and
Kruszka rose and remained standing for some time, amid shouts of "Sit
down!" Finally, a resolution was introduced calling for his exclusion,
but Kruszka continued to defend himself. He had obeyed Messmer's
1907 orders about the *Kuryer*, he asserted, and had written to *Dziennik
Narodowy* only a few times to defend himself against the Resurrectionists.

At this point Bishop Rhode intervened to accuse Kruszka of siding
with the bad press and the federation. He was privately inspiring the
policies of the *Kuryer*, Rhode contended, and his actions indicated that
"he is not a priest according to the spirit of God." Rhode pleaded with
Kruszka to break decisively with the "masonic press," but Kruszka
replied that the clerical press was guilty of hypocrisy. To lend weight to
his charges, Rhode read, as a specimen of Kruszka's writing, a strong

antipapal attack from a book Kruszka recognized as one he himself had repeatedly condemned. Kruszka reported in his memoirs that a number of sympathetic delegates later told him they knew he had not written the passage in question. Nevertheless, a strong majority of the 300 priests voted to exclude him. Kruszka made a dramatic departure, described in a partisan fashion by the *Nowiny* correspondent:

> The silence of the grave, a silence gloomy and at the same time threatening, remained in the meeting room when Father Kruszka left. Nobody even glanced at him as he was going out, so angry and depressed were they at finding among the Polish clergy a priest who, having a great opportunity to turn from the evil path, who had only to utter one "yes" to join and unite with them, refused . . . in his insolence and presumptuousness. Everybody deplored this immensely, deplored it from the heart.[5]

More isolated than ever in his quest for Polish equality, Kruszka claimed that the experience strengthened his determination to persevere.

After he had left, the clergymen passed a number of resolutions, including one which condemned eleven newspapers. Among them were Michael Kruszka's journals in Milwaukee and Chicago. The delegates appealed to the bishops for assistance in combating the enumerated papers.

In Milwaukee, the exclusion was featured in large headlines by the English-language press. When he returned to the city on February 8, Kruszka told the *Free Press* that the meeting was a factional gathering of priests, opposed to the federation, who had been planning all along to exclude him. The comment in the restaurant, he said, was the first sign that he would be singled out for harsh treatment. But Boleslaus Goral disagreed. In a letter published by the *Free Press* one week later, he stated that the *Ave, Rex Judaeorum* comment had been treated as a joke by all concerned, even Kruszka, who "joined the rest in the merriment that followed, and seemed to enjoy the joke as well as the others." Goral condemned Kruszka's use of the comment as an effort to slur the Polish priests by alleging anti-Semitism. As late as April 19, the *Nowiny* was keeping the story of the Detroit meeting alive, comparing Kruszka with Martin Luther and suggesting that he had become bitter because his ambition to become a bishop had not been honored.

The archbishop was kept informed on the convention's actions by Paul Rhode, who wrote to him that Kruszka's expulsion resulted from his refusal to sever connections with his brother's paper and with "movements among our people, that led directly to schism."[6] But Kruszka protested to Messmer about the *Nowiny*'s description of his exclusion, which prompted Messmer to ask Rhode for more details.

The reply stated that the convention had voted for severance without dissent because Kruszka had insulted the priest-delegates and had written a letter to *Dziennik Narodowy,* a representative of the "yellow press," which incited Poles to oppose church authority. Moreover, Rhode wrote, Kruszka had refused the opportunity to apologize. He advised only that Messmer direct the *Nowiny* to issue a clarification.[7] It was hardly surprising that Messmer chose to believe Rhode's version of the proceedings and to keep the pressure on Kruszka. Bishop Fox supported him in this determination by expressing his satisfaction that Kruszka "got the grand bounce" in Detroit. He urged Messmer to remain firm.[8]

The archbishop's conviction that Kruszka was defying church authority led to a third hearing on the Kenosha speech on March 4. Once again, Kruszka refused to sign the statement unless a similar demand were placed on the other priests. But this time Messmer refused to yield, and Kruszka wavered. At that moment, he wrote, he felt like William Tell immediately after he had been told to shoot the apple from his son's head:

> The cause of Polish bishops, as if it had been my own son, was close to my heart. And upon this cause . . . now rested the apple of disagreement over the signing of this statement. It was necessary to shoot it in such a way as not to damage the cause.

The pastor traveled to Washington to make a last appeal to the interim delegate. Cerretti advised him to sign because Rome was well informed in the matter and would not regard the statement as evidence of a desire for non-Polish bishops.[9]

When he arrived back in Milwaukee, Kruszka went directly from the depot to the Chancery Office, where he signed a statement designed to "undo the scandal given and the harm done" by the "false report" in the *Kuryer* of his Kenosha speech. It had three main parts:

> 1. I solemnly affirm . . . that I did not use the phrase attributed to me, namely, that I would not allow a foreign or non-Polish bishop to enter my church except over my dead body or corpse. I positively affirm that I never intended to express any such sentiment as contained in the phrase as reported.

> 2. I acknowledge that I did use such language and phraseology which might easily be misunderstood by the ordinary people and thus convey a meaning which would be quite contrary to Catholic faith and obedience. I am sincerely sorry if any of those that listened to me, took any anti-catholic meaning out of my words, as this was entirely against my intention.

3. Hence, to remove any misunderstanding, I hereby solemnly declare and promise that I shall, at any and all times, receive with due respect and honor any and every Catholic bishop of whatever nationality he may be, who is in communion with the See of Rome and who may come to my house or church vested with lawful ecclesiastical authority, and that I will also induce my parishioners to do the same when the occasion arises.[10]

The statement was published in *Nowiny* and *Miesięcznik Franciszkański,* and Messmer required Kruszka to read it at each service of his parish church on Easter Sunday. Kruszka complied resentfully, adding that he still trusted the pope and believed that additional Polish bishops would soon be appointed.[11]

Although he was insistent in exercising his jurisdiction over Wenceslaus Kruszka, Archbishop Messmer had something more drastic in mind for Michael Kruszka and the federation: a pastoral letter from the bishops of the Milwaukee ecclesiastical province to impose the ban on Kruszka's papers and forbid membership in the federation. Messmer had been considering the measure for some time. After the formation of the federation, he called a meeting of the bishops on December 19, 1911; they authorized preparation of the letter, which was completed and signed by February 1, 1912, although publication was withheld until after the meeting of Polish priests in Detroit. The fact that Paul Rhode wrote Messmer immediately after the convention about the condemnation of certain newspapers suggests he may have been deputized to put the Polish priests on record ahead of time. Now that the scene was set, the letter was released and ordered read at every Polish church in the five dioceses on February 11, the first Sunday after the Detroit meeting.[12] Bishop Fox wrote to Messmer on the day of publication: "It is grand. It fully covers the ground and will create a sensation but in the end will be effective. . . . Having done our duty let us now quietly await results."[13]

The sensational quality of the letter stemmed more from its content than its rhetoric. Somberly, the bishops argued that their action was justified by the admonition of Jesus against false prophets. They professed to understand the desire of the Poles for bishops but warned that national sentiment had degenerated into "blind passion" among some Poles in the state, alienating them from their religious leaders and sowing "the seed of strife and hatred" within the community. The present ferment, they predicted, would end in schism, the result of an "uncatholic and unchristian nationalistic spirit" which went beyond mere preaching of falsehood to "organize the misled masses into combined bodies of agitation, even at the risk of incurring the censures and excommunications of the Church." They accused the *Kuryer* of proceeding in a stealthy way to alienate the unsuspecting Poles from their Catholic affiliation. Thus the battle against "German" bishops was only a pretext for fighting for ecclesiastical independence—"a Polish church within the Catholic Church of America." Furthermore, the pope's statement to Wenceslaus Kruszka was shamefully misused by making the pope appear to be unfaithful to his word and by suggesting that the bishops were his opponents for preventing fulfillment of the promise. In short, under the guise of Catholicism the *Kuryer* and the federation were subverting the principles of loyalty and authority within the Church. That was the reason for the condemnation.

> We hereby solemnly condemn the said Kuryer-Polski . . . and the Dziennik Narodowy . . . as publications greatly injurious to the Catholic faith and discipline and falling under the rules and prohibitions of the Roman Index. Therefore, should any Catholics still dare in the face of this solemn warning to read or keep or subscribe to or write for the said Kuryer-Polski and Dziennik Narodowy, as long as these papers continue their present course and attitude in ecclesiastical affairs, a matter to be decided by Ourselves, let them know that they commit a grievous sin before God and the Church.

The letter also forbade Catholics to join the federation, a society "full of danger to Catholic loyalty and discipline and in its very purpose tending to create great disorder and even a schism." The letter concluded with an appeal that Polish Catholics receive the warnings in a proper spirit and follow their true religious leaders.

Messmer discussed his reasons for the pastoral letter in a long interview which was placed in the chancery archives. He stated that he had begun receiving complaints about the *Kuryer* while he was the bishop of Green Bay and that he, and especially Bishop Fox, had kept a careful watch on the paper. His main concern in the campaign for bishops was that Poles were apparently interested in bishops only for themselves, independent of other Catholics. The federation had added an additional facet to the problem, particularly in its move to transfer church property to lay ownership, in violation of the decrees of the Third Baltimore Council. He cited the Don't Pay campaign, too, as a violation of the church law which required lay persons to support the Church according to their financial means. Thus the bishops of the province had issued the letter in accordance with the laws of the Church and their own responsibility.

Most of the Polish priests supported the letter. Several wrote to Messmer from the Green Bay Diocese to express their willingness to cooperate.

> The Generals have declared war, we the officers are ready to carry
> it into the end through thick and thin provided we are not left to
> ourselves; we know the battle shall be fierce even unto blood.[14]

To consider implementation of the letter's provisions, Messmer summoned the Polish clergy to a meeting on February 22. According to
Wenceslaus Kruszka, a few priests argued for softening the impact of
the decree but the majority wanted strong measures. In the end, they
prevailed upon the archbishop to make the forbidden actions "reserved
sins," meaning that a confessor could not grant absolution from them
without special permission from the ordinary.[15] But in supporting their
bishops, the priests had no intention of abandoning the crusade for
equality within the Church. Acting on the impetus of the Detroit
convention, thirty-three clergymen met at Stevens Point in June to set up
an organization of Polish priests for Wisconsin. With approval, the
group received an address urging them to seek the support of their
parishioners and of the bishops in Poland for the cause. Then they
endorsed a resolution to form a movement for advocating the appointment of Polish bishops in ways which paralleled some of the efforts of
the federation.[16]

Outside the province, bishops reacted to the letter in a variety of
ways. Expressions of support came from several places, and in Winona,
Toledo, Peoria, Grand Rapids, and Detroit the bishops issued letters of
their own to condemn selected Polish newspapers. Cardinal Farley of
New York cautioned the Polish Catholics under his jurisdiction not to
read the papers, although he did not place them on the Roman Index.[17]
More significant was the fact that Archbishop Quigley declined to
introduce the measures in Chicago, a reaction that created a difficulty
for Messmer, whose critics began to ask: "Why is it sinful to read the
Kuryer in Milwaukee, but not in Chicago?"

Michael Kruszka was evidently caught off guard by the letter. The
Kuryer said little about it on the next day, but it printed the text.
Kruszka, however, released statements to the *Free Press* on Monday
and Tuesday, calling the condemnation "a foolish step" and predicting
that the *Kuryer*'s readers would do without the sacraments, if necessary,
to uphold their rights. He claimed that the bishops were naive in
thinking that one letter would make the Poles abandon their causes and
newspapers after their 120 years of persecution under German authority. Instead, he predicted, the people would stand by the *Kuryer*, and the
measures that were aimed at him would rebound against the bishops.
"Our people wish to be Catholics in their own way," he said. "Five
German bishops cannot control our people in this city."

But Kruszka was more worried than he pretended. At the annual
meeting of the *Kuryer* stockholders on February 20, he delivered an

emotional address, describing the paper as his second child and pledging the remainder of his life to serving Poles through the printed word. Many stockholders voted to return their dividends to the Central Committee for current and anticipated legal actions, and the capital stock was increased to $100,000. The meeting passed a long resolution of protest against the pastoral letter, denying that the *Kuryer* had ever been anti-Catholic and insisting on proportional representation for the Polish clergy. The resolution predicted that the ban on the paper would be "the death knell of confession among the Polish people, especially the younger element," and accused the bishops of taking the first steps toward an anti-Polish and un-American theocratic government. Those who were present also authorized a legal appeal to recover the loss of advertising revenue which resulted from the ban.

Kruszka carried his campaign for noncompliance with the letter to the English-speaking public in two pamphlets, written in 1912. The first, "Polish-Americans," described the efforts of the *Kuryer* to correct the "outrageous conditions" which had been uncovered by the questionnaires on Polish congregations in 1911. The second brochure, "The Polish Church War,"[18] was published under the auspices of the Central Committee of Polish Parishioners in America, which, Kruszka explained, was distinct from the federation because it concentrated on reforming the financial administration of parishes. Its object was to overturn the "funny corporations" which permitted bishops to dominate every Catholic parish and institution. Distorting the truth, Kruszka charged that the pastor of a Milwaukee parish had, with the archbishop's approval, squandered $500,000 collected for a church on "reckless speculation in gold mines, stock exchanges, gambling and high living." Most of the clergy, Kruszka claimed, were unfit to handle finances because they were unacquainted with the hard work by which their parishioners earned money for contributions. To rectify this situation, the Central Committee had four demands: the return of church property to lay ownership, representation for church taxation, better schools, and autonomy for the Poles within the structures of the Church. With united action, the Poles would be victorious.

> It is a gigantic struggle between medieval feudalism and enlightened progress. On one side four million oppressed Polish people fighting for their rights; on the other side—selfish bishops and part of the clergy trying to down the spirit of enlightenment, progress and freedom.

> But these are times of emancipation of the people from all serfdom and slavery; these are times of enlightenment of the people, of progress, of attaining full rights and happiness for the people who

like Atlas have to carry the burden of the whole world on their shoulders.

And the people will win!

Pressing his opposition on another front, Michael Kruszka supported the federation's efforts to resist the letter. The *Kuryer* gave extensive coverage to a mass meeting in Milwaukee on February 25, at which a crowd, reportedly numbering 5,000, passed a resolution similar to that of the Kuryer Publishing Company. Other protest gatherings, held throughout the state in March, were also publicized extensively by the *Kuryer*. In August, a federationist delegation visited John Bonzano, the new apostolic delegate. In two meetings, the delegate refused to receive the petitioners as representatives of the Polish Catholics or as Federationists. He addressed them only as "private Catholics." The discussions were inconclusive, and Bonzano's only promise was that he would speak with Messmer about the matter. The Federationists returned to Milwaukee claiming that Bonzano's reception of them amounted to a recognition of the organization. But the delegate specifically denied this to Messmer in a report which sustained both the propriety of the pastoral letter and the penalties it imposed.[19]

Wenceslaus Kruszka, too, resented the bishops' action, though he was less able than his brother to oppose it. In his memoirs, he identified fourteen reasons for the issuance of the letter and refuted each to his own satisfaction. Prejudice and fear of exposure, he insisted, were the real reasons, since the federation was fighting only for Polish recognition and improvement of the disastrous financial arrangements which had led to such problems as the Josaphat debt.[20] The affidavits of Kruszka's parishioners, collected by the Milwaukee Chancery Office, indicate that he expressed his opinions publicly during 1912. He complained that national papers were forbidden but that those that were issued under church auspices, often just as extreme, were allowed. He also noted that Joan of Arc had been burned by Catholic bishops, and warned: "It is no schism to demand one's rights."[21] Kruszka's attitude was especially crucial because his parish shared a boundary with Goral's. When it became clear that professed Federationists were to be denied the Church's sacraments and Catholic burial, a number of disputes between the two pastors over parish membership flared into the open. Messmer finally wrote to Kruszka, warning him to accept into his parish only those who lived within its territorial boundaries.

For his efforts, Kruszka was increasingly isolated within the Catholic community of the area. During 1912 he was denied faculties to exercise his priestly ministry in the dioceses of Green Bay, Marquette, and Peoria, and on Memorial Day the chaplain of the Polish orphanage refused him permission to enter when he led the school children and teaching sisters of his parish there, on their way home from visiting the cemetery.[22] The personal attacks also continued in the *Nowiny*. But instead of breaking his resistance, such reactions only intensified his sense of persecution.

By the end of 1912, the effect of the pastoral letter upon the Poles of Wisconsin was becoming clear. Indications are that pastors differed in their eagerness to impose the penalties. Some, for instance, asked each penitent about reading the *Kuryer* and membership in the federation before giving absolution; others did not. Annual reports from the Green Bay Diocese, although incomplete, show a sharp rise in the number of noncommunicating Polish Catholics for 1912 and a steady decline thereafter.[23] But even at the peak of resistance, the best indications are that only about 4 percent of adult parishioners failed to receive Communion during the Easter season, as required by church law. The pastor of the parish at Alban, who in 1912 had complained that some *Kuryer* readers had gone over to the more tolerant pastor at Polonia, reported a year later that resistance to the bishops was almost dead:

> The spirit favoring *the forbidden newspapers* is lost; also we did not have here *the condemned federation* and [it] never will be here; only five obstinate men still read the paper and you know them. Generally the people here are good.

Gwiazda Polarna (The North Star) printed a similar report from Stevens Point on August 10, 1912, noting that federation organizers sent to the small towns in central Wisconsin were failing to follow up their early initiative. But another pastor complained of Federationist victories in parish elections and reported that neighboring pastors were granting absolution to such people. So there were ways, even immediately after the letter's appearance, to continue to participate in the Church without taking the prohibitions too seriously.

Nevertheless, some did drop their *Kuryer* subscriptions, and the paper claimed that the episcopal ban had hurt its business. Michael Kruszka attested that he had lost 2,771 subscribers between February 1912 and May 1913. But business volume was up during 1912, and the absolute number of subscribers rose by 668. In mid-1915, the *Kuryer* reported daily circulation at 23,370, with several thousand more on Sundays. Week-day *Nowiny* subscribers averaged 5,240 at the same time.[24] Thus Kruszka's enterprise was not crippled by the bishops' ban, nor, it seems, did the letter have much effect on the publishing corporation except, perhaps, to slow its growth. And even with his chief competitor under a ban, Goral could not raise the *Nowiny*'s circulation to a competitive level.

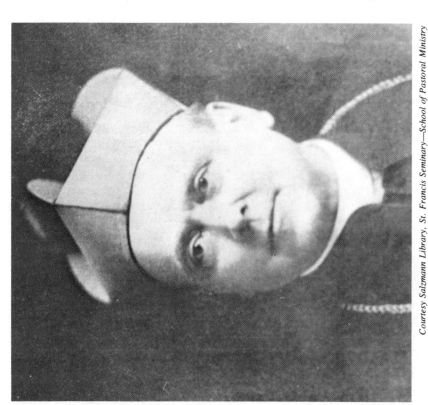

Edward Kozlowski, appointed auxiliary bishop of Milwaukee in 1913 as a concession to the Poles.

Joseph Koudelka (and an unidentified group), appointed auxiliary bishop of Milwaukee in 1911 in an effort to placate the Poles.

Sebastian Messmer, archbishop of Milwaukee at the time of the Polish Church War.

Paul Rhode, first Polish bishop in the United States, designated bishop of Green Bay in 1915.

Goral's effort to defeat a Federationist with the Nowiny ends when the Kuryer becomes a stumbling block (Kuryer, April 11, 1913).

Michael Kruszka strikes with a club marked "truth" a donkey eating from a bin marked "lies" (Kuryer, October 19, 1912).

Messmer fiddles while Goral dances on the graves of two Federationists denied burial in the Catholic cemetery (Kuryer, April 9, 1913).

Entrance to St. Adalbert's Cemetery in 1913 at the time of sanctions following the pastoral letter of 1912.

Nevertheless, the pastoral letter had a number of far-reaching and permanent effects on the common life of the state's Poles. One arose from the fact that Federationists were excluded from the Polish Association of America, whose constitution limited participation to practicing Catholics. Three Federationists tested the restriction by obtaining a court injunction, which temporarily halted the PAA convention in Kenosha in September 1912. But the court ultimately upheld the PAA, whose membership reached 8,500 in 1911.[25] Partly as a gesture to those who had been excluded from the PAA, the federation introduced a noncompulsory insurance plan at its first national convention in Milwaukee in November. The 176 delegates gave a twenty-minute ovation to Michael Kruszka and passed resolutions that aimed at protecting Poles from parochial maladministration and saving them from perishing in a "sea of Americanism." They asked for state certification of teaching sisters, more Polish bishops, and improvement of parish schools. The program was not as extreme as it might have been, but neither did it yield much to the authority which the bishops had claimed in February. Delegates elected to national offices a Kuryerite slate, headed by Martin Cyborowski, thereby maintaining Michael Kruszka's dominance in the organization. The officers claimed a national membership of at least 50,000, but a truer estimate of active members, based on the number of delegates who attended, would probably be 10,000 to 15,000, with perhaps 4,500 in the Milwaukee area.[26]

Another effect of the bishops' decrees was a separate Polish cemetery in Milwaukee for Federationists. Cemeteries had been an issue in the city since the beginning of 1912, when the *Kuryer* attacked St. Adalbert's Cemetery, which was operated by the archdiocese under the administration of Boleslaus Goral. On January 13 an article complained that the income from the sale of lots was not being used for improvements, and it predicted that the German owners might eventually sell the land to the Chinese for a chop-suey restaurant or "a pen for raising cats or rats." Wenceslaus Kruszka was also critical, claiming that some of the graves were so full of water that the remains of people were drowned, not buried.[27] When it became clear that regulations in the pastoral letter did not allow Federationists to be buried at St. Adalbert's, a group associated with the outcasts started plans for a new cemetery, which were extensively publicized by the *Kuryer* throughout the summer of 1912. By Memorial Day, 1913, the new Polish National Cemetery was ready for formal dedication, in ceremonies which included a procession to transfer several exhumed bodies from St. Adalbert's.

But just as Federationists were excluded from the old cemetery, Catholics were excluded from the new. In October 1912, Messmer issued a circular letter to tell the Polish Catholics that anyone who requested burial in the new cemetery "would by the very fact show that he rejects the authority and the law of the Church." He also forbade priests to conduct services there or to accompany bodies to the cemetery.[28] He wrote a separate letter to Wenceslaus Kruszka to warn him that the penalty for disobeying the ruling would be automatic suspension.[29] At the same time the older burial ground was improved. On September 28, 1913, the archbishop dedicated a new chapel there in the presence of 5,000 spectators who heard an address about the modern enemies of the Church. Both Goral and Ignatius Czerwinski, Michael Kruszka's old adversary, were singled out as donors in the *Nowiny*'s report on the following day.

Because it made Federationists ineligible to stand for parish office, the pastoral letter led to difficulties in the election of trustees. There were several problems with parish elections in the Green Bay Diocese in 1912, and in December Messmer warned the Polish Catholics under his jurisdiction not to vote for federation members. The issue, he said, was not a Polish but a Catholic question, and if they wanted more bishops, the Poles had to give "strong and universal proof of a true Catholic spirit and loyalty."[30] The *Kuryer* injected mischief into the situation, however, by printing a false report on January 4, 1913, the day before the Milwaukee parishes were to hold their annual meetings. The article stated that Messmer was planning to resign in favor of a Pole; for that reason, Federationists were eligible for parish office. The ploy was unsuccessful, except at St. Hedwig's, where the meeting had to be postponed because of the objections of Federationists, and at St. Adalbert's in South Milwaukee, where Federationists won the election. As a result of the South Milwaukee decision, Messmer placed an interdict on the church, writing that he prayed God to "open the eyes of the blinded and misled members of the parish and bring them back to a sense of their Catholic duty." When new elections resulted in another Federationist victory, the church remained closed.[31] Even Wenceslaus Kruszka's parish obeyed the rules, though one parishioner reported that, in reading Messmer's prohibition against the election of Federationists to his congregation, Kruszka added that such people were eligible to pay their assessments. Laughter followed.[32]

In general, there was little humor as Poles institutionalized their differences in the wake of the pastoral letter. During the summer of 1912, picnics supported by the *Nowiny* and the *Kuryer* became occasions of public rivalry. When the *Nowiny* sponsored an outing in June to benefit the Polish orphanage, the *Kuryer* urged people not to attend, as a test of its Don't Pay campaign. And Federationists, marching to city parks in June and August, were greeted with shouts of "Long live the *Nowiny*!" from the bystanders. The following January, the business manager of the *Nowiny* assaulted Michael Kruszka in a Milwaukee restaurant, and eventually settled the publisher's suit out of court by agreeing to make contributions to specified charities.[33] Federationist proposals on parochial schools and the ownership of church properties were introduced in the Wisconsin legislature later in 1913. All were eventually defeated, but the arguments for and against increased the rancor as rival delegations, headed by Goral and prominent Federationists, carried the battle to Madison.[34] And early in 1914, when Milwaukee churches sponsored a citywide "Church Sunday," the *Kuryer* used the occasion to accuse the Catholic bishops of driving people out of the churches. For that reason, the paper claimed on January 31, the appropriate name of the event for the Poles was not "Go to Church Sunday," as its sponsors stated, but "Go to Hell Sunday."

The quality and intensity of the disputes that followed the pastoral letter placed a heavy burden on the Polish clergy who undertook to defend and support the bishops' actions. Although most of them willingly entered the battle on the side of the prelates, they had made an act of faith that their wishes for greater recognition would ultimately be recognized. Thus the issue of a Polish bishop for Wisconsin remained prominent. Early in 1913, *Nowiny* began publishing rumors of the imminent resignation of Augustine Schinner from the Superior Diocese and his probable replacement by Koudelka. By February 13 Schinner's resignation had been confirmed and on August 3 Koudelka's transfer was announced. In the meantime, speculation had been building that Rev. Edward Kozlowski of Bay City, Michigan, would follow Koudelka in Milwaukee. Even the *Kuryer* printed the rumors, which soon proved to be true. On October 13 a cable from Rome announced that he had been chosen as the new auxiliary bishop for Milwaukee. Fifty-three years old at the time, Kozlowski had immigrated to the United States in 1885 and, like Rhode, had attended St. Francis Seminary. After ordination, he had worked in the Diocese of Grand Rapids, where he gained the reputation of peacemaker by settling troublesome parish disputes.[35]

Various groups claimed credit for the welcome news. The *Nowiny* immediately attributed the appointment to the 1911 petition of Milwaukee's Polish priests. The secretary of the association of Polish priests in Wisconsin disclosed that his group had petitioned all the bishops of the province in 1912 to urge support at Rome for a Polish bishop.[36] And Joseph Schrembs, the bishop of Toledo, who had previously worked with Kozlowski in Grand Rapids, wrote to the Vatican secretary of state, at Messmer's request, to support the nomination, which would alleviate the "most trying position" in which the archbishop found himself and "do much to bring him the needed support to solve the Polish problem."[37] Clearly, the bishops had cooperated with the Polish priests in working for the appointment and insisting to the Roman authorities that it was essential. Cardinal Cajetan De Lai, of the Congregation of the Consistory, contacted Messmer while Kozlowski's nomination was pending. The archbishop, he wrote, was to stress to the people that the regular procedures of the Church would be followed in appointing bishops, not extraordinary methods resulting from public clamor. He also asked Messmer to remind the Poles that Rome had their concerns at heart and that additional bishops might be granted "according to time and place and persons."[38]

The new bishop met with general approval. On the day after the announcement, the *Free Press* found that loyal *Nowiny* supporters were "unanimous in believing that his appointment means everything to the Polish members of this diocese." Wenceslaus Kruszka expressed gratification, and Jan Szukalski, Kruszka's best friend among the Milwaukee clergy, predicted that the new bishop would "do much to heal the breach in the church between the Poles and the church authorities." But one week later the *Kuryer* expressed a dissenting view: the appointment fell short of the federation's goal of obtaining Polish bishops with full authority. Although the paper praised Kozlowski as more intelligent and understanding than Rhode, it predicted that he would be forced to promote the policies of the Messmer-Goral group against the Kuryerites.

At the start, there seemed to be substance to the prediction. Despite Kozlowski's request that all the Polish priests of the province be invited to a banquet that was being arranged by Boleslaus Goral for the clergy on the day of installation, Wenceslaus Kruszka was excluded. When they challenged this ruling, Kruszka's parishioners were told that the cause was their pastor's refusal to apologize after his expulsion from the organization of Polish priests in 1912.[39] Despite the pettiness which surrounded the preparations, both the priests' banquet at midday and the public gathering in the evening provided occasions for displays of harmony between Messmer and his new suffragan. At noon, the archbishop told the audience of 7 bishops and 250 priests: "I shall receive him as a younger brother and those who will be under him should receive him as another father." Kozlowski replied: "He is my father and I will be his loving son. He is the head and I am the arm. He will lead and I will follow."

Afterward, an estimated 50,000 lay people waited in the January cold along Mitchell Street and in front of St. Stanislaus Church to get a glimpse of their new leader. At the community banquet in the evening, the theme of good will and subsidiarity was repeated when Messmer told the gathering: "I have done more for the Poles in this archdiocese

than for other nationalities." Thus the celebrations enabled the archbishop to display benevolence toward the Poles and to stress that, even
with a Polish bishop, the lines of authority and loyalty were to be
unchanged. In their jubilation at achieving a goal long sought, most of
the city's Poles would have agreed heartily to the terms of the appointment. So there was an aptness to the *Sentinel*'s report that January 14 had
been "a memorable day—memorable to the new bishop, memorable to
the Roman Catholic Church, and memorable to the Polish people of the
city."

The most important event of the day was Kozlowski's inaugural
sermon—a frank address, intended to set the tone for his work in
Milwaukee and to introduce his episcopal motto: "Everything for God
and Fatherland, through Love."[40] Kozlowski admitted at the outset that
he had been hesitant to accept the appointment. He disclosed that his
nomination had encountered difficulties from the enemies of the Poles
and from some of the Poles themselves. Nevertheless, he came to
Milwaukee because failure to do so would have damaged a cause he had
long endorsed. Furthermore, the conditions in Wisconsin dictated that
he accept:

> My decision and reflections were affected in no small way by the
> thought that it would be faint-hearted and cowardly to decline
> because the conditions among which I come to work in Milwaukee
> are unusually difficult.

Factionalization was intensifying, he said, and faith had become mean-
ingless for many of the city's Poles. He encouraged those who had
abandoned Catholicism to use this opportunity to begin practicing their
faith again so that he might be the leader of all in a spirit of charity.
"Yes, charity towards everyone, towards friends and enemies, towards
Poles and others—love always and everywhere."

As a bishop for everybody, he pledged that his position would
represent "the quintessence of all existing sides and parties." He
promised to share the good fortune and the sorrow of his people and
urged them to seek his help at all times: "The door will be open, the
heart even more so." He asked the Polish clergy to be his closest friends
and advisers and reminded them that theirs were common goals: the
salvation of souls, the good of the people, and the repair of the
deplorable conditions. Kozlowski granted acknowledgment to the
Polish lay people for their efforts on behalf of his consecration: "You
did not agitate in vain for so many years for a Polish bishop for
Milwaukee." He expressed appreciation for their welcome and asked
for their obedience and prayers. He concluded with a plea that criticism

formerly directed against priests be replaced by prayer, and he pledged himself again to his motto.

The sermon was moderate and realistic. Kozlowski did not minimize the difficulties which beset the community nor did he pretend that they would be easy to resolve. In acknowledging that his appointment had been the result of efforts by Messmer, the Polish clergy, and the people, he communicated to all three groups his belief that their best hope lay in cooperation and that he himself was a symbol of their united effort. And although the address was implicitly critical of the *Kuryer* and the federation, Kozlowski left the door to reconciliation open.

After the consecration ceremony, reactions to the new bishop indicated how far he had succeeded in sharing his convictions. The *Nowiny* cited the appointment as proof that the aspirations of Poles would be acknowledged by the Church, and it urged gratitude to Rome for granting the request. Wenceslaus Kruszka agreed, using the occasion to take a special collection to send to Rome with the thanks of his congregation. When Kozlowski visited St. Adalbert's in March, he compensated for the snub at the banquet by praising Kruszka as the first Polish priest to work for Polish bishops. Only the *Kuryer* refrained from joining in the general praise, repeating that the new appointee would have no real authority.[41]

As if to prove the *Kuryer* wrong, Kozlowski convoked a council of the Polish priests of the archdiocese early in March to announce that Messmer had given him "extensive authority" to handle Polish parishes and affairs. He proposed a number of reforms for the administration of Polish parishes and promised to consult with the priests regularly. When Messmer left in April to visit Rome, he announced in a widely publicized letter that Kozlowski would be in charge of the administrative affairs of the archdiocese during his absence.[42] While the archbishop was away, Kozlowski published the new rules for Polish parishes and parishioners in a pastoral letter, designed to counter some of the criticism from the anticlerical elements in the community. He characterized the critics as "apostles of perversity" who were attempting to destroy the confidence of the people in their priests and said that only parish members had full rights as Catholics. He defended the Polish priests of Milwaukee, who received less of parish funds than priests in other places, and he introduced norms for clerical salaries, as well as other rules and reforms. The letter closed by expressing hope that the new regulations would bring peace to the shattered community.[43]

Kozlowski exercised broader leadership over the Polish and Catholic forces through *Przegląd Kościelny* (The Ecclesiastical Review), the journal of the Polish Priests' Association, which began to appear in January 1914. The first issue carried a full-page picture of the new bishop and the text of his inaugural sermon. Later, he wrote a long article on the connection between language and faith, in which he showed himself to be a strong opponent of forced Americanization, while arguing that a priest must be "not only a servant of God, but also a priest of the holy duty of love of country." In that spirit, he expressed opposition to the language decrees issued by Messmer and Eis in 1901 and he urged parish priests to increase their efforts to inculcate love for the Polish language in the younger generation. He deplored the fact that Polish parishioners were joining non-Polish Catholic organizations which harmed them by hastening the process of Americanization. And he spoke strongly for the appointment of many more Polish bishops, presenting statistics with all the verve of Wenceslaus Kruszka. Although he was careful to say that Polish bishops would not work independently of existing diocesan structures, he was unhappy about the small number of appointments: "Clearly, an injustice is being done to us!"[44]

Thus Kozlowski demonstrated his willingness to develop a line at variance with Messmer's. His dedication to the Polish heritage and the aspirations of Polish-Americans could only please many Poles who had been disaffected with their Church. In that sense, he was a good choice for the place and the times.

As salutary as Kozlowski's appointment was for the troubled conditions, it did not completely relieve the tension in the community nor put an end to the criticism being directed against Catholic leaders. The appearance of the Polish National Catholic Church in the state in 1914 and the continuing opposition of Michael Kruszka proved that Kozlowski had not won over all the dissidents. Confronting this situation, the bishops brought another Polish prelate to the state in 1915, when Paul Rhode was named to succeed the ailing Joseph Fox as bishop of Green Bay. By helping make Rhode the ordinary of a diocese which was 30 percent Polish, the other bishops directly challenged the *Kuryer*'s charge that Polish bishops had no jurisdictional authority in the American Church. In response, the paper belittled Rhode's accomplishments and his dedication to the Polish cause. Also, it suggested that Archbishop Quigley's confidence in him as auxiliary had been so low that he had not implemented the pastoral letter's provisions in Chicago.[45]

Nevertheless, the announcement of the new appointment generated great enthusiasm among Wisconsin's Poles. Rhode's journey from Chicago to Green Bay in September 1915 was triumphal. Archbishop Messmer and Fathers Goral and Traudt accompanied him on the train, witnessing the joyful demonstrations at each stop in Rhode's new diocese.[46] No doubt the archbishop enjoyed the reception, but he may also have pondered the irony of his new popularity among Polish Catholics. True, he had earned it, by bringing the first two Polish-American bishops to his province. But he had done so in the knowledge that the Poles would regard these bishops as their own, precisely as he had predicted before the onset of the Church War. This was a compromise he liked no better than the Kruszkas, since it made the Church's catholicity too broad for his taste and too narrow for theirs. But it did preserve the dedication and enthusiasm of most Poles toward their Church. And the maintenance of authority had been his goal all along.

With Rhode's appointment, Messmer's counteroffensive came to an end. In general, it was a success. After asserting his authority over Wenceslaus Kruszka, he had condemned Michael Kruszka's papers and the federation. When it became clear that these actions had not automatically alienated Poles from the forbidden papers and movements, he had been instrumental in appointing bishops. It was fortunate, in a way, that vacancies opened in Superior and Green Bay in 1913 and 1915. One wonders what he would have done to demonstrate good faith if those opportunities had not presented themselves. In any event, he had maintained discipline and had granted major concessions to the national pride and desires of Poles. In the process, he mollified Wenceslaus Kruszka's anger somewhat and, perhaps to his surprise, left Michael Kruszka's publishing enterprise largely intact.

The enduring popularity of the Kruszkas indicated that their issues were not totally specious, as Messmer liked to insist. But the popular enthusiasm for the two bishops demonstrated the importance of these appointments compared with other federation causes, even the problems with parish administration, which Kozlowski's new rules tacitly acknowledged. It is likely that many Poles understood the issues in a more sophisticated fashion than the bishops thought. Obviously, many continued to favor Kruszka's arguments without endorsing all of his tactics. In the context of their anti-German feelings and their experiences with the American Church, they probably even enjoyed them. But their loyalty to the Church remained, and the appointment of Polish bishops cemented it. In time, Messmer's concessions and the outbreak of the European war helped to divert attention from the problems which had transformed a model community into a community in conflict. Even then, however, the troubles could not be forgotten. Unresolved issues and lingering resentment delayed a truce as the contestants sorted out the consequences of division.

7. The Aftermath

LIKE A STORM WHICH BRINGS a sudden end to the heat and activities of a summer afternoon, the European war interrupted the conflict which was besetting Wisconsin's Poles and their Catholic leaders. Quickly and decisively, it altered the conditions which had supported disagreement. At the time of the assassin's act in Sarajevo, Sebastian Messmer was in the midst of his counteroffensive and a half dozen lawsuits relating to Michael Kruszka's papers and the pastoral letter were providing new outlets for old animosities. By the time of the Armistice, the permanent nature of the ideological and religious differences had largely been accepted and individuals were learning to live with division.

Clearly, the outbreak of the Great War had caught the Poles in a contradiction. In the effort to promote the restoration of Poland and aid their suffering countrymen along the Eastern Front, they discovered that they could not easily support the Polish cause abroad while fighting one another at home. America's war effort hastened the trend toward abandoning church disputes by placing stronger emphasis on common loyalty to the adopted country. Slowly, courtroom trials and vituperative journalism gave way to discussions about the development of postwar Poland and an updated understanding of Polish-Americanism. The air was filled with concerns which did not so much replace the older questions as adapt them to another context. And a new generation was eager to search for answers.

Before the Church War subsided, lawsuits had become a principal means by which both sides sought redress. Unable to find acceptable referees within their community, the Poles turned to civil courts for vindication. Between 1909 and 1918, Kruszka's opponents brought five suits against him for statements in his papers, and Kruszka sued the bishops of the Milwaukee Province for $100,000 for conspiracy and boycott in the issuance of the pastoral letter. As each case wound its way through the courts, heavily biased reports in the press ensured that the old antagonisms would burn bright. Although the cases were primarily an outlet for the frustration and anger of the various parties, they were conducted on neutral ground before judges who presumably were trained to value reason above emotion. For that reason the trials became an important "stage" in the conclusion of the Church War; they made it necessary for each side to distill its arguments and to reckon seriously with the position of the antagonist. After that had happened, it was easier to abandon hope for total reconciliation or total victory and to accept the more pluralistic Polish-American life which had been developing all along.

Two libel suits were directed against the *Kuryer* by enemies of Michael Kruszka who hoped to settle old scores by taking advantage of the turbulence in the community. The first, a $50,000 damage suit filed in 1911, disputed the paper's description of an incident of embezzlement in 1905. Throughout the trial the *Kuryer* complained that the plaintiff was being directed by church authorities, and when the court ruled in Kruszka's favor, early in 1913, he brought out an English-language report to claim a victory of enlightenment over despotism.[1] The second suit was filed by Ignatius Czerwinski in 1911, protesting a story that he had been guilty of fraud against the Polish Roman Catholic Union in 1896. The trial, conducted in March 1914, was followed with intense interest as partisans of the two opponents packed the courtroom, sitting on opposite sides of the center aisle. The jury's verdict found that Czerwinski had known about wrongdoing by others but had received none of the embezzled funds. Thus it awarded no punitive damages. When he appealed the decision in an effort to clear his name, Czerwinski won a token judgment of six cents. Afterward, he claimed he had received "full satisfaction," and the *Nowiny* proclaimed Michael Kruszka's defeat in a large headline. The *Kuryer* retaliated by scoffing at Czerwinski's "six-cent honor."[2]

In addition to the Milwaukee cases, three suits were filed against Kruszka's *Dziennik Narodowy* by clerics in Chicago. The first, similar to the Czerwinski case, ended December 4, 1913, when the defendant was awarded damages of $1 because of an article that attacked his private life. The second complaint, brought by the Resurrectionists, led to Kruszka's indictment before a federal grand jury on charges of violation of federal mail laws against printing lewd and obscene articles in attacking his opponents. Returning the indictment, federal officials claimed that the articles were of such character that no English-language newspaper in the country would have dared print them. But Kruszka angrily branded the suit another instance of his persecution at the hands of Catholic officials:

> My God, who is not against Kruszka by now and the Kuryer! First was the Prussian government,then all the German bishops with the addition of their court jester Goral! Among them came forth also a half dozen lawsuits. And if neither the Prussians, nor the

hakatistic bishops, nor the "priests' conference" in Detroit, nor Goral, nor the Resurrectionists, nor the Nowiny crowd with boycotts and lawsuits cannot handle Kruszka they apparently have invited the "federal government" to help, including the whole army and navy of the United States. If such powers cannot overcome Kruszka, then perhaps no one can![3]

The case remained in court until January 8, 1917, when the district attorney moved that the charges be dismissed.

The most sensational of the Chicago lawsuits—and ultimately the shabbiest—resulted from a suit filed by Bishop Rhode in December 1911. The case was the result of an article printed by *Dziennik Narodowy* after Rhode had preached a strong sermon in condemnation of it. The bishop alleged that the editors questioned the legitimacy of his birth by writing: "Some spiritual . . . dignitary, not only did not know his father, but changed his mother's name in order to wipe out traces of his illegitimacy."[4] In an effort to prove the paper wrong, the bishop brought his mother to the stand to testify about the circumstances of his birth, and then Rhode was forced to submit to cross-examination by Kruszka's lawyers. In the end, the publisher was acquitted.

Although the article's implications were reasonably clear, it was nearly impossible to prove, as a technical point of law, that they referred to a specific individual in the Polish original. The Catholic press interpreted the proceedings as another instance of Kruszka's slyness and pointed out that the paper had at least been forced to retract its innuendoes about Rhode. But the *Kuryer* concluded that the decision reflected shame on all the Polish clergy in the country and had destroyed Rhode's honor.[5] It was an odd moment for one of Kruszka's papers to print a lecture about honor.

Irritated by the series of lawsuits against him and by the issuance of the pastoral letter, Michael Kruszka initiated a legal battle of his own on February 21, 1913. The action, filed by the Kuryer Publishing Company, charged Messmer and the bishops of the Milwaukee Province with conspiracy and boycott by issuing a letter in violation of the Wisconsin statutes which covered injury to business, restraint of will, and pursuit of work.[6] Kruszka asked for damages of $100,000. When the case opened, the chief issue became Messmer's refusal to testify and supply documents concerning the background of the pastoral letter, as Kruszka's attorneys wished. Although the judge eventually ruled that Messmer had to appear in court, he was exempted from disclosing his private correspondence pertaining to the letter and information relating to his connection with the *Nowiny*.[7]

The archbishop's appearance before the court commissioner in March 1914 set the stage for the second part of the suit. He refused to

answer most of the questions asked by Kruszka's lawyers, necessitating
a further ruling on the extent of personal testimony which could be
required from him. After eleven months, the judge ruled that the
archbishop had to testify because the matter was civilly adjudicable, but
that he could not be examined on privileged affairs of the Church,
including his personal role in preparing the pastoral letter.[8] Kruszka
appealed this decision to the Wisconsin Supreme Court, but the justices
upheld the bishops after a hearing in February 1916:

> Recommending to the members what they should read, under pain
> of expulsion from the church, is within the jurisdiction of every
> pastor and prelate of every church which professes to leave such
> matters to the determination of its clergymen.[9]

Although the *Kuryer* said it would resubmit the case, the appeal
was dropped on August 5, 1918. The editors explained that the
publishing company had recovered so quickly from the financial blow
dealt by the pastoral letter that it would be difficult to prove an actual
loss had occurred. They also claimed that anti-German war hysteria
would have made a fair trial unusually difficult, given the character of
the *Kuryer*'s attacks. So the last of the cases arising from the Church
War ended in a weary willingness to let the issue rest.

The briefs prepared for the Supreme Court are still interesting
because they contain the most precise discussion of the issues under-
taken by the two sides at any time during the controversy. Attorneys for
the bishops generally cited precedents based on freedom of religion and
the separation of church and state, while the *Kuryer* rested its claims on
cases involving labor unions and the use of boycotts unacceptable in
law. But appeals to precedent were almost an afterthought, compared to
the rhetorical insistence that each side had acted in response to provoca-
tion and abuse from the other. Even after ten years, the temptation to
deny responsibility was strong.

The *Kuryer*'s appeal rested on the assumption that, because of the
"tremendous influence and power" of bishops over Catholics, the
letter's directives constituted a malicious plot to destroy the newspaper.
According to Catholic doctrine, the lawyers argued, *Kuryer* readers
and associates had been denied the possibility of "a happy hereafter"—a
form of coercion stronger than holding a pistol at a person's head. "Can
it be said," they asked, "that its newspaper field is free when ninety
percent of its readers are threatened with everlasting punishment . . . ?"
Furthermore, advertisers, suppliers, and laborers had been so affected
by the ban that it posed an illegal threat to the reputation, good will, and
financial standing of the paper. Although the appellants conceded that
the *Kuryer* had published a number of regrettable attacks upon the

Church and clergy, they insisted that the paper had generally been conducted on a high level. In his affidavit, Michael Kruszka stressed that the *Kuryer*'s chief purpose had been to elevate the welfare of Polish-Americans by seeking to improve parochial schools and the financial administration of church property. His criticism of church leaders, he claimed, had been motivated by a desire for the proper pastoral care of Poles. He had avoided attacks on the Church as such, and its dogma and creed.[10]

The bishops' brief countered with a long recitation of specific acts of the *Kuryer* against the Church which had aroused episcopal opposition. The defendants charged that the paper had endangered the faith, attacked the position of the hierarchy, and seduced its readers into schism, all under the guise of national interest. To deny their right to protect their members against such protracted attacks, they asserted, would have threatened the right of the Church to exist and function. "Only petty, self-willed agitators," they concluded, "following the dismal light of their egotism and malice, determined to rule or ruin, would fail to . . . appreciate that the Bishops spoke concerning a subject matter most obviously within their jurisdiction." Rather than being motivated by malice in issuing the letter, the prelates claimed their abiding purpose had been to protect Polish Catholics from the danger posed by Kruszka's paper:

> This splendid document speaks for itself. It breathes the spirit of charity. It expresses the solicitude of the Church for her children; it points the offending and the danger; in virtue of the authority of the Church, it commands, and it points the consequence to its members, of disobedience.

The bishops insisted that they had only been doing their duty in issuing a letter to persons who, as voluntary members of the Church, expected and desired ecclesiastical leaders to issue warnings like those in the pastoral letter.[11]

Much of what the two briefs argued was true. There were problems with the administration of Polish parishes, the quality of the parish schools, and the failure of Polish-Americans to achieve positions of leadership within the Church. And the bishops' fears of schism and Polish separatism were hardly contrived. But in their impatience, both groups failed to appreciate the limits of their arguments. Kruszka, for instance, oriented his papers increasingly in the direction of an ethnocentric ecclesiology which was unacceptable in the American context. Although many of his goals were praiseworthy, he tended to belittle the resistance his efforts raised among scarred veterans of the Cahensly and Americanist disputes and thus failed to achieve some of the reforms whose need he had so ably demonstrated. The bishops' problem was their misjudgment of the Polish-Americans, whose attachment to their Church was not as voluntary as the prelates suggested in their statement to the court. Bound by social, psychological, and historical pressures to Roman Catholicism, Poles experienced advancement within the Church as a test of acceptance. In resisting the campaign for Polish bishops, the prelates did not alienate the allegiance of Poles to the institutional Church as much as their loyalty to leaders who seemed unsympathetic and even anti-Polish. Thus the letter's effort to assert authority over the Poles through threats of punishment was not nearly as effective in promoting peace as the subsequent appointment of bishops. It was fortunate, in the end, that the court refused to prolong the case by compelling Messmer to divulge the Church's inner workings. The decision allowed the period of litigation to end without an unqualified endorsement for either side.

The final, determining factor in ending the lawsuits was their expense. The problem was less severe for those who attacked Michael Kruszka, since the cost was borne by a number of individuals. The *Kuryer's* costs, however, ran to thousands of dollars, and the corporation was constantly collecting funds for legal defense, with records of contributions printed under the heading "Defend Yourself." On March 28, 1914, Kruszka sold the *Dziennik Narodowy* to help pay his legal expenses, according to a report in the *Nowiny*. Inevitably, the unwillingness of Poles to contribute for further legal action, especially during the war, functioned as a brake on the litigation. The fact that no plaintiff in the seven cases won more than a token victory also made continued appeals to the courts unappealing. Eventually, everybody had to admit that the lawsuits were not worth the cost.

The decline of interest in the lawsuits coincided with the arrival of the Polish National Catholic Church in Wisconsin. The new congregations probably helped reduce tension in the long run by providing a permanent refuge for those who were unhappiest with the Roman Catholic leaders and policies. Francis Hodur, the leader of the PNCC, made an open appeal to the state's dissident Catholics on December 12, 1913, when he suggested in a *Straż* article that Michael Kruszka was in an untenable position. Since the Catholic Church in America was not likely to grant further concessions beyond auxiliary bishops, he wrote, Poles would remain subservient. Kruszka had to accept that reality or form a free church. Although the publisher rejected Hodur's challenge, a number of Polish Milwaukeeans were persuaded. In March 1914 they announced formation of an independent church. As leader of the group, Hodur sent the Rev. Francis Bończak, a competent and hard-working man who had studied at the universities of Vienna and Chicago and had filled a number of important responsibilities in his church, including designation as bishop-elect.[12] Under his leadership, the original group of 100 grew large enough to construct a church in Milwaukee, and a new congregation was organized in South Milwaukee. In a short time, efforts were made to found a third parish in the state, at Pulaski.[13]

The *Kuryer* took a friendly interest in the new parishes, judging that their prosperity was due to the actions of the Messmer-Goral faction in resisting Polish aspirations. The paper praised the use of Polish for worship services and predicted that Bishop Hodur would send a permanent Polish National bishop to Milwaukee with full authority—something the Roman Church had not been willing to do. Bończak nearly destroyed this good will, however, when he criticized Wenceslaus Kruszka in an article he wrote for *Straż* in April 1915. The *Kuryer* made it clear that the new pastor had committed a tactical mistake when it denounced him as a spreader of lies and warned that he would not have a bright future in Milwaukee unless he could verify the authenticity of what he wrote. In time, Bończak was able to repair the damage, and within a year he was writing occasional articles for the *Kuryer*.[14] The paper provided extensive coverage of the dedication of his new church on September 2, 1917, and Hodur's address.

By then it was clear that the movement had been successfully launched. Despite the *Nowiny*'s denigration of Bończak as a "preacher" and a chameleon of unstable loyalties,[15] the group claimed nearly 1,000 members in Milwaukee in the federal census of religious bodies in 1916.[16] Although only 1 or 2 percent of the city's Poles were initially involved, they had found a stable means for expressing some of their deepest values.

The arrival of the national church challenged the federation to accommodate itself to the desire of non-Catholics for unrestricted membership. Francis Bończak spoke at a federation meeting in the city on March 1, 1916; and at their national meeting later that year, on November 28–29, Federationists endorsed the new spirit of cooperation by dropping the pretense of a special attachment to the Roman Catholic Church. The *Kuryer* explained the change on July 15 by denying that the federation's purpose was still to combat the Church. Instead, the federation was pledged to maintain a good system of insurance, to promote the welfare of all Poles in America, and to encourage interest in the language and culture of the Old Country. Having thus altered its goals, in 1924 the organization even changed its name, to Federation Life Insurance of America. It took fewer than fifteen years for the federation to acknowledge defeat in trying to win concessions from the Roman Catholic Church in the United States. Thus an emotional crusade for Polish rights became, instead, an effort to provide financial security and preserve the Polish identity after the end of the great migration.

Obviously, neither the waning of enthusiasm for lawsuits nor the transformation of the federation can be understood outside the context of the First World War. The war was crucial, not only in forcing Poles to acknowledge how many concerns they still shared but also in helping them discover how to work for common ends in parallel, rather than unified, ways. National organizations furnished a handy pattern. Early in 1913, various Polish-American organizations and leaders attempted to band American Poles together as the "Fourth Partition of Poland" in a unified organization known as the Committee of National Defense. Catholics soon became dissatisfied, however, because of the participation of socialist groups. Under the leadership of Edward Kozlowski, Paul Rhode, and others, they withdrew six months later to form the National Council.[17] By the summer of 1914, the principal factions in Wisconsin had taken sides on the issue, with the *Kuryer* supporting the Committee and the *Nowiny* and the Polish priests generally backing the Council.

The disagreement subsided briefly after the outbreak of the war, when cooperation was explored. At the first group meeting, in January 1915, the Kuryerites expressed suspicions that the Catholics would donate money for rebuilding churches, rather than for alleviating human suffering. When the differences proved insurmountable, the parties conducted separate collections and sent the receipts to different organizations.[18] Four months later, a successful united effort resulted from formation of the Polonia Committee, which united Michael Kruszka and other leaders of both factions under the honorary chairmanship of Bishop Kozlowski. The group raised $8,000 by a citywide tag day on May 22, and wired President Wilson to express the loyalty of the Polish-Americans of the city and county.[19]

Although it had been a success, the coalition quickly crumbled. Four days after the collection, the *Nowiny* refused suggestions that the committee be left intact, arguing that Catholics could not work with Federationists on a permanent basis. And Michael Kruszka, still enmeshed in his suit against the bishops, repeatedly explained to readers (in English) that Poles did not hate Germans but refused to be dominated by them.[20] Hopes for unity received a further setback at the time of Paderewski's benefit concert in Milwaukee on January 4, 1916. Each faction sent its own delegation to greet the pianist and afterward vied in demonstrating which had received the warmer reception. The *Kuryer* had the last word, however, when at the end of the month it announced that the Paderewskis had invited Michael Kruszka's daughter and son-in-law to dinner in their private railway car after a concert in Ann

Arbor. "Whether anything of great public importance was discussed there is not known," the paper reported archly, "because this was a private dinner, and the Zwierzchowskis were the only guests."[21]

And so the efforts to aid Poland remained divided. In February 1916, two separate bazaars were held. The first was sponsored by the Catholic loyalists and the second by the Polonia Committee, which now combined the efforts of the Polish National Alliance, the Polish National Catholic Church, and the federation. Although the newspapers quibbled over the ultimate destination of the funds, both events were successful.[22] Indeed, it is likely that more money was raised in the spirit of rivalry than would have been collected in a harmonious undertaking.

It was a sign of the times that even Archbishop Messmer's desire to help the cause engendered debate. On January 6, 1916, he announced that a collection would be taken for Polish relief at the pope's request, and he advised all Catholics to regard a contribution as part of their Christian responsibility. The *Kuryer* advised its readers to withhold their donations until the archbishop divulged the name of the agency to which the money would be sent. Nevertheless, the collection raised over $25,000. Afterward, the *Nowiny* concluded that Messmer's actions were further proof of his willingness to work with and for the Poles.[23]

However, many would have disagreed with that conclusion. Despite the *Nowiny*'s optimistic view of the archbishop's good will toward Poles, the prelate had made clear, early in the war, exactly where his sympathies lay. He was in Europe when the war broke out and had written to Bernard Traudt that Belgium was "paying a just punishment for its treacherous conduct against Germany." He added that he was praying for "the victory of the just cause of Austria and Germany." Traudt released the letter to the English dailies of Milwaukee for publication on September 30, thereby furnishing the *Kuryer* an immediate opening to attack Messmer for adopting a double standard in insisting to the Poles that the Church recognizes no nationality while defending Germany's invasion of Belgium. The *Nowiny* refrained from comment.

The archbishop embarrassed his Polish supporters again when he returned to Milwaukee on November 14. Restating his views to a *Free Press* reporter, he said: "The spirit with which the Germans have entered the conflict is one that will win. I can see nothing else but that the German causes for war were just." In response, the *Kuryer* predicted a new pastoral letter ordering Catholics to pray for a German victory, and even the *Nowiny* argued that there was no basis for believing that either the pope or a majority of church leaders favored the German cause.[24] Whatever the archbishop's purpose in making the statement, it was inopportune from the point of view of his Polish allies in Wisconsin. It forced them to dissociate themselves from him and it lent credence to the old charges that he was a "German" bishop. Thus the tendency of the state's Poles to keep somewhat apart from their ecclesiastical leaders was again reinforced.

After America's entry into the war, the archbishop was constrained to find reasons to support the national effort against Germany. He presented his rationale in a pastoral letter which he issued six months after the declaration of war. Private judgment alone, he contended, could not ascertain the rightness or wrongness of the war; that responsibility rested with Congress. Since it could not be demonstrated that Washington had erred in judging the causes for war, all Americans were obliged to support the war effort, "willing or unwilling . . . for that is God's will."[25]

The prelate's conversion to the Allied cause induced him to describe the implications of American loyalty for the Poles in an article he wrote for the Easter 1917 issue of the *Nowiny*. In it, he defended the Poles' right to cherish their traditions but insisted that assimilation was the ultimate goal. He viewed American society as moving toward a unity in which excessive national exclusiveness would be eliminated:

> It would . . . be a great detriment to the Polish-American citizens were they to keep aloof from their fellow citizens and to refuse accepting from them anything good merely on the plea that it was not Polish.

In this spirit, he told the Poles not to "keep themselves walled up against the rest of us" but to learn English and adopt the common customs of America. Only in this way could they promote their own welfare while contributing their best gifts to the development of the United States. Messmer's new emphasis on Americanism was a natural response to the turns the war had taken, but it also helped explain his unwillingness to favor the aspirations of the Poles after Rhode's appointment to Green Bay. To his earlier fears about the unity of the Church he now added his conviction that steady assimilation would safeguard the unity of the nation. In short, the war reinforced his earlier stance against Polish advancement in the Church.

Messmer's opposition to further concessions for Polish Catholics—as Polish—first became clear after Bishop Kozlowski's death on August 8, 1915. When the archbishop presided at the funeral a few days later, he heard Bishop Rhode, recently designated for the See of Green Bay, tell the 30,000 mourners: "How difficult it was for us to obtain a second Polish bishop, and how easy to lose him!"[26] If there was a hint in Rhode's eulogy that a new Polish auxiliary would be welcome in Milwaukee, Messmer was unwilling to recognize it. Instead, he gave the Polish priests of his archdiocese standing permission to invite Rhode to their parishes for confirmation and other activities, exactly as if he had been their ordinary. Perhaps Messmer was motivated in this decision by Kozlowski's failure to restore peace during his short tenure in Milwaukee. Perhaps he was uncomfortable with Kozlowski's militant statements on the role of Poles in the American Church. However, the clearest indication of his reasoning appeared in 1924, in a letter admitting that he had obtained Kozlowski's appointment not so much from principle or sympathy for the Poles as under pressure from his critics:

> Some years ago, before Bishop Rhode came to Green Bay, I asked the Holy See for a Polish Auxiliary because of the troubles caused here by the Polish independent movement, which threatened to lead many Poles away from the faith. That movement is practically dead. But even under those conditions, the movement gave little satisfaction even to the Poles, not to speak of the Irish and German[s]. When poor Bishop Kozlowski died in 1915 it was felt like a relief by all, and no one wished for another Polish auxiliary.[27]

Messmer's return to the "hard line" included opposition to the appointment of Polish bishops in general, as he made clear in his reaction to a petition for more bishops that the Polish ambassador at the Vatican submitted in 1920.[28] Resisting the proposal, the archbishop argued that such appointments would work to the detriment of the Church, the nation, and Polish Catholics themselves. The new request, he warned, would jeopardize the Church's unity, provoke Protestant Americans to mistrust and suspicion, and undermine Americanization, a policy so strongly established that "anything opposed to it would be considered as bordering on treason." Messmer also insisted that encouraging the Poles to be separatistic would make them "aliens among their own brethren in the faith," whose attachment to the Church would easily die if, later, they happened to live among non-Polish Catholics. The prelate blamed the anticlerical immigrant press for earlier difficulties, but suggested that the Polish priests were also at fault because of their high incomes and ambitiousness for higher office:

> One thing is certain, the Polish Catholics do not clamor for Polish bishops when they are properly and faithfully served by their Polish priests. In many cases the demand for Polish bishops on the part of the people arose from the unpriestly, money-grabbing and tyrannical attitude of Polish priests toward their parishioners. They thought Polish bishops could give them more efficient

protection against such priests than other bishops would. On the
other hand there were Polish priests who expected more liberty of
action and independence if they were placed under bishops of their
own nationality, on the plea that those bishops would know better
than others how to treat Polish Catholics.

Within a few years of the war's end, therefore, Messmer had reached his
final position on Polish Catholics. Only as Americans could persons of
Polish descent hope to share the authority of the Church. They would
have to prove their acceptability by conforming to the customs and
expectations of the New Land.

The archbishop was not alone in maintaining an unbending position on the Polish question after the First World War. His old antagonist, Wenceslaus Kruszka, had also become inflexible, as he
continually demonstrated in his actions and writings. In 1915, for
instance, Kruszka refused to send delegates from his parish to a meeting
called by Messmer to establish a local federation of Catholic societies,
and the following year, St. Adalbert's was cited as one of five parishes
substantially in arrears in payment of the Josaphat assessment.[29] In
1918, Kruszka wrote to the archbishop that the American bishops were
the "declared enemies" of the Polish people, while posing as their
friends. Several years later, he advised Messmer openly to segregate
Poles in the Catholic life of the state: "You will make your name
immortal by creating a distinct Polish diocese in your Milwaukee
Province." As late as 1926, he was still trying to sway the archbishop,
this time by adopting a bellicose tone: "The Poles are entitled to their
own Catholic Bishops *and they demand them*. Please inform the Roman
authorities immediately!"[30]

All the appeals were in vain. Messmer was not likely to be moved
by threats or cajolery or a logic which, as Kruszka grew older, became more contorted and less compelling. Nevertheless, the priest remained a popular orator and an eager advocate of Polish and Polish-
American causes. His insistent crusade for national dioceses probably
strengthened Messmer's opposition to the Poles; and the end of the
archbishop's Polish appointments doubtless intensified Kruszka's sense
of injustice and desire to resist. There was little common ground
between the two old warriors, except their mutual antipathy. In the years
before Messmer's death in 1930, the stalemate was unbroken.

Boleslaus Goral, Messmer's best ally in the Polish community,
ultimately arrived at a position on religion and nationality between those
of the archbishop and Kruszka. He indicated some of his ideas at the
time of the Silver Jubilee of the Polish society at St. Francis Seminary,
warning that those who place allegiance to country ahead of loyalty to

God risk a narrow nationalism which can destroy the common bonds of
humanity that are emphasized by religious faith.[31] In 1918 he clarified
his stand in a report prepared for the Polish Priests' Association on the
section of the new code of canon law requiring strictly territorial
parishes. Resisting blind application of the statute, Goral cited the prior
principle that the salvation of souls is the highest law.[32] He noted that
American Poles were maintaining their attachment to the language and
customs of the Old Country and suggested that these tendencies be
utilized to remind them of their Catholic heritage and their duty to be
faithful to it. As Wenceslaus Kruszka had done in 1901, he argued from
the Good Shepherd text that a pastor and his people must be able to
understand one another. Although he stopped short of advocating Polish
bishops, he recommended concerted efforts to prevent abolition of the
national parish. In effect, he was bowing to experience in speaking only
in terms of Polish participation in the life of the Church at the parish
level. The enthusiastic reception that was given to the report indicated
widespread agreement among the Polish clergy for Goral's position. By
implication, his plan included both the subsidiarity which the Kruszkas
resented and the resistance to assimilation which Sebastian Messmer
deplored, but it is a good indication of the path which was actually taken
in the years after the war.

Michael Kruszka, too, continued to concern himself with Polish
questions during the war. The remarkable quality about his leadership
was the fact that his popularity and flexibility were so little affected by
the Church War and its aftermath. In 1916 the *Kuryer*'s circulation in
Milwaukee was still twice that of the *Nowiny*, a fact which politicians
and advertisers were quick to recognize in continuing to associate with
him, despite the archbishop's ban. A large number of Polish dignitaries
and politicians turned out for a surprise banquet, celebrating the thirtieth
anniversary of his journalistic career in Milwaukee, on June 23, 1915;
and the candidate who was backed by the *Kuryer* defeated the *Nowiny*'s
contender in a lively race for city comptroller the following spring.[33]

Maintaining his imaginative grasp of the journalistic possibilities
associated with the evolving nature of the Polish community, Kruszka
turned increasingly to the use of English in his papers. In 1917 he even
experimented with an English-language weekly, the *American Courier*,
in an effort to extend his market to English-speaking Polish-Americans.
And his willingness to allow the federation to drift away from the
militance of its early years, like his decision to drop the suit against the
bishops, indicated his ability to admit defeat if the circumstances
warranted it.

His preoccupation after 1914 was the cause of his homeland. While
the war lasted, he published signed articles almost every day about the

reestablishment of Poland. The culmination of the series was a column, written under the influence of the False Armistice of November 7, 1918, titled "Te Deum Laudamus." The piece revealed a man over-joyed because Poland was being reborn. His contentment at that moment must have been especially strong. From the time of his arrest as a youth for advocating Polish freedom, he had never abandoned his commitment to the fatherland. His preoccupation with plans for the development of Poland and the part the Polish-Americans could play undoubtedly neutralized a good deal of the disappointment he must have felt over his lack of success in suing the bishops. Thus there was a certain poignancy to the report carried by a black-bordered *Kuryer* on December 2, 1918, that Michael Kruszka was dead. A man who had often characterized himself as a fighter, he died precisely at the moment when the most important issues of his life had finally been decided.

Kruszka's passing elicited expressions of respect from his enemies and praise from his friends. Mayor Daniel Hoan ordered flags in Milwaukee to be flown at half-staff until the funeral on December 5, and the *Kuryer* printed a long biography. The *Nowiny* noted that under Kruszka's direction the *Kuryer*'s policies had been "extremely liberal and progressive . . . and at the same time anti-Catholic." But in examining the meaning of his life, the editors demonstrated respectful forbearance:

> Today we state that it is not for us to judge him, because the Highest has already judged him, and before Him there are no secrets.

About 1,000 persons at the funeral heard eulogies from Governor Emmanuel Philip and from John Kleczka, a young politician just elected, with Kruszka's support, as the first Polish-American con-gressman from Wisconsin. On December 20 *Rolnik* reported that Kruszka had left an estate of $18,000—a small amount, considering his remarkable service to his countrymen.

Kruszka's legacy, however, involved more than his financial estate. It was composed, in part, of the lessons a community learned about the methods and limits of public disagreement and debate. It included an understanding that it is better to take arms against evils, even at the risk of being wrong, than to let the fear of mistakes cow one into inactivity. It involved awareness of the limits which a less-than-universal view can impose upon an individual or a group. And it influenced the nature of Polish participation in American life for decades. Whatever his weaknesses, Kruszka died a man respected, not so much for what he did or pretended to be, as for what he was.

As his successor in the presidency of the Kuryer Publishing

Company the directors chose Kruszka's son-in-law, Stanislaus Zwierzchowski, a teacher of hydraulic engineering at the University of Michigan.[34] Because of his academic background and reserved temperament, Zwierzchowski could not manage the papers in the same image as Michael Kruszka. But perhaps that was just as well. The end of the great migration, the establishment of Polish independence, the new emphasis on Americanism, and other factors were bringing into being a new phase in the development of Polish-American life. The old issues were still important, but in the end the original immigrants could not give satisfactory answers to their children. Increasingly, it was up to the children to puzzle out answers for themselves. However difficult that process might have been, they did best when they proceeded upon an understanding of the lessons which their parents' lives had taught.

8. In Retrospect

AFTER THE DEATH OF Michael Kruszka, the other contestants in the great dispute passed slowly from the scene. Behind them, these early leaders and the people who watched and followed them in the Church War left testimonials of their accomplishments in America. Rows of large houses on small lots on the South Side of Milwaukee, prosperous farmsteads in central Wisconsin, monumental churches, successful commercial enterprises—all demonstrated that traditional values had served them well as they began to establish roots in the New World.

But the men and women of that first generation left another legacy, which bespeaks the pain and uncertainty of their lives and the price which settlement cost. The written records and oral traditions of the community speak to the point. Their descriptions of the difficulty in reconciling the often contradictory claims of religion and nationality and in sorting out questions of personality and claims of authority from fundamental principles form an important part of the Polish immigrant heritage. Here, in the area of community dissent, the Poles grappled most intensely with issues and problems that are common to all people. Here, too, they pressed their claims most forcefully against the resistance of other Americans. It is here, therefore, that the search for the meaning of their lives properly begins.

Part of the problem in understanding the Polish Church War is the difficulty of recapturing its context. In those days, the idea of pluralism was in competition with the goal of assimilation. Wisconsin experienced the tension most clearly in 1890, when the Bennett Law and its consequences pitted the two social models against one another in what proved to be an unequal contest. The state's citizens pondered the same issues again during World War I, when the debate took a different turn. Despite the shifting circumstances, however, the Poles appear to have suffered little discrimination because of their nationality in participating in civil government. As their numbers increased, they were nominated, elected, and appointed to various offices with great regularity. Given their length of stay in America and the limitations in their educational, economic, and social opportunities, they probably did as well as any other group. Even in their relationships with German-American officeholders, Poles experienced little serious difficulty. Elected from their own districts and wards and areas, they took their places at Washington, Madison, and city and village halls as respected participants.

But things were different in the Church. Despite the clarifications which the Vatican rulings of the 1890s attempted to provide, experience taught that there was no precise conception of what the "American" Catholic Church should be like. Under the circumstances, Germans, Irish, Poles, and others were able to justify different—and sometimes opposing—positions, based on the heritage of the particular group, its experience in America, and the particular ecclesiologies associated with each. Insecurity and mistrust led not to the appointment of the best man, but the most suitable Irishman, or German, or American-born churchman.

In Wisconsin, that confusion encouraged the historical antipathy between Germans and Poles. For the Germans, exercising authority in their traditional stronghold within the American Church, that amounted to unwillingness to grant Polish-Americans the same consideration which had once been accorded to themselves. And for the Poles, arriving with long memories of the *Kulturkampf,* it bred a growing impatience with the leadership and a temptation to draw parallels between the ecclesiastical authorities they had left behind in Germany and those who administered the Church in Wisconsin.

Increasingly, many of those who found the Church's intermediate leaders unresponsive focused their attention on the pope. Despite his promise to help, however, the pope proved relatively powerless in altering the situation. The old-guard leaders, particularly the Irish, exerted their influence to deny or delay the aspirations expressed by Catholic immigrants from partitioned Poland. Fearful of the nativists and outspoken in their loyalty to the United States, many of these prelates, in the interest of acceptability, deemphasized the universality of their Church. More attuned to questions of power and influence outside the fold, they sacrificed some of the legitimate interests of those (like the Poles) whose loyalty could be taken for granted because they had no real alternative. Furthermore, in the difficult circumstances of the immigrant Church, they trusted those whose experiences and attitudes were closest to their own. In this, the German-American prelates concurred.

Under the circumstances, the early hopes that ecclesiastical recognition would come to Wisconsin's Poles as a "normal" result of their participation in Catholic life began to wither. And when Frederick Katzer died, Poles lost their best advocate within the state's hierarchy.

His successor, Sebastian Messmer, was not inclined to favor the Polish cause. He made his position amply clear before and after the Church War. He found the Poles "aloof," their pastors independent and avaricious, and their finances a source of worry and even embarrassment, as when he journeyed to Rome, hat in hand, to find help for St. Josaphat's. As long as he could, he resisted their efforts to obtain a bishop. His obstruction of the movement indicated how far he was willing to go in blocking achievement of the Polish goal. He was especially harsh in his judgment of Wenceslaus Kruszka, a Pole who refused to stay in his place. Under Messmer, Kruszka suffered the indignity of prolonged "exile" in Ripon and attacks in *Nowiny* without a regular opportunity to reply or press a complaint. Ultimately, Kruszka was able to return much of the disapprobation and to do it within the Church, for his actions, like Messmer's, were technically permissible and the archbishop had no grounds for suspension. The contest was between resolute authority and imaginative determination. Both emerged bloody but unbowed.

Ultimately, Messmer gave the Poles much of what they wanted. The appointments of Kozlowski and Rhode palpably relieved the tension and contributed to the restoration of peace. True, Messmer granted the requests only in response to pressure and in the context of the calamitous atmosphere of Wisconsin Catholicism in the years between 1910 and 1915—but this differentiated him from other American bishops of the day. Only Quigley and Katzer came close to conceding as much to the Poles, and Messmer differed even from them. He bent in response to far more concerted efforts. He also accepted responsibility, at least in the short run, for a situation partly of his own making. More importantly, he made it possible for Poles to fulfill some of their most crucial aspirations within the Church. In the process, he demonstrated that some of the decisions that were reached during the Cahensly controversy were still open to interpretation.

To emphasize Sebastian Messmer and Wenceslaus Kruszka as the protagonist and antagonist of the Church War, however, is to neglect too much the roles of Michael Kruszka and Boleslaus Goral, for it is hard to imagine that the war would have taken place without the constant criticism (some constructive, some not) which the *Kuryer* directed against the Church and its role in the life of Polish immigrants. It is also hard to imagine that a man of less stature than Kruszka could have survived the Church War and the episcopal ban and maintained such a strong position. That he did was a tribute not only to his hard work for the cause of Polish progress but also to the fact that he had become a symbol of Polish success and independent judgment in the New World. None of his opponents, from Casimir Neuman to Archbishop Messmer, was able to resist the temptation to attack him, personally and often. But none of the assailants hurt him very much; in fact, they probably added to his stature as a resilient and resourceful leader. Even ultra *Nowiny*-ites would have admitted as much. Words like "sly" and "dangerous," on the lips of an antagonist, carry connotations of respect, and that was something Kruszka never lost.

Boleslaus Goral, too, was important in the Church War, not only because of his willingness to be Messmer's spokesman in addressing the Polish Catholics, but also because Messmer had to take his opposition to the Koudelka appointment most seriously. Between 1911 and 1918, Goral helped chart the path subsequently followed by most Polish-American Catholics in the state. His model allowed for national-language parishes and access to a Polish bishop. It permitted the Poles to be somewhat independent within the life of the Church and thus reduplicated a number of features which had marked the religious life of earlier Catholic immigrants. Although the plan delayed the full integra-tion of Polish-Americans into the mainstream of Catholic life, it accorded respect to legitimate differences without compromising au-thority or catholicity in the Church.

Despite the compromises in the plan, assimilation was under way. The influence which the Kruszka brothers had marshaled was clear evidence that Polish pastors in Wisconsin could not easily play the traditional, unchallenged role of priests in the Old Country. There would be no more Josaphat scandals, but neither were there new church riots. At the same time, Michael Kruszka had to concede that the bonds which united Poles to the Catholic Church were deep and abiding. It was—and remained, for the most part—an institution they supported, despite its problems. The result was a healthy tension in which the religious and secular leaders strengthened one another by mutually warding off the others' worst temptations. Unexpectedly, a process filled with anger and pettiness resulted in a gain for accountability and integrity.

In retrospect, the Church War was not so much the destroyer of the model community as its final act. Habituated by their early, unusual success to believe that they would enjoy a wide field for free expression and participation in American life, Wisconsin's Poles were receptive to arguments that advocated equal status within the Church. Although they were told they had to become "more American" to share in Catholic leadership, not everyone believed it. Certainly the Kruszkas did not, and, in time, most of the others agreed. The debate over the best means to achieve equality presented many difficulties, and the resulting split in leadership was at first perceived as a defect in the community rather than as a broadening of its base. But in the end, concerted efforts won concessions as unusual as their earlier successes in civic and economic life. Perhaps their ultimate faith that they could carry their point gave these people the fortitude to persevere long after Polish-Americans in other places might have given up or turned to the independents. If that was the case, it bespoke the self-assurance of individuals whose only guarantee in advance of the outcome was a sentence spoken by the pope.

The Church War also marked the beginning of a new era in the history of Wisconsin's Poles. By 1918 the newcomers and their children had a wider range of choices than in the days of joint control by Kruszka and Gulski. Unwittingly, Messmer helped them discover more than their exclusion from the hierarchy. He showed them their diversity. As their Americanization slowly continued, its first gift was the ability to accept those differences.

Appendix

Text of the Pastoral Letter of February 1912

To Our beloved Brethren of the Clergy and the Laity Greeting and Blessing.

When St. Paul addressed the ancients of Ephesus he told them: "Take heed to yourselves and to your whole flock, wherein the Holy Ghost hath placed you bishops to rule the church of God, which he hath purchased with his own blood. I know that after my departure ravening wolves will enter in among you, not sparing the flock. And of your own selves shall arise men speaking perverse things, to draw away disciples after them. Therefore watch." Acts, XX, 28 ff. With these words the Apostle pointed to the sacred duty of bishops to watch over the purity of faith and the bond of unity among the faithful of their flocks. Bishops were not only to preach the word of divine truth and to administer the mysteries of eternal salvation, but wherever there was danger of false doctrines spreading among the believers and of disorder and dissension arising in the Church, they were in conscience bound, as watchful shepherds of the flock of Christ, to warn the faithful of that danger and to take the necessary measures of guarding the faithful against it. Our Lord Jesus Christ foretold that false prophets and seducers would arise in the Church. His prophecy was fulfilled even in the time of the Apostles who had to raise their voices against teachers of false doctrines and self-appointed leaders causing disruption and schism. That prophecy was fulfilled in nearly every century of the Church, when the successors of the Apostles, the Popes and bishops of the Catholic Church, had to contend with the same scandals of heresy and schism. The few years of our present century have repeatedly heard the voice of the Supreme Shepherd of the Church, Pius X., warning Catholics all over the world against the insidious errors of Modernism and condemning in its first stages an uncatholic and rebellious movement against the disciplinary authority of Pope and bishops.

To our great sorrow duty compels Us to warn our faithful flock against a similar movement in our own country which threatens to

129

mislead the people into false doctrines regarding ecclesiastical authority and to direct its passions into the path of schism and separation. The agitation for Polish bishops in the United States has assumed such a character, especially in our province, that it becomes positively subversive and destructive of Catholic faith, loyalty, discipline and order. No sensible person will blame the Polish Catholics of America for being desirous of having bishops who can preach to them the word of God in their own mother-tongue. Rome with its wisdom gathered from the experience of over a thousand years and guided by the Spirit from on high, will know the time and the way to solve this important problem confronting the Church in America. Whenever and wherever the Holy See shall see fit to appoint Polish bishops in the United States, whether to residential sees or to the office of auxiliaries, the other bishops of the American Catholic Hierarchy will receive them with sentiments of a true and loyal Catholic love and reverence. In the meantime Polish Catholics may rest assured that the bishops of our hierarchy will be just as solicitous and zealous for the spiritual and ecclesiastical interests of the Polish faithful as they must be for all the other children of the Church whatever their nationality or race. But Polish Catholics must also be persuaded that love of one's nation or race or tongue can not be allowed to degenerate into blind passion and narrow-minded sentiment, and that blind nationalism has been the cause of all the great and disastrous schisms in the history of the Church. Nationalism of this kind has no place whatever in God's Holy Church of which St. Paul says: "There is neither Jew nor Greek; there is neither bond nor free; there is neither male nor female. For you are all one in Christ Jesus." Gal. III, 28. Of whatever race or nationality we may be, in the Church we are all members of the same mystic body of Christ, children of the same spouse of Christ, being animated and sanctified by the same Holy Spirit of Christ. "For in one Spirit were we all baptized into one body, whether Jews or Gentiles, whether bond or free; and in one Spirit we have all been made to drink. . . . Now you are the body of Christ and members of member." I. Cor. XII. 13, 27. Where nationalism and nationalistic passions strive to become the leading and ruling principles in the affairs of the Church, general or local, they breathe and beget the spirit of disobedience and rebellion and very soon of heresy itself. When men of this spirit systematically attack the public acts of ecclesiastical superiors in the exercise of their lawful authority, they undermine that ecclesiastical authority itself and shatter the very foundation of rule and order in the Church. When in that same spirit they claim for the lay people the power of government in ecclesiastical affairs, and the right of management of the church properties, independent of the lawfully appointed bishops, they attack the very constitution and fundamental law upon which the visible organization of the Church is built. When this same spirit becomes a common scandal-monger and blackmailer by spreading broadcast before the masses all kinds of reports of so-called clerical scandals, it destroys effectively the reverence and love of the people for the priesthood and for the religious institutions of the Church. Again, when this uncatholic and unchristian nationalistic spirit denounces as traitors to the holy cause and as apostates from their nation whosoever refuse to submit to its dictates and to follow its call, then it sows the seed of strife and hatred among the children of that same race, it sets up father against son, brother against brother, children against parents, to the great scandal of Catholics and non-catholics and to the great detriment of religion and nationality. Finally, when that same spirit, not satisfied with merely preaching its false doctrines, begins to organize the misled masses into combined bodies of agitation, even at the risk of incurring the censures and excommunications of the Church, then it will soon attain its last object, namely, independence from the authority of the Church, separation and complete schism.

Unfortunately this spirit of revolt and disorder is at present being fostered to a dangerous degree among our Polish Catholic brethren. The highest interests of their Catholic faith and religion are at stake. Unbeknown to themselves, they are gradually being led away, by a clever and cunning agitation, from the path of Catholic obedience and allegiance to the Church and their rightful superiors. The fight against what they maliciously call the "German" bishops of this province of Milwaukee, is but a sham battle to cover the real fight for ecclesiastical independence from non-Polish bishops; the proposed appeal to the Holy Father himself as against the American bishops is but a device to deceive the unwary Polish faithful; even the words of the Pope, reported by a clergyman as having been spoken to him some eight years ago, are being most shamefully misused for the purpose of poisoning the minds of Polish Catholics against the Pope as being untrue to his word and against American bishops as stopping the Pope from keeping his promise.

The true spirit of this whole agitation has been most clearly set forth in the call and program for "The American Federation of Polish Catholic Laymen", issued by the Kuryer Polski of Milwaukee and the Dziennik Narodowy of Chicago. This program calls upon the Polish lay people to organize a national federation embracing parish, county and state federations all over the United States. The purpose of this federation is, first, to demand of the Holy See Polish bishops for the Polish Catholics, a phrase well calculated to convey to thousands of Polish Catholics the idea of separate Polish bishops independent of the other American bishops, so that the Polish Catholics of the United

States would form a separate religious body under its own episcopal jurisdiction distinct from the other American hierarchy, a Polish church within the Catholic Church of America. Secondly, to obtain civil laws by which the control and management of church property and the money affairs of the parishes shall be placed in the hands of the laity. Thirdly, to induce Polish voters to arise as one man against all civil officers and judges who show themselves overbearing and unjust against Polish citizens. The program calls upon Polish Catholics to keep up this agitation even if they had to suffer persecution and excommunication from the Church. Meetings of these Polish federations have already been held in different places. A plan for raising a fund of money for the defense of Polish priests against persecution from non-Polish bishops is also being discussed among Polish laymen.

For several years the Kuryer Polski has in its columns openly advocated the same doctrines and demands subversive of ecclesiastical order; it has without ceasing, at all times, openly and by mere insinuation, attacked Catholic bishops of the United States, particularly the bishops of this province; it has repeatedly reviled and caluminated [sic] priests, especially Polish priests who condemned its uncatholic tone and teaching. Notwithstanding all this it has the effrontery to sail under the Catholic flag, pretending to be a Catholic Polish paper, to speak for the Polish Catholics and to defend and promote the religious interests of the Polish Catholic people. No wonder that thousands of otherwise well-meaning and good Polish Catholics have unconsciously come under the evil influence of this paper, not knowing or even suspecting whither it leads them. The same is true of the Dziennik Narodowy of Chicago, Ill.

Under such conditions We would, indeed, be grossly neglectful of our sacred duty, as shepherds and leaders of the Christian souls entrusted to our charge, did We not loudly and solemnly condemn public papers which fill the minds of their readers with false religious doctrines and excite in their hearts sentiments of rebellion and hatred against ecclesiastical authority. Speaking of similar occurrences in his own time, St. Paul writes to St. Titus, bishop of Crete: "There are also many disobedient, vain talkers, and seducers . . . who must be reproved; who subvert whole houses teaching things which they ought not, for filthy lucre's sake. . . . Wherefore rebuke them sharply." Tit. I. 10, 11.

Obedient to this apostolic command We hereby solemnly condemn the said Kuryer Polski, published in the city of Milwaukee, and the Dziennik Narodowy, published in Chicago, as publications greatly injurious to Catholic faith and discipline and falling under the rules and prohibitions of the Roman Index. Therefore, should any Catholics still dare in face of this solemn warning to read or keep or subscribe to or write for the said Kuryer Polski and Dziennik Narodowy, as long as these papers continue their present course and attitude in ecclesiastical affairs, a matter to be decided by Ourselves, let them know that they commit a grievous sin before God and the Church. Should any such Catholics dare to go to confession and communion without confessing or telling to the priest that they still read or keep or subscribe to the papers mentioned, let them understand that by such confession and communion they commit a horrible sacrilege. This solemn warning will also hold good in case that the aforementioned papers should in future be conducted under changed names though still in the same anti-catholic spirit.

Moreover, We strictly forbid any Catholic of our province to join the above mentioned "American Federation of Polish Catholic Laymen," established according to the program published by the Kuryer Polski. As such a society is evidently full of danger to Catholic loyalty and discipline and in its very purpose tending to create great disorder and even a schism, it must be considered a forbidden society, and no Catholic belonging to it can be admitted to the sacraments of the Church.

In conclusion, We urgently appeal to all the faithful of our flock, especially our Polish brethren, to be truly mindful of the repeated warnings of Our Lord and His apostles, namely, to beware of false prophets departing from sound doctrines and from false brethren causing dissension and disunion among the faithful. "Be not seduced. Evil communications corrupt good manners," St. Paul tells the Corinthians (I. Cor. XV. 33). This applies to bad books and papers just as much as to bad talk and speech. The tongue, as St. James tells us (III. 3 ff.), may do a great deal of harm and become a world of iniquity. But greater harm can be done by the pen and press. It has been well said that the modern press speaks with a hundred thousand tongues. Thousands have lost their faith because of reading books or periodicals dangerous to religion. The danger has become greater and more widespread in our days. Hence the great Popes Pius IX., Leo XIII., Pius X. have repeatedly and most solemnly warned Catholics of this growing danger; they have renewed the rules and laws of the Church forbidding the faithful to read such dangerous publications; they have insisted on the grave duty of Catholics to abstain from such books and papers not only because of the prohibition by the Church, but also because of the law of God which forbids every soul to expose itself knowingly and willingly to dangers of faith or good morals. Hence the 21st rule of the Roman Index clearly says:

"Daily journals, newspapers and periodicals which of set purpose attack religion or good morals are prohibited not only by the natural law, but also by the ecclesiastical law. Ordinaries are bound, when necessary, to carefully and properly warn the faithful of the danger and injury that such reading entails."

Therefore We beseech you all to listen to the voice and warning of the Church and keep away from yourselves and your houses all newspapers, periodicals and books that might hurt and weaken in your souls the spirit of holy Faith and of Christian virtue. Rather strengthen in your minds and hearts a loyal Catholic faith and the spirit of Christian piety by the reading of good Catholic literature and by listening attentively to the words of eternal truth preached to you by your priests and pastors, that thus you may grow in the charity of our heavenly Father, in the knowledge of Our Lord Jesus Christ, and in the unity of the Holy Spirit. With the apostle We admonish you: "Let not evil speech proceed from your mouth; but that which is good, to the edification of faith, that it may administer grace to the hearers. . . . Let all bitterness and anger, and indignation, and clamour, and blasphemy, be put away from you, with all malice. And be ye kind one to another; merciful, forgiving one another, even as God hath forgiven you in Christ." (Eph. IV. 29 ff).

Bestowing upon you all, dearly beloved brethren, our episcopal blessing, We greet you with the salutation of St. Paul: "The grace of Our Lord Jesus Christ be with you all. Amen."

Given on the feast of St. Ignatius, bishop and Martyr, Febr'y 1st, 1912.

SEBASTIAN G. MESSMER, Abp. of Milwaukee.
JAMES SCHWEBACH, Bp. of La Crosse.
FREDERICK EIS, Bp. of Marquette.
JOSEPH J. FOX, Bp. of Green Bay.
AUGUSTINE F. SCHINNER, Bp. of Superior.

P.S. This pastoral letter is to be read in all churches where Polish Catholics worship, on Sunday Sexagesima, Febr'y 11th, A.D. 1912.

Notes

Introduction

1. Wacław Kruszka, *Historya Polska w Ameryce* (13 vols.; Milwaukee, 1905–1908).

2. For information on the German Catholic position see Colman Barry, *The Catholic Church and German Americans* (Milwaukee, 1953). The standard source on the Americanist controversy is Thomas T. McAvoy, *The Great Crisis in American Catholic History, 1895–1900* (Chicago, 1957). See also Robert Cross, *The Emergence of Liberal Catholicism in America* (Cambridge, Mass., 1958), pp. 88–105, 182–205.

3. John Tracy Ellis, *American Catholicism* (Chicago, 1956), pp. 116–21, 146–47; Will Herberg, *Protestant, Catholic, Jew* (rev. ed.; Garden City, N.Y., 1960), pp. 136–71; Winthrop Hudson, *Religion in America* (2nd ed.; New York, 1973), pp. 258–59, 393–94; Sydney Ahlstrom, *A Religious History of the American People* (New Haven, Conn., 1972), pp. 1001–3, 1007.

4. William Thomas and Florian Znaniecki, *The Polish Peasant in Europe and America* (reprint ed.; 2 vols.; New York, 1974), 2:1523–74.

5. Daniel Buczek, *Immigrant Pastor* (Waterbury, Conn., 1974).

6. Andrew Greeley and Peter Rossi, *The Education of Catholic Americans* (Garden City, N.Y., 1968), pp. 3–4, 36–41.

7. Józef Miąso, *Dzieje oświaty polonijnej w Stanach Zjednoczonych* (Warsaw, 1970).

8. Kruszka, *Historya,* 2:58–59, 66–79.

9. See, for instance, Karol Wachtl, *Polonja w Ameryce* (Philadelphia, 1944), pp. 101–11; Joseph A. Wytrwal, *America's Polish Heritage* (Detroit, 1961), pp. 168–71; Eugene Kusielewicz, *Reflections on the Cultural Condition of the Polish American Community* (New York, 1969), pp. 11–13.

10. *Immigrant Pastor,* p. 149.

11. Paul Fox, *The Polish National Catholic Church* (Scranton, Pa., n.d.), pp. 65–73; Hieronim Kubiak, *Polski Narodowy Kościół Katolicki w Stanach Zjednoczonych Ameryki w Latach 1897–1965* (Wrocław, 1970), pp. 99–101.

12. Victor Greene, *For God and Country: The Rise of Polish and Lithuanian Ethnic Consciousness in America* (Madison, 1975).

13. *Historya,* 2:66–79.

14. *Polonja w Ameryce,* pp. 109–10.

15. *For God and Country,* p. 142.

16. Andrew Greeley, "Catholicism in America: Two Hundred Years and Counting," *The Critic,* 34 (Summer 1976), 17–18.

17. Anthony J. Kuzniewski, Jr., "Faith and Fatherland: An Intellectual History of the Polish Immigrant Community in Wisconsin, 1838–1918" (unpublished Ph.D. dissertation, Harvard University, 1973 [hereafter cited as "Dissertation"]), pp. 12–28.

18. Barry, *Catholic Church,* pp. 44–50, 128–30.

1. The Setting

1. The public documents of the council were published as *Acta et Decreta Concilii Plenarii Baltimorensis Tertii* (Baltimore, 1886). Biographies of the participants, sermons delivered at the council, and the pastoral letter issued at the conclusion may be found in *The Memorial Volume: A History of the Third Plenary Council of Baltimore, November 9–December 7, 1884* (Baltimore, 1885). On the rules for administration, see Peter Guilday, *A History of the Councils of Baltimore (1791–1884)* (New York, 1932), pp. 242, 268–69. On the rules for the nomination of bishops, see *Acta et Decreta,* pp. 12–14, and Guilday, *History,* p. 231. From 1833 to 1884, episcopal nominations were the responsibility of the American archbishops. Guilday, pp. 271–72.

2. Peter Leo Johnson, *Crosier on the Frontier: A Life of John Martin Henni* (Madison, 1959), pp. 123–24; Mileta Ludwig, *Right-Hand Glove Uplifted: A Biography of Archbishop Michael Heiss* (New York, 1968), pp. 444–48; Henry H. Heming, *The Catholic Church in Wisconsin* (Milwaukee, 1896), pp. 891–95; "Decreta Legenda in Synodo" of the Second Diocesan Synod of Green Bay, 1889, Milwaukee Archdiocesan Archives (hereafter cited as MAA), 65. In citations of the MAA, the numbers refer to the file.

3. *Handbook for Catholic Parishioners of the Archdiocese of Milwaukee* ([Milwaukee] 1907), pp. 23–27.

4. Johnson, *Henni,* pp. 38–52; Ludwig, *Heiss,* p. 145.

5. Johnson, *Henni,* pp. 124–25.

6. Peter Leo Johnson, *Halcyon Days: Story of St. Francis Seminary, Milwaukee* (Milwaukee, 1956), pp. 27, 68.

7. Barry, *Catholic Church,* pp. 45–50; Johnson, *Henni,* pp. 191–97; David Francis Sweeney, *The Life of John Lancaster Spalding, First Bishop of Peoria, 1840–1916* (New York, 1965), pp. 113–17.

8. Ludwig, *Heiss,* p. 433.

9. John Henni, for instance, utilized the statement "Language saves faith," and Bishop John Neumann of Philadelphia agreed (Barry, *Catholic Church,* pp. 10–11). Others objected. George Willard, pastor in Fond du Lac, Wisconsin, protested strongly to Gibbons in 1878 about the German policies in the state: "Their great endeavors are to make everything foreign and German, to make them obnoxious to Americans" (Archives of the Archdiocese of Baltimore, 73-5-1, cited in Barry, *Catholic Church,* p. 46). See also Johnson, *Henni,* pp. 134–35.

10. The best source on the St. Louis Petition and the Abbelen Memorial is Barry, *Catholic Church,* pp. 50–85. For specialized accounts of certain participants, see Ludwig, *Heiss,* pp. 511–25; James H. Moynihan, *The Life of Archbishop Ireland* (New York, 1953), pp. 57–59; John Tracy Ellis, *The Life of James Cardinal Gibbons, Archbishop of Baltimore, 1834–1921* (2 vols.; Milwaukee, 1952), 1:347–53.

11. John Cardinal Simeoni (prefect of the Congregation for the Propagation of the Faith) to Gibbons, Rome, June 8, 1887, copy in MAA, 40.

12. Letter of April 21, 1890, Archives of the Archdiocese of Baltimore, 87–J–5, cited in Sweeney, *Spalding,* p. 194; Heming, *Church in Wisconsin,* p. 307.

13. Sweeney, *Spalding,* pp. 195–96. Spalding wrote, in *The Religious Mission of the Irish People and Catholic Colonization* (New York, 1880), p. 62: "No other people could have done for the Catholic faith in the United States what the Irish people have done. Their [qualities] enabled them . . . to accomplish what would not have been accomplished by Italian, French, or German Catholics." Cited in Sweeney, *Spalding,* p. 123.

14. Circular letter, April 5, 1891, MAA, 73.

15. Barry gives the most complete account of the Cahensly controversy; see his *Catholic Church,* pp. 131–82.

16. James Gibbons, *A Retrospect of Fifty Years* (2 vols.; Baltimore, 1916), 2:151–52; Ellis, *Gibbons,* 1:378.

17. Ellis, *Gibbons,* 1:374–75; Barry, *Catholic Church,* pp. 163–65; Heming, *Church in Wisconsin,* p. 578.

18. McAvoy, *Great Crisis,* p. 361. See the same source (pp. 94–153), for the best description of the period between the Cahensly and the Americanist crises. Barry's account, *Catholic Church,* pp. 183–236, is also excellent. On the enthusiasm of the liberals for fostering contact with American civic and religious leaders, see Cross, *Liberal Catholicism,* pp. 51–105, 130–45.

19. John Tracy Ellis (ed.), *Documents of American Catholic History* (2 vols.; Chicago, 1967), 2:538–47. The letter was issued in large part because of a furor which developed in French Catholic circles over a biography of Isaac Hecker, founder of the Paulist Fathers. The book intensified a long-standing division between the monarchists and liberals, since the liberals used the book in an effort to demonstrate that Catholicism can enjoy greater success when it encounters democratic governments. McAvoy, *Great Crisis,* pp. 163–203.

20. McAvoy, *Great Crisis,* pp. 281–86.

21. The letter was dated Pentecost Sunday, 1899. MAA, 79.

22. Letter to Denis O'Connell, October 21, 1899, Richmond Diocesan Archives, in McAvoy, *Great Crisis,* pp. 332–33.

23. Richard M. Linkh, *American Catholicism and European Immigrants* (1900–1924) (Staten Island, N.Y., 1975), pp. 13–14.

24. Franz Loidl, *Erzbischof Friedrich Xaver Katzer, Ebensee–Milwaukee, 1844–1903* (Vienna, 1953), p. 54.

25. Monica Gardner, "The Great Emigration and Polish Romanticism," in W. F. Reddaway et al. (eds.), *The Cambridge History of Poland* (2 vols.; Cambridge, 1941). 2:321–23, 326; Wincenty Urban, *Ostatni Etap Dziejów*

Kościoła w Polsce przed Nowym Tysiącleciem, 1815–1921 (Rome, 1966), pp. 91–93.

26. Marian Kukiel, *Dzieje Polski Porozbiorowe, 1795–1921* (London, 1961), pp. 257, 259–60.

27. R. Dybowski, "Literature, Art and Learning in Poland since 1863," in Reddaway, *Cambridge History of Poland*, 2:535–36.

28. Kukiel, *Dzieje Polski*, p. 415; Jan Slomka, *From Serfdom to Self-Government: Memoirs of a Polish Village Mayor, 1842–1927*, trans. William J. Rose (London, 1941), pp. 14ff., 36–37.

29. Ibid., pp. 42, 95, 141; Thomas and Znaniecki, *Polish Peasant*, 1:205–84.

30. Thomas and Znaniecki, *Polish Peasant*, 1:285–86, 2:1309–11.

31. Slomka, *From Serfdom to Self-Government*, p. 142.

32. Łucja Borodziej, *Pruska polityka oświatowa na ziemiach polskich w okresie Kulturkampfu* (Warsaw, 1972), p. 47. Borodziej uses literacy statistics for army recruits in 1866–67, which she takes to be more representative than the much lower rate of illiteracy for naval recruits.

33. Lech Trzeciakowski, *Pod pruskim zaborem, 1850–1918* (Warsaw, 1973), pp. 134–42; Stefan Kieniewicz, *The Emancipation of the Polish Peasantry* (Chicago, 1969), pp. 197–98, 222.

34. U.S. Department of the Interior, Census Office, *Twelfth Census of the United States, 1900: Population*, 1:clxxiv–clxxv.

35. Only about 5,000 of the approximately 300,000 Poles who entered the United States in the first five years of the twentieth century went to Wisconsin (Dissertation, pp. 91–92).

36. See especially Victor Greene, *God and Country*, pp. 1–6. Stefan Kieniewicz, in *Polish Peasantry*, p. 197, supports this view while admitting the differences among the three partitions (p. 5).

37. Kukiel, *Dzieje Polski*, p. 461; Borodziej, *Pruska polityka oświatowa*, pp. 11–12, 33.

38. William J. Rose, "Prussian Poland, 1850–1914," in Reddaway, *Cambridge History of Poland*, 2:416.

39. Ibid., pp. 419–20; Kukiel, *Dzieje Polski*, pp. 395–98; Urban, *Ostatni Etap*, pp. 306–11.

40. Trzeciakowski, *Pod pruskim zaborem*, pp. 113–23.

41. Ibid., pp. 193, 285–314; Kukiel, *Dzieje Polski*, pp. 407–11. The term *ausrotten* was adopted by the philosopher Edward Hartmann in an article of 1885 ("Rückgang des Deutschtums") which encouraged greater stability within the German Empire through elimination of alien elements. For Poles, the expression carried the same emotional connotations as Hakatism. Piotr S. Wandycz, *The Lands of Partitioned Poland, 1795–1918* (Seattle, 1974), pp. 236, 284.

42. Mieczysław Szawleski, *Kwestja Emigracji w Polsce* (Warsaw, 1927), p. 32; Borodziej, *Pruska polityka oświatowa*, pp. 43–47.

43. Fałkowice was a village of 500 in the regency of Opole. Józef Madeja, *Dzieje szkoły w Fałkowicach* (Katowice, 1962), pp. 43–47, 50–51, 68–69.

44. Borodziej, *Pruska polityka oświatowa*, p. 139.

45. The cartoon appeared in *Diabel* (1887, no. 24). Trzeciakowski, *Pod pruskim zaborem,* illustration 23, following p. 160.

46. Borodziej, *Pruska polityka oświatowa,* pp. 227–28.

47. Trzeciakowski, *Kulturkampf w zaborze pruskim* (Poznan, 1970), pp. 274–78.

48. Szawleski, *Kwestja,* p. 32; Kieniewicz, *Polish Peasantry,* pp. 222, 225–26; Urban, *Ostatni Etap,* p. 231; Wandycz, *Lands of Partitioned Poland,* pp. 279–80.

49. *From Serfdom to Self-Government,* p. 157; Kieniewicz, *Polish Peasantry,* pp. 203–14; Krystyna Duda-Dziewierz, *Wieś Małopolska a Emigracja Amerykańska* (Warsaw, 1938), pp. 20–32. Slomka says that national consciousness developed slowly from newspapers, books, and by word of mouth. Some feared a restored Poland would mean a return to serfdom (pp. 171–73).

50. Szawleski, *Kwestja,* p. 53.

2. The Model Community

1. William F. Raney, *Wisconsin, a Story of Progress* (New York, 1940), pp. 199–209, 231–34; Bayrd Still, *Milwaukee: The History of a City* (Madison, 1948), pp. 186–91, 194–95, 324–40, 476–77, 483, 486; Paul Wallace Gates, *The Wisconsin Pine Lands of Cornell University* (Ithaca, 1943), p. 248.

2. Theodore C. Blegen, "The Competition of the Northwestern States for Immigrants," in *Wisconsin Magazine of History,* 3 (September 1919), 4–29; John G. Gregory, "Foreign Immigration to Wisconsin," in Wisconsin State Historical Society *Proceedings* (1901), pp. 138–40; Albert H. Sanford, "The Polish People of Portage County," in WSHS *Proceedings* (1907), pp. 270–71.

3. U.S. Department of the Interior, Census Office, *Eighth Census of the United States, 1860: Population,* 1:544; *Fourteenth Census, 1920: Population,* 2:983. Constantine Klukowski, in *A History of St. Mary of the Angels Catholic Church, Green Bay, Wisconsin, 1898–1954* (Pulaski, Wis., 1956), pp. 28, 35–38, presents a good discussion of the difficulties in attempting to get accurate statistics on the number of Polish immigrants.

4. *Kuryer Polski,* July 10, 1890; November 7, 1896; June 11, 1902; June 23, 1913; May 31, 1915.

5. Still, *Milwaukee,* pp. 268, 464. A more thorough discussion of the number of Polish Wisconsinites may be found in "Dissertation," pp. 87–97, 482–91.

6. *Twelfth Census, 1900: Population,* 1:clxx–clxxv.

7. Wisconsin Department of State, *Census Enumeration, 1905,* pt. 1, Enumeration of the Inhabitants, pp. 266–67; U.S. Congress, Senate, *Reports of the Immigration Commission,* vol. 26, *Immigrants in Cities* (S. Doc. 633, 61st Cong., 2d sess., 1911), pp. 266, 692.

8. *Fourteenth Census, 1920: Population,* 2:714, 766, 794, 983–95, 1036.

9. Kruszka, *Historya,* 7:21–25; Johnson, *Henni,* p. 136; Sanford, *Proceedings,* pp. 260–64.

10. Sanford, *Proceedings,* pp. 265, 272, 279–80.

11. U.S. Congress, Senate, *Reports of the Immigration Commission*, vol. 22, *Immigrants in Industries*, pt. 24, *Recent Immigrants in Agriculture*, 2:191.

12. Sanford, *Proceedings*, p. 280.

13. Ibid., pp. 267–87; *Kuryer*, April 9, 1892; November 10, 1894; November 16, 1898; Kruszka, *Historya*, 7:21–69.

14. "Dissertation," pp. 104–6.

15. Constantine Klukowski, *History of St. Stanislaus, Bishop and Martyr, Church, Hofa Park, Wisconsin* (Pulaski, Wis., 1958), pp. 11–17, 31–46; "Osada Pulaski," in *Kalendarz Franciszkański* (1913), pp. 114–27. See also Hof's obituary in *Miesięcznik Franciszkański*, 4 (November 1910), 128.

16. "Kolegium św. Bonawentury w Pulaski, Wis.," in *Kalendarz Franciszkański* (1916), pp. 93–102; Dacian Bluma and Theophilus Chowaniec, *A History of the Province of the Assumption of the Blessed Virgin Mary* (Pulaski, Wis., 1967), pp. 19ff.

17. Robert G. Carroon, "Foundations of Milwaukee's Polish Community," in *Historical Messenger of the Milwaukee County Historical Society*, 25 (September 1970), 89, 94; Kruszka, *Historja Polska w Ameryce* (rev. ed.; Milwaukee, 1937), 1:549–51, 687–90. At the time of his death in 1937, Wenceslaus Kruszka was preparing the second volume of a projected two-volume revision of the work, originally published between 1905 and 1908. Despite the variant spelling of the title's first word, the later work was a revision and not a completely new history. Unless otherwise noted, all subsequent citations refer to the original, unrevised book.

18. Edward S. Kerstein, "The Kaszubas of Milwaukee's Jones Island," in Thaddeus Borun (ed.), *We, the Milwaukee Poles* (Milwaukee, 1946), pp. 121–22; Frank K. Raniszewski, "Milwaukee Poles in Business," in ibid., pp. 217–28; Still, *Milwaukee*, pp. 269–73, 454; *Kuryer*, January 1 and October 16, 1895. See also Martin Cyborowski's article, "Polacy w Milwaukee," in *Kuryer*, June 27, 1908.

19. June 27, 1903. See also the various parish histories in Borun, *We, the Milwaukee Poles*.

20. John E. Kalupa, "The Fourteenth Ward," in *We, the Milwaukee Poles*, p. 157; Cyborowski, "Polacy in Milwaukee," in *Kuryer*, June 27, 1908.

21. Stanisław Osada, *Prasa i Publicystyka Polska w Ameryce* (Pittsburgh, 1930), pp. 21–40; Edmund G. Olszyk, *The Polish Press in America* (Milwaukee, 1940).

22. Peter Piasecki, Frank Krukar, and Leo Kosak, "History of Company K," in Borun, *We, the Milwaukee Poles*, pp. 123–24; Cyborowski, "Polacy in Milwaukee," in *Kuryer*, June 27, 1908.

23. Still, *Milwaukee*, pp. 273, 454–55.

24. "Dissertation," pp. 122–24.

25. Aleksander Syski, *Ks. Józef Dąbrowski: Monografia Historyczna* (Orchard Lake, Mich., 1942), pp. 54–55, 68–72; [Józef Dąbrowski], "Historia Coloniae Poloniae, Portage Co., Wis.," MS in Green Bay Diocesan Archives (hereafter cited as GBDA).

26. Syski, *Dąbrowski*, pp. 74–75; Kruszka, *Historya*, 7:40–43.

27. Michael Stoltz to Messmer, Ellis, December 9, 1893, GBDA. Stoltz

hardly helped his case by fabricating a statement he attributed to Matthew 16:18–19: "A bishop's words are hard."

28. Kruszka, *Historja* (rev. ed.), pp. 666–67; Thomas Grenbowski to Messmer, Polonia, January 23, 1895, GBDA. A number of protest letters against the pastors at Polonia are in GBDA and have been translated by Charles Lepich.

29. Syski, *Dąbrowski*, pp. 80–91.

30. Ibid., pp. 96, 219–21; Kruszka, *Historja* (rev. ed.), p. 667.

31. Milwaukee *Sentinel,* February 1, March 16 and 19, 1875.

32. Ibid., October 19, 1895; *Kuryer,* October 17, 1896; Kruszka, *Historja* (rev. ed.), pp. 689–90.

33. Edward A. Masalewicz, *History of St. Hedwig's Congregation, Thorp, Wisconsin* (n.p., 1966), pp. 19ff., Klukowski, *St. Mary of the Angels,* pp. 68–80; *Kuryer,* April 16, 1892; May 13, 1893; March 23, 1894.

34. *Kuryer,* November 5, 1895.

35. Ibid., July 29, 1890; September 11 and November 28, 1891; Heming, *Church in Wisconsin,* p. 340; Kruszka, *Historya,* 7:153–55.

36. Wenceslaus Kruszka, *Siedm Siedmioleci czyli Pół Wieku Życia* (2 vols.; Poznan and Milwaukee, 1924), 1:35, 63; *Historya,* 5:38–42, 45–46.

37. Olszyk, *Polish Press,* p. 56; *Kuryer,* June 23, 1898.

38. *Kuryer,* June 23, 1898; Reuben Gold Thwaites, *Wisconsin: The Americanization of a French Settlement* (Boston, 1908), pp. 401–3; Frank H. Miller, "The Polanders in Wisconsin," Parkman Club *Publications,* 10 (1896), 241–44; Jerry M. Cooper, "The Wisconsin National Guard in the Milwaukee Riots of 1886," *Wisconsin Magazine of History,* 55 (Autumn 1971), 31–48.

39. A good ten-year history of the paper appeared in the anniversary issue of June 23, 1898. See also Olszyk, *Polish Press,* pp. 56–57.

40. *Kuryer,* March 17 and August 12, 1890; September 7, 1893.

41. See especially the issues of September 10, October 18, 20, and 27, 1890. An editorial on March 20 emphasized the fact that the *Kuryer's* opposition to the Bennett Law was an independent judgment and not the result of clerical pressure. But by fall, close association with the priests was good politics. On the 1890 election in Wisconsin generally, see William F. Whyte, "The Bennett Law Campaign," *Wisconsin Magazine of History,* 10 (June 1927), 363–90; and Roger E. Wyman, "Wisconsin Ethnic Groups and the Election of 1890," *WMH,* 51 (Summer 1968), 269–93.

42. *Kuryer,* November 5, 1890; March 6, 1891.

43. Ibid., January 8, March 24, April 23, and December 26, 1891.

44. Ibid., October 17, November 7–11, 1892; January 17 and April 22, 1893; May 7, 1895. There was also a short-lived attempt to boost Kruszka for mayor of Milwaukee in 1893. See issues of February 3 and 4, 1893.

45. Ibid., January 25, 1893; May 7, 1895.

46. See various issues of the *Kuryer,* September 9–October 2, 1893. *Przegląd Emigracyjny* condemned Neuman in the issue of February 15, 1894 (p. 45).

47. Kruszka, *Historya,* 5:21–22.

48. Kruszka, *Siedm,* 1:36–195, 205–6; *Kuryer,* June 19, 1895. The *Kuryer* published articles and addresses of Wenceslaus Kruszka beginning late in 1893. For samples of those early efforts, see Kruszka, *Siedm,* 1:206–10, and *Kuryer,* April 28, May 1, 2, and 4, 1894.

49. *Wiarus,* December 22, 1892.

50. *Kuryer,* December 14, 1893.

51. Ibid., July 13, 1895; Joseph Swastek, "Kardynał Ledóchowski," in *Sodalis,* 38 (March 1957), 68–70.

52. *Kuryer,* September 18, 1891.

53. Ibid., August 20–27, 1892.

54. Ibid., October 9 and 28, 1895; January 6–7, 1896.

55. Ibid., May 3, 1894.

3. The Emergence of Factions

1. *Kuryer,* January 6, 13 and May 6, 1896.

2. Ibid., May 26 and 27, 1896.

3. "Kazanie Ks. Szukalskiego, 31. Maja. [1896]," MAA, Kruszka Correspondence; *Kuryer,* June 1, 1896; Milwaukee Board of School Directors, *Proceedings,* May 1896–May 1897 (Milwaukee, 1897), p. 37.

4. *Kuryer,* June 1, 1896.

5. Ibid., June 3, 1896.

6. Ibid., June 3–5 and 30, 1896.

7. Kruszka told the committee that he had first proposed the introduction of Polish into the public schools to several local pastors in 1891, but that they had opposed the scheme as a possible detriment to parish schools. At that time, he had deferred to their wishes. Now he claimed to support the PES proposal because the parish schools had not improved in the interval. Ibid., June 12, 1896.

8. Milwaukee Board of School Directors, *Proceedings,* pp. 89–90.

9. *Kuryer,* July 3, 1896; August 8, 1900; October 3, 1906; and February 11, 1908. Wenceslaus Kruszka estimated that there were 6,000 children in Polish parochial schools in Milwaukee in 1900 and 9,000 in Wisconsin. They were taught by 200 lay teachers and 800 religious sisters. Although he admitted that many of the teaching sisters did not have college training, Kruszka maintained that they had sufficient preparation for work in elementary schools, where, with classes sometimes as large as 130, one did the work of three. *Historya,* 2:87–88, 101; see also Miąso, *Dzieje oświaty,* pp. 112–26.

10. *Kuryer,* November 4–6, 1896.

11. Ibid., April 16 and October 17, 1898.

12. Kruszka, *Historya,* 5:77; *Kuryer,* January 17 and December 9–31, 1897; *Wiarus,* January 21, 1897; January 5, 1899.

13. Kruszka, *Historya,* 5:80–81.

14. *Kuryer,* May 20, July 3–8 and 21, 1899; Kruszka, *Siedm,* 1:216. The friendship between Kruszka and Czerwinski had been so close that Kruszka cast a complimentary vote for Czerwinski for U.S. senator when the state's

Democratic caucus became deadlocked early in 1893. *Kuryer*, January 25, 1893.

15. Kruszka, *Historya*, 5:25–26.

16. *Kuryer*, June 14, 1897; July 7, 1900.

17. Kruszka, *Historya*, 7:9–10; *Kuryer*, June 29, 1901; May 24, 1902; *Souvenir Album of the Golden Jubilee of the Dedication of St. Josaphat's Basilica, 1901–1951* (Milwaukee, 1951), pp. 34–37.

18. Letter of Hyacinth Fudzinski, *The Catholic Citizen* (Milwaukee), January 29, 1910. The *Kuryer* (August 13, 1896) put the cost of the stone at $85,000. See also the *Kuryer*, June 17, 1896, and May 24, 1902.

19. *Kuryer*, May 2, 1899. The mine came into Polish hands in 1894, when it was purchased by a corporation headed by Casimir Midowicz and including Grutza and Rev. Vincent Barzynski of Chicago. Midowicz left the mine after two years to work on his invention, the "wave motor," which was to propel ships by using the force of ocean waves. Kruszka, *Historya*, 3:109–10.

20. *Kuryer*, August 20, 1901; Kruszka, *Historya*, 8:10.

21. Kruszka, *Siedm*, 1:359–60. See also the section of Kruszka's history which appeared in the *Kuryer*, May 24, 1902, and his description of a conversation with Martinelli (*Historya*, 8:10–11).

22. Kruszka, *Siedm*, 1:324–29.

23. Ibid., 1:268, 290, 335–40, 349.

24. Kruszka, *Historya*, 1:25–47.

25. Kruszka, *Siedm*, 1:376–80, 468–84.

26. Karol Wachtl, *Dzieje Zjednoczenia Polskiego Rzymskiego-Katolickiego w Ameryce* (Chicago, 1913), pp. 260–61; Greene, *God and Country*, pp. 130–31; *Kuryer*, December 13–14, 1900; Kruszka, *Siedm*, 1:481–84.

27. Kruszka, "When the Firmaments Shook," *Kuryer*, December 29, 1900. See also the statements of Augustine Schinner and Frederick Eis, in *Kuryer*, November 23, 1900, and January 30, 1901.

28. Kruszka, *Siedm*, 1:329–34.

29. The article's title, "Anyone Who Does Not Care for His Own Has No Faith," was taken from 1 Timothy 5:8, but Kruszka used 1 Corinthians 14 as a theological basis. Kruszka, *Siedm*, 1:385–89.

30. Ibid., 1:389–95, 397.

31. Ibid., 397–404.

32. Ibid., 549–50.

33. Ibid., 419–29; Kruszka, *Historya*, 2:42–46; *Kuryer*, September 24–October 1, 1901.

34. Executive Committee to the American Catholic Archbishops, Chicago, November 10, 1901, MAA, *Kurjer Polski* File.

35. Keane to Casimir Sztuczko, Dubuque, December 16, 1901, in Kruszka, *Siedm*, 1:445.

36. Ibid., 1:448.

37. Ledóchowski to Katzer, Rome, March 22, 1902, MAA, 55.

38. Kruszka, *Siedm*, 1:507–9, 513; *Kuryer*, April 5, 1902.

39. Milwaukee *Free Press*, October 10, 1902.

40. Kruszka, *Siedm*, 1:546, 552–54.
41. Victor Greene, *God and Country*, p. 134, interprets Pitass's motives as arising from loyalist tendencies which dampened his enthusiasm for the mission, but clearly the Buffalo pastor was indispensable in other ways. Kruszka, *Siedm*, 1:596–99.
42. Ibid., 1:572, 574–77, 593, 601.
43. Kruszka, *Historya*, 2:129–37; *Kuryer*, June 4, 1903; *Pamiątka: 25-Letnej Rotniczy Założenia Parafii Świetego Piotra* (Stevens Point, Wis., 1901), pp. 81, 99. The full title of the congregation is Sisters of St. Joseph of the Third Order of St. Francis.
44. *Kuryer*, August 21 and November 15, 1897; January 19, April 9, and August 29, 1898. Specific information on the South Milwaukee controversy is in Kruszka, *Historya*, 8:30–32. Details on the Thorp conflict are in Masalewicz, *Thorp*, pp. 21–25. The prevalence of the independent movement among Polish Catholics prompted Cardinal Ledóchowski to warn American bishops that Kozlowski had been excommunicated. Letter of May 2, 1898, MAA, 55.
45. *Kuryer*, April 11, 1903.

4. The Promise

1. Kruszka, *Siedm*, 1:596, 599; *Historya*, 2:68–71. Kruszka described his stay in Rome in *Siedm*, 1:635–708, 731–816.
2. Jan Piekoszewski speculates that Cardinal Puzyna's veto on behalf of Francis Joseph in the papal conclave of 1903 created an unfavorable climate in Rome for Polish aspirations. "Kościół i Polonia w Stanach Zjednoczonych Ameryki," in Hieronim Kubiak and Andrzej Pilch (eds.), *Stan i Potrzeby Badań nad Zbiorowościami Polonijnymi* (Wrocław, 1976), pp. 387–88. The point is interesting, but I can find nothing to substantiate it. See, for instance, Kruszka's discussion of the matter in *Siedm*, 1:687.
3. *Siedm*, 1:708–32.
4. Sztuczko's letter was dated October 23, 1903 (ibid., 1:760–61). For information on expenses and funding, see Kruszka's discussion, ibid., 1:742–43.
5. Ibid., 1:748–50. The responses are on pp. 750–52.
6. Ibid., 1:796. Sebastian Messmer was one of those who wrote, probably unfavorably, though the nature of his statement is unclear. Diomede Falconio, the papal delegate, wrote to Messmer from Washington on December 5, 1903: "I thank you for the information you gave me [about Wenceslaus Kruszka] and I shall at once notify the Most Eminent Prefect of Propaganda. I would furthermore ask you that if new evidences of the case should be brought to you, you would let me know in order that I may keep informed the S. Congregation." MAA, Messmer Correspondence.
7. Petition of Pitass and Kruszka to Pius X, February 25, 1904, MAA, 55. Trans. Nelson Minnich.
8. Kruszka, *Siedm*, 1:803–6; *Kuryer*, April 28, 1904.

9. *Kuryer*, May 10–12, 1904; Kruszka, *Siedm*, 2:7–13.

10. *Siedm*, 2:23–29. See also the articles on Kruszka's mission in *Straż* (Scranton), December 19, 1903 and April 9 and July 9, 1904.

11. Kruszka, *Siedm*, 2:15, 61. Messmer showed his unwillingness to bend to pressure from the Poles in nominating his successor to Green Bay. Kruszka had written him from Rome to urge Messmer to show his love for the Poles "not only in word but in deed," and to remind him of the Polish independents' argument that "Rome is careless about her children." (Kruszka to Messmer, January 26, 1904, MAA, Kruszka Correspondence.) Other Polish and Irish interests also promoted candidates for the vacant see, but in the end Joseph Fox was appointed, keeping Green Bay within the German sphere (Kruszka, *Siedm*, 1:785–86). See also a letter from the Association of the Secular Polish Roman Catholic Clergy in the United States of America to the Diocesan Consultors of the Green Bay Diocese, January 29, 1904 (MAA, "Kurjer Polski" File).

12. Kruszka, *Siedm*, 2:21–22.

13. Ibid., 2:48–49.

14. Kruszka reprinted a number of these letters in *Siedm*, 2:31–81, passim.

15. Ibid., 2:87–88; *Kuryer*, March 6 and May 2, 1905.

16. Kruszka, *Siedm*, 2:91, 102.

17. Roosevelt's statement is taken from Symon's official report to Pius X. Ibid., 2:107.

18. Ibid., 2:115–19, 125; *Kuryer*, June 19, 1905.

19. *Kuryer*, June 20, 1905; Kruszka, *Siedm*, 2:142.

20. Polish translations of the two reports are in Kruszka, *Siedm*, 2:171–74, 188–99.

21. Letter of October 5, 1905, *Kuryer*, November 18, 1905.

22. Kruszka, *Siedm*, 2:179–83.

23. *Kuryer*, August 22, October 2, 6, and 10, 1903; April 16, 1904.

24. Ibid., April 25, 1904; April 13, 1905.

25. Ibid., April 6 and November 9, 1904.

26. Ibid., April 30, 1906, and January 16, 1907.

27. *Siedm*, 2:58.

28. Dated at Milwaukee, January 19, 1905, Archives of the Archdiocese of Baltimore, 102-A (in Barry, *Catholic Church*, p. 275n.).

29. Kruszka, *Siedm*, 2:61, 177.

30. Ibid., 2:178. There was both truth and exaggeration in Kruszka's view. Colman Barry called Messmer "an advocate of slow yet consistent assimilation" (*Catholic Church*, p. 165). Yet Messmer was not above defending the cause of German-American Catholics. When he wrote to congratulate Denis O'Connell on assuming the rectorship of the Catholic University of America, he urged him to add some Germans to the faculty (dated at Milwaukee, January 26, 1904, Archives of the Catholic University of America, O'Connell Papers; *Catholic Church*, pp. 248–49n.). Evidently Messmer saw the Poles in another light. He remained suspicious of their campaign for equality in Church leadership, and particularly of Wenceslaus Kruszka's tactic of appealing directly to Rome.

31. The letters, dated at Ripon on February 25, 1905, and February 6, 1906, are in MAA, Kruszka Correspondence.

32. Ibid., Messmer's letter is dated March 15, 1905.

33. Kruszka reprinted the exchange of letters in *Siedm*, 2:147–60.

34. Ibid., 2:204. The entire set of articles, which started on December 6, 1905, were reprinted in the same volume, pp. 206–577.

35. See especially the columns of February 3, March 3, 8, 15, 17, 1906; January 24 and March 16, 1907, in the *Kuryer*.

36. Ibid., December 5, 1904, and March 25, 1905.

37. *Free Press*, October 15, 1906.

38. *Siedm*, 2:494. The column appeared October 25.

39. *Free Press*, October 29, 1906. A copy of the resolution is in MAA, Kruszka Correspondence.

40. *Kuryer*, September 13, 1906.

41. Michael Kruszka's letter was dated January 13. The chancellor, Joseph Rainer, wrote from Fond du Lac on January 20, 1906. *Siedm*, 2:253.

42. Pociecha to Messmer, Pine Grove, Wisconsin, February 16, 1906, MAA, Kruszka Correspondence.

43. Simon to Wenceslaus Kruszka, Ostrowity Prymasowski, March 2, 1906, and Symon to Kruszka, Rome, March 1, 1906, in Kruszka, *Siedm*, 2:342–44.

44. Dated at Milwaukee, April 16, 1906 (ibid., 2:370–71). See also Pociecha's letter of February 16.

45. *Siedm*, 2:371.

46. Ibid., 1:764–67.

47. Kruszka reprinted the entire *Dziennik Chicagoski* column. Ibid., 2:517–19.

48. Ibid., 2:520–21.

49. "Rev. Boleslaus Edward Goral," in *Memoirs of Milwaukee County*, edited by Jerome A. Watrous (2 vols.; Madison, 1909), 2:438–39. On Goral's opposition to Kruszka, see the letter of Jan Szukalski to Kruszka, Milwaukee, February 16, 1904, in *Siedm*, 1:781–82.

50. *Siedm*, 2:560.

51. Goral to Messmer, St. Francis, Wisconsin, January 9, 1907, MAA, Messmer Correspondence. The letter was a strange contrast to the editorial claim of the *Nowiny* on February 27, 1907, that the priests had acted as one in their support for the new paper. As late as March 1, 1908, Goral wrote to Messmer to complain of the lack of cooperation from the priests because they were afraid the enterprise would not succeed or because "they are either open or at least secret friends of the Kruszkas." Dated at St. Francis, MAA, Messmer Correspondence.

52. Messmer to the Polish priests of the Milwaukee Archdiocese, Milwaukee, February 20, 1906, MAA, 75.

53. Issue of December 19, 1906.

54. Kruszka, *Siedm*, 2:555. See also his *Kuryer* columns of March 14 and 16, 1907.

55. March 6 and 8, 1907.

56. Kruszka, *Siedm*, 2:572–73, 576.

57. Dated at Ripon, March 29, 1907, Kruszka Correspondence.

58. Dated at Ripon, April 4, 1907 (ibid.). Messmer had been considering the measure for some time. Diomede Falconio wrote to him on July 9, 1906, that he could order Kruszka to stop the agitation on the Polish question if he thought it prudent. MAA, Messmer Correspondence.

59. May 1, 1907.

60. Kruszka, *Siedm,* 2:62–65, 82–83, 338–40.

61. *Kuryer*, April 11, 1907.

5. From Resistance to Revolt

1. *Nowiny* and *Kuryer*, May and June, 1907. The charges are specified in the minutes of the extrajudicial inquiry into the case of W. Kruszka against *Nowiny,* October–December, 1907, MAA, Kruszka Correspondence. See also Michael Kruszka's letter to Sebastian Messmer, Milwaukee, June 13, 1907 (private collection of Szymon Deptuła, Milwaukee).

2. *Kuryer*, January 31 and June 27, 1908.

3. See the letters in Kruszka, *Siedm*, 2:603–8; also W. Kruszka to Messmer, Ripon, June 19, 1907, MAA, Kruszka Correspondence.

4. The hearings were held October 4 and 29, December 4, and 13, 1907. Minutes in MAA, Kruszka Correspondence.

5. See Kruszka's letters of October 14, November 2 and 16, 1907. By July 22, 1908, Kruszka wrote: "I want justice. Either I am a briber, an atheist, a rebel, a heretic, a hypocrite, as the 'Nowiny,' approved by Your Grace, represented me to the reading public—then I ought to be suspended without delay; or I am not—and then the libelers ought to be punished without delay." All dated at Ripon, in MAA, Kruszka Correspondence.

Letters of Falconio (Washington, January 27, 1908) and Messmer (Milwaukee, March 11, 1908) to Kruszka attempt to explain the delay. See Kruszka, *Siedm*, 2:619–21.

6. Report of R. J. Smith, Kenosha, October 22, 1908, MAA, Messmer Correspondence.

7. Dated at St. Francis, January 2, 1908, in Kruszka, *Siedm*, 2:618–19.

8. Messmer's letters were dated at Milwaukee, March 11 and April 22, 1908, ibid., 2:620–21, 623.

9. Antonucci to Kruszka, Rome, May 23, 1908, ibid., 2:625–26.

10. Goral to Messmer, St. Francis, March 1, 1908, MAA, Messmer Correspondence.

11. Kruszka to Messmer, Ripon, November 11, 1908, MAA, Kruszka Correspondence.

12. *Sentinel,* November 8, 1908. W. Kruszka's comment on the archbishop's statement was "Long live consistency!" *Siedm,* 2:638.

13. Goral to Messmer, March 1, 1908, MAA, Messmer Correspondence. Goral acknowledged that the paper was in an "awful plight" due to the shortage of funds and the difficulty of finding an editor who was not openly or secretly

sympathetic to the Kruszkas. He admitted soliciting funds from "nearly all the Polish priests in America," and stated that he was considering offering shares to non-Polish priests secretly "so that nobody . . . would know anything about it."

14. Kruszka, *Siedm*, 2:639–47.

15. *Kuryer*, June 18 and July 29, 1908; *Nowiny*, June 17, 1908; *Miesięcznik Franciszkański*, 1 (July 1908), 326.

16. Greene, *God and Country*, pp. 168–70; Kruszka, *Historya*, 13:187–89; Mieczysław Haiman, "J. E. Ks. Biskup Paweł Rhode, Jego Życie i Czyny," in *Przegląd Katolicki*, 9 (March–April 1934), 14, 19.

17. Kruszka, *Siedm*, 2:633, 650–56.

18. Kruszka wrote to Messmer from Ripon on June 2, 1909 and from Milwaukee on March 2, 1910. His appeal to Falconio was dated at Ripon on April 6, 1909. MAA, Kruszka Correspondence.

19. The cited passage is from the letter of March 17, 1909. See also letters of June 30, September 17, and November 19, 1907, January 15 and August 22, 1908, and April 13, 1909, all of which urged Messmer to greater speed in the matter. MAA, Messmer Correspondence.

20. Messmer to Kruszka, Milwaukee, September 18, 1909, ibid.; Kruszka to Messmer, Ripon, November 16, 1907 and June 20, 1909, MAA. Kruszka Correspondence.

21. Kruszka, *Siedm*, 2:663–66.

22. The letter was dated at Ripon, September 30, 1907 (MAA, Kruszka Correspondence). See also *Handbook,* pp. 62–63.

23. Sztuczko to Messmer, Chicago, August 30, 1907 (MAA, *Kurjer Polski* File); *Kuryer*, August 29, 1907.

24. The best discussion to date on the Polish parochial schools is Joseph Miąso's *Dzieje oświaty polonijnej,* recently published in English translation under the sponsorship of the Kościuszko Foundation. See also Kuzniewski, "Boot Straps and Book Learning: Reflections on the Education of Polish Americans," in *Polish American Studies*, 32 (Autumn 1975), 14–26. Typical discussions in the Milwaukee press may be found in *Nowiny*, November 2 and 16, 1907, and *Kuryer*, June 7, 1907.

25. *Kuryer*, May 5, 1908; *Free Press*, April 21, 1908; *Nowiny*, December 17, 1908 and January 25, 1909.

26. The committee's chairman was Bernard Traudt. Its Polish-American members included Gulski and Goral. Its reports and Messmer's circular are in MAA, 107.

27. *Nowiny*, January 14, 1910; *Kuryer*, January 18, 1910.

28. *Siedm*, 2:701–5, 712–13. Kruszka's parish was not the only one to fall behind in Josaphat payments. By 1916 the situation had become so serious that Messmer threatened to impose a partial interdict on several parishes, including St. Adalbert's, if payments were not received within a month. It was "the most drastic letter of his whole career." Benjamin J. Blied, *Three Archbishops of Milwaukee* (Milwaukee, 1955), p. 120.

29. The first article was reprinted in the *Kuryer*, May 31, 1909. The second is in *Siedm*, 2:658–61.

30. *Siedm*, 2:688, 691–93.

31. Ibid., 2:681–86, and Milwaukee papers for July 18, 1910. Kruszka's speech was later printed as a brochure, *Krzyżackie plemię* (The Teutonic Race).

32. *Kuryer*, March 2, 1909, and January 3, 1911. The paper was ruthless in presenting historical arguments for not trusting Germans. An article of July 19, 1911, cited the example of Gero, graf of Brandenburg, who invited twenty Polish princes to his court and then had them murdered. It also discussed the brutality of the Teutonic Knights and the policies of the Prussians: "Thus it has always been and always will be. Poles are obliged always to remember this—and enough of them do remember. . . . ."

33. Conflicting reports on the convention in *Nowiny* and *Kuryer* between September 13 and 17 indicated that the meeting was a test of strength between the two parties. Neither achieved total victory, but the "*Nowiny*-ites" clearly had a majority. See also *Nowiny*, December 23, 1910, and *Kuryer*, February 20 and March 28, 1911.

34. *Nowiny*, March 5, 1909; *Tygodnik Polski*, January 26, 1911; *Miesięcznik Franciszkański*, 4 (September 1911), 746–48, and 5 (October–December 1911), 63–64, 126–28, 186–91.

35. *Kuryer*, July 22, September 29, and October 11, 1911.

36. The *Free Press* gave front-page coverage to the organizational meeting in its issues of August 13 and 14. Wenceslaus Kruszka commented on the 13th: "When Archbishop Messmer's place becomes vacant, trouble on account of national feelings is bound to come, unless the Poles, who constitute a large fraction of the Catholics of this diocese, have their own bishop."

37. Ibid., September 11, 1911; *Kuryer*, October 2, November 7, December 12 and 18, 1911; Kruszka, *Siedm*, 2:693–94.

38. *Free Press*, August 17, 1911.

39. *Kuryer*, September 6, 1911; *Nowiny*, September 14, 1911; Barry, *Catholic Church*, p. 253.

40. The document was dated October 10, 1911. MAA, untitled file.

41. Kruszka's *Free Press* interview was quoted in the *Kuryer*, September 6, 1911. Rainer's letter, dated at Evanston on September 26, and Kruszka's reply, Milwaukee, September 28, are in *Siedm*, 2:705–7.

42. Letter dated at Milwaukee, November 4, 1911, *Siedm*, 2:709–11.

43. Kruszka, "Sketch of what and why I spoke at Kenosha, Wis., Dec. 10th, 1911," Milwaukee, January 27, 1912, MAA, untitled file.

44. W. G. Miller to Messmer, Waukesha, June 17, 1911, MAA, Messmer Correspondence. See also *Kuryer*, May 6, June 24, and August 3, 1911.

6. The Archbishop's Counteroffensive

1. *Kuryer*, January 22, 23, 29, 1912; Manel, "Walka na Śmierć," in *Miesięcznik Franciszkański*, 5 (January 1912), 252–56. *Wiarus*, January 4, 1912, reprinted the priests' letter.

2. Kruszka described the first and second hearings in *Siedm*, 2:724–33. See

also "Sketch of what and why I spoke at Kenosha, Wis., Dec. 10th, 1911" (MAA, untitled file).

3. For a firsthand account of Rhode's organizing activities, see Władysław Krakowski, "J. E. Ks. Biskup Rhode a Zjednoczenie Kapłanów Polskich," in *Przegląd Katolicki,* 9 (March–April 1934), 54–55, 58.

4. *Rolnik,* February 16, 1912. (After preparation of this manuscript, I was informed that the Wisconsin State Historical Society has a complete set of *Rolnik.* Since it has not proved to be a particularly rich source on the Church War, I have not examined the issues of 1915, the one crucial year not previously consulted for this work.)

5. Kruszka's account of the Detroit meeting is in *Siedm,* 2:736–51. The *Nowiny* excerpts appeared on February 12, 1912. See also Stanisław Osada, *Jak się Kstałtowała Polska Dusza Wychodźtwa w Ameryce* (Pittsburgh, 1930), p. 56.

6. Rhode to Messmer, Chicago, February 9, 1912. MAA, Kruszka Correspondence.

7. Kruszka to Messmer, Milwaukee, February 9, 1912, and Rhode to Messmer, Chicago, February 12, 1912. Ibid.

8. Fox to Messmer, February 11, 1912. MAA, Messmer Correspondence.

9. Kruszka, *Siedm,* 2:773–75.

10. The statement was dated March 4, 1912. MAA, Messmer Correspondence.

11. Kruszka, *Siedm,* 2:779.

12. Messmer discussed the background of the letter in an undated interview (MAA, *Kurjer Polski* File). The pastoral letter is reprinted in the appendix.

13. MAA, Messmer Correspondence.

14. S. Elbert, W. Polaczyk, L. Peścinski, and J. Pociecha to Messmer and Fox, February 19, 1912. MAA, Messmer Correspondence.

15. *Siedm,* 2:767–68; circular letter of Messmer, February 29, 1912 (MAA, 116). Bishop Frederick Eis, writing to Messmer from Marquette on February 25, argued that it was unnecessary to treat violations as reserved sins. Bishop Fox, however, endorsed the imposition of the sanction in a letter of February 24. But in a letter written to Bishop James Schwebach of La Crosse on the previous day, Messmer noted that the prelates had originally desired to impose such a sanction but had dropped it on the advice of their lawyers. Now, at the request of the Polish priests, he asked that pastors of all nationalities be informed of the sanctions, lest violators attempt to receive absolution at a non-Polish church. MAA, Messmer Correspondence.

16. *Miesięcznik Franciszkański,* 5 (June and July, 1912), 573–74, 621–32.

17. Ibid., 5 (April 1912), 466–68, and (June 1912), 564–67. Responses to the letter from a number of bishops are in MAA, Messmer Correspondence.

18. Both pamphlets are in MAA, *Kurjer Polski* File.

19. *Kuryer,* August 26, 1912. Bonzano to Messmer, Washington, February 18, 1913, cited in *Nowiny,* February 3, 1914.

20. *Siedm,* 2:761–67.

21. Affidavits of Michael Kwasniewski and Michael Kowalski, October

16, 1912, and of Jadwiga Janukanis, October 17, 1912. MAA, Messmer Correspondence.

22. Kruszka, *Siedm*, 2:778–89, 795–97.

23. The *Kuryer*, in March and April 1912, printed a number of letters from readers who were willing to discuss experiences with their confessors over the provisions of the pastoral letter. If the reports are reliable, enforcement of the penalties varied widely. That impression was supported by Rev. Joseph Schulist in a personal interview in Polonia, Wisconsin, in August 1970. For an overview of the statistics from the Green Bay Diocese, see "Dissertation," pp. 385–87, 498–99.

24. Kuryer Publishing Co., *vs.* Messmer *et al.*, Wisconsin Supreme Court, Second Circuit (August Term, 1915), No. 76, *Case*, pp. 81–82; *Kuryer*, January 15, 1913, and October 31, 1915.

25. *Kuryer* and *Nowiny*, September 11–13, 1912.

26. *Kuryer*, November 17–20, 1912. For a discussion of membership figures for the federation, see "Dissertation," p. 382n.

27. *Siedm*, 2:688–89.

28. Circular letter of Messmer, Milwaukee, October 11, 1912, MAA, 113.

29. Messmer to Kruszka, Milwaukee, November 2, 1913. MAA, Messmer Correspondence.

30. Messmer's letter was dated December 12, 1912 (MAA, 116). On the difficulties in Green Bay, see the *Nowiny*, September 24, 1912, and annual parish reports in GBDA.

31. *Nowiny*, January 6, 18, and April 1, 1913; Messmer's letter to the members of St. Adalbert's Congregation in South Milwaukee was printed in the issue of January 20.

32. Affidavit of Jadwiga Janukanis, December 18, 1912. MAA, Messmer Correspondence.

33. *Kuryer*, January 14 and June 28, 1913.

34. The *Nowiny* covered the bill extensively from March 10 until its defeat on May 21.

35. *Życiorys Przew. Ks. Edwarda Kozłowskiego, Proboszcza parafii św. Stanisława K. w Bay City, Michigan* (n.p., 1912), passim.

36. *Nowiny*, October 13 and November 6, 1913.

37. Schrembs to Merry del Val, Toledo, November 14, 1913. Copy in MAA, Messmer Correspondence.

38. Cajetan De Lai to Messmer, Rome, August 20, 1913. MAA, 55.

39. *Kuryer*, December 12, 1913; *Nowiny*, December 13, 1913.

40. *Nowiny*, January 17, 1914, carried the full text.

41. Ibid., January 14, 1914; *Kuryer*, March 25, 1914; Kruszka, *Siedm*, 2:799–800.

42. *Nowiny*, March 4, 1914; Messmer to the Clergy of the Milwaukee Archdiocese, April 15, 1914 (ibid., April 20, 1914).

43. Kozlowski to the Polish Clergy and Parishes of the Milwaukee Archdiocese, July 10, 1914. MAA, St. Hedwig File.

44. "Postulaty Naszego Społeczeństwa pod Względem Zachowania Wiary

Św. Naszego Ludu," in *Przegląd Kościelny*, 2 (March–April 1915), 157–59, (June 1915), 236, 241–46.

45. *Kuryer*, July 12, 1915.

46. *Przegląd Kościelny*, 2 (September–October 1915), 325–27.

7. The Aftermath

1. *Kuryer*, January 11, 1913.

2. Ibid., April 6 and July 15, 1914; *Nowiny*, July 16, 1914.

3. *Kuryer*, October 17, 1912.

4. Ibid., April 19, 1913.

5. Ibid., April 4–7, 1913; *Miesięcznik Franciszkański*, 6 (May 1913), 509–12.

6. Wisconsin, *Statutes* (1911), ch. 182, sec. 4466 a and c.

7. *Kuryer*, July 10–12, 1913; Kuryer Publishing Co. *vs.* Messmer *et al.*, Wisconsin Supreme Court (August Term, 1915), No. 76, *Case*, pp. 83–87.

8. *Case*, pp. 87–114.

9. *Kuryer*, March 19, 1916.

10. Kuryer Publishing Co. *vs.* Messmer *et al.*, Wisconsin Supreme Court (January Term, 1916), No. 17, *Brief for Appellant*, pp. 30, 46, 64–65; *Case*, pp. 5–6, 11–12, 81–83.

11. Kuryer Publishing Co. *vs.* Messmer *et al.*, Wisconsin Supreme Court (August Term, 1915), No. 76, *Respondent's Brief*, pp. 18–19, 28–38, 106.

12. *Kuryer*, September 2, 1917; *Album Jubileuszowy: Srebrny Jubileusz Kapłaństwa Ks. Prob. F. N. Kaczmarczyka, 1929–1954* (n. p., 1954), p. 24.

13. For information on the congregation in South Milwaukee, see *Po Drodze Życia* (Scranton, 1922), pp. 174–76, and the *Kuryer*, June 16, 1914. On the Pulaski group, see *Miesięcznik Franciszkański*, 7 (August 1914), 701–2.

14. *Kuryer*, July 3, 1914, and April 17, 1915. Bończak's articles included "The Idea of the National Church in Poland," in the issues of June 21 and 25, 1916, and "The National Church in Milwaukee," September 2, 1917.

15. *Nowiny*, March 25 and December 2, 1914.

16. U.S. Department of Commerce, Bureau of the Census, *Religious Bodies, 1916*, part 1, *Summary and General Tables*, p. 348.

17. Osada, *Jak się Kształtowała*, pp. 71–81.

18. *Kuryer*, January 16 and 17, 1915; *Nowiny*, January 18, 1915.

19. *Nowiny*, May 18, 1915; *Kuryer*, March 10, April 3, June 12, 1915.

20. One reason for Kruszka's outburst may have been the issuance of a circular letter by Messmer on December 18, 1914, stressing that all prohibitions and sanctions of the pastoral letter of 1912 were still in effect (MAA, 116). *Kuryer*, January 6 and 10, 1915.

21. January 29, 1916.

22. *Kuryer*, January 13, 1916; *Nowiny*, January 10 and 14, 1916.

23. *Nowiny*, January 7–8, 1916; *Kuryer*, January 14, 1916.

24. *Kuryer*, November 14, 1914; *Nowiny*, December 11, 1914.

25. Cited in Blied, *Three Archbishops,* pp. 136–37.

26. *Nowiny,* August 14, 1916.

27. Messmer to "A. D.," Milwaukee, May 9, 1924. MAA, Messmer Correspondence.

28. "Notes on the Polish Memorial." Ibid.

29. Kruszka to Messmer, Milwaukee, November, 1915 (ibid.); Milwaukee Archdiocesan circular letter, November 21, 1916 (MAA, untitled file).

30. Kruszka's letters to Messmer were dated at Milwaukee on August 3, 1918, May 25, 1921, and August 14, 1926 (MAA, Kruszka Correspondence). Signing himself "The Delegate of the Second Polish-American Congress," Kruszka petitioned Pius XI for Polish bishops and national dioceses in 1923 (printed copy, MAA, untitled file). See also Kruszka's discussion of faith and nationality in *Wiara i Mowa Ojców Naszych* (Milwaukee, 1928).

31. *Nowiny,* July 17, 1915.

32. Goral, "Nowy Kodeks prawa Kanonicznego jako środek zaradczy przeciw szereniu się niedowiarstwa między Polakami w Ameryce," in *Przegląd Kościelny,* 5 (March 1918), 202–4. (April 1918), 221–35.

33. *Kuryer,* March 19 and 22, 1916.

34. J. A. Kapmarski, "The Kuryer Polski," in Borun, *We, the Milwaukee Poles,* p. 55.

Bibliography

I. Primary Sources

A. *Archives*

Green Bay Diocesan Archives. In the Chancery Office of the Diocese of Green Bay, DePere, Wisconsin.

La Crosse *Times-Review* Parish History Files. In the offices of the *Times-Review*, La Crosse, Wisconsin.

Milwaukee Archdiocesan Archives. In the Chancery Office of the Archdiocese of Milwaukee, Milwaukee, Wisconsin.

B. *Published Sources*

1. *Books*

Acta et Decreta Concilii Plenarii Baltimorensis Tertii. Baltimore, 1886.

Ellis, John Tracy, ed. *Documents of American Catholic History*. 2 vols. Chicago, 1967.

Gibbons, James. *A Retrospect of Fifty Years*. 2 vols. Baltimore, 1916.

Handbook for Parishioners of the Archdiocese of Milwaukee. Milwaukee, 1907.

Kruszka, Michael. *The Polish Church War*. Milwaukee, 1912.

[————]. *Polish-Americans*. Milwaukee, 1912.

Kruszka, Wacław (Wenceslaus). *Historya Polska w Ameryce*. 13 vols. Milwaukee, 1905–1908.

————. *Historja Polska w Ameryce*. Rev. ed. Milwaukee, 1937.

————. *Neapol, Wezuwiusz, i Pompeji*. Milwaukee, 1898.

————. *Siedm Siedmioleci czyli Pół Wieku Życia: Pamiętnik i Przyczynek do Historji Polskiej w Ameryce*. 2 vols. Poznan and Milwaukee, 1924.

————. *Wiara i Mowa Ojców Naszych*. Milwaukee, 1928.

Slomka, Jan. *From Serfdom to Self-Government: Memoirs of a Polish Village Mayor, 1842–1927*. William J. Rose, tr. London, 1941.

2. *Articles*

Goral, Boleslaus. "Nowy Kodeks prawa Kanonicznego jako środek zaradczy przeciw szereniu się niedowiarstwa między Polakami w Ameryce,"

154

Przegląd Kościelny, 5 (February 1918), 126–31; (March 1918), 202–4; (April 1918), 218–35.

Kozlowski, Edward. "Postulaty Naszego Społeczeństwa pod Względem Zachowania Wiary Św. Naszego Ludu," *Przegląd Kościelny,* 2 (March–April 1915), 149–60; (June 1915), 236–46.

Krakowski, Władysław. "J. E. Ks. Biskup Rhode a Zjednoczenie Kapłanów Polskich," *Przegląd Katolicki,* 9 (March–April 1934), 54, 55, 58–60.

Manel, Franciszek (Francis). "Walka na Śmierć," *Miesięcznik Franciszkański,* 5 (January 1912), 252–56.

3. *Newspapers and Periodicals*

The Catholic Citizen (Milwaukee), 1904–1918.

The Free Press (Milwaukee), 1906–1918.

Gwiazda Polarna (Stevens Point, Wisconsin), 1908–1918. The set in the possession of Worzalla Brothers Publishing Company in Stevens Point omits the issues of October 28–December 30, 1911.

Kalendarz Franciszkański, 1912–1919.

Kuryer Polski, 1888–1918.

Miesięcznik Franciszkański, 1907–1919.

Nowiny Polskie, 1906–1910, July 1912–December 1918. The set in the possession of St. Anthony Friary, Detroit, omits the issues of September 2–October 6, 1909; March 4, April 1–5, December 24–31, 1910; and the first half of 1912.

Przegląd Emigracyjny (Lwów), 1892–1894.

Przegląd Kościelny, 1914–1918.

Rolnik (Stevens Point, Wisconsin), 1899, 1901, 1904–1914, 1916–1918.

The Sentinel (Milwaukee), 1875–1918.

Straż (Scranton), April 17, 1897–December 1898, 1900–1907, 1910, 1913, 1917.

Tygodnik Polski (weekly edition of *Nowiny Polskie*), 1911. The set in the possession of St. Anthony Friary, Detroit, omits the issues of July 20, August 10, and December 14–28.

Wiarus (Winona), February 11, 1886–May 25, 1893, January 2, 1896– February 22, 1917.

4. *Public Documents*

Kuryer Publishing Co. *vs.* Messmer *et al.* Wisconsin Supreme Court, Second Circuit, August Term, 1915. No. 76, *Case.*

————. Wisconsin Supreme Court, August Term, 1915. No. 76, *Respondent's Brief.*

————. Wisconsin Supreme Court, January Term, 1916. No. 17, *Brief for Appellant.*

Milwaukee, Board of School Directors. *Proceedings: May, 1896–May, 1897.* Milwaukee, 1897.

U.S. Congress. Senate. *Reports of the Immigration Commission.* Sen. Doc. 633, 61st Cong., 2d sess., 41 v., 1911.

U.S. Department of the Interior. Census Office. *Eighth Census of the United States, 1860: Population,* vol. I.
———. *Ninth Census of the United States, 1870: Population,* vol. I.
———. *Tenth Census of the United States, 1880: Population,* vol. I.
———. *Eleventh Census of the United States, 1890: Population,* vol. I.
———. *Twelfth Census of the United States, 1900: Population,* vol. I.
U.S. Department of Commerce, Bureau of the Census. *Thirteenth Census of the United States, 1910: Population,* vol. I.
———. *Fourteenth Census of the United States, 1920: Population,* vol. II.
———. *Religious Bodies, 1916.* Pt. I, *Summary and General Tables.*
Wisconsin. Department of State. *Census Enumeration, 1905.* Pt. I, *Enumeration of the Inhabitants.*
Wisconsin Historical Records Survey. *Directory of Churches and Religious Organizations in Wisconsin.* Madison, 1941.
Wisconsin. Statutes (1911).

5. *Personal Interview*

Schulist, Rev. Joseph J. Personal Interview, Polonia, Wisconsin, August 1970.

II. Secondary Sources

A. *Books*

Ahlstrom, Sydney. *A Religious History of the American People.* New Haven, 1972.
Balch, Emily. *Our Slavic Fellow Citizens.* New York, 1910.
Barry, Colman J. *The Catholic Church and German Americans.* Milwaukee, 1953.
Blied, Benjamin J. *Three Archbishops of Milwaukee.* Milwaukee, 1955.
Bluma, Dacian, and Chowaniec, Theophilus. *A History of the Province of the Assumption of the Blessed Virgin Mary.* Pulaski, Wisconsin, 1967.
Borodziej, Łucja. *Pruska polityka oświatowa na ziemiach polskich w okresie Kulturkampfu.* Warsaw, 1972.
Buczek, Daniel S. *Immigrant Pastor: The Life of the Right Reverend Monsignor Lucyan Bójnowski of New Britain, Connecticut.* Waterbury, Connecticut, 1974.
Cross, Robert D. *The Emergence of Liberal Catholicism in America.* Cambridge, Massachusetts, 1958.
Curti, Merle. *The Making of an American Community.* Stanford, California, 1959.
Drewniak, Bogusław. *Emigracja z Pomorza Zachodniego, 1816–1914.* Poznan, 1966.
Duda-Dziewierz, Krystyna. *Wieś Małopolska a Emigracja Amerykańska.* Warsaw, 1938.
Ellis, John Tracy. *American Catholicism.* Chicago, 1956.

————. *John Lancaster Spalding: First Bishop of Peoria, American Educator*. Milwaukee, 1961.

————. *The Life of James Cardinal Gibbons, Archbishop of Baltimore, 1834–1921*. 2 vols. Milwaukee, 1952.

Fox, Paul. *The Polish National Catholic Church*. Scranton, n.d.

Gates, Paul Wallace. *The Wisconsin Pine Lands of Cornell University*. Ithaca, 1943.

Greeley, Andrew M., and Rossi, Peter H. *The Education of Catholic Americans*. Garden City, New York, 1968.

Greene, Victor. *For God and Country: The Rise of Polish and Lithuanian Ethnic Consciousness in America*. Madison, 1975.

Guilday, Peter. *A History of the Councils of Baltimore, 1791–1884*. New York, 1932.

Halecki, Oscar. *A History of Poland*. Chicago, 1966.

Handlin, Oscar. *The Uprooted*. Boston, 1951.

Heming, Henry H. *The Catholic Church in Wisconsin*. Milwaukee, 1896.

Herberg, Will. *Protestant, Catholic, Jew*. Rev. ed. Garden City, New York, 1960.

Hudson, Winthrop. *Religion in America*. 2d ed. New York, 1973.

Johnson, Peter Leo. *Crosier on the Frontier: A Life of John Martin Henni*. Madison, 1959.

————. *Halcyon Days: Story of St. Francis Seminary, Milwaukee*. Milwaukee, 1956.

Kieniewicz, Stefan. *The Emancipation of the Polish Peasantry*. Chicago, 1969.

Klukowski, Constantine. *A History of St. Mary of the Angels Catholic Church, Green Bay, Wisconsin, 1898–1954*. Pulaski, Wisconsin, 1956. (Because of the unusual length and scholarly approach of this book it is listed here, rather than in section C.)

Kubiak, Hieronim. *Polski Narodowy Kościół Katolicki w Stanach Zjednoczonych Ameryki w Latach 1897–1965*. Wrocław, 1970.

Kukiel, Marian. *Dzieje Polski Porozbiorowe, 1795–1921*. London, 1961.

Kusielewicz, Eugene. *Reflections on the Cultural Condition of the Polish-American Community*. New York, 1969.

Linkh, Richard M. *American Catholicism and European Immigrants (1900–1924)*. Staten Island, New York, 1975.

Loidl, Franz. *Erzbischof Friedrich Xaver Katzer, Ebensee–Milwaukee*. Vienna, 1953.

Ludwig, Mileta. *Right-Hand Glove Uplifted: A Biography of Archbishop Michael Heiss*. New York, 1968.

McAvoy, Thomas T. *The Great Crisis in American Catholic History, 1895–1900*. Chicago, 1957.

Madeja, Józef. *Dzieje Szkoły w Fałkowicach*. Katowice, 1962.

Miąso, Józef. *Dzieje oświaty polonijnej w Stanach Zjednoczonych*. Warsaw, 1970.

Moynihan, James H. *The Life of Archbishop Ireland*. New York, 1953.

Olszyk, Edmund G. *The Polish Press in America*. Milwaukee, 1940.

Osada, Stanisław. *Jak się Kształtowała Polska Dusza Wychodźtwa w Ameryce*. Pittsburgh, 1930.

———. *Prasa i Publicystyka Polska w Ameryce*. Pittsburgh, 1930.

Raney, William F. *Wisconsin, a Story of Progress*. New York, 1940.

Reddaway, W. F., et al., eds. *The Cambridge History of Poland*. 2 vols. Cambridge, 1951.

Still, Bayrd. *Milwaukee: The History of a City*. Madison, 1948.

Sweeney, David F. *The Life of John Lancaster Spalding*. New York, 1965.

Syski, Aleksander. *Ks. Józef Dąbrowski: Monografia Historyczna*. Orchard Lake, Michigan, 1942.

Szawleski, Mieczysław. *Kwestja Emigracji w Polsce*. Warsaw, 1927.

———. *Wychodźtwo Polskie w Stanach Zjednoczonych Ameryki*. Lwów, 1924.

Thomas, William I., and Znaniecki, Florian. *The Polish Peasant in Europe and America*. 2 vols. 2d ed., reprint. New York, 1975.

Thwaites, Reuben Gold. *Wisconsin: The Americanization of a French Settlement*. Boston, 1908.

Trzeciakowski, Lech. *Kulturkampf w zaborze pruskim*. Poznan, 1970.

———. *Pod Pruskim Zaborem, 1850–1918*. Warsaw, 1973.

Urban, Wincenty. *Ostatni Etap Dziejów Kościoła w Polsce przed Nowym Tysiącleciem, 1815–1965*. Rome, 1966.

Wachtel (Wachtl), Karol. *Dzieje Zjednoczenia Polskiego Rzymskiego-Katolickiego w Ameryce*. Chicago, 1913.

———. *Polonja w Ameryce*. Philadelphia, 1944.

Wandycz, Piotr S. *The Lands of Partitioned Poland, 1795–1918*. Vol. 7, *A History of East Central Europe*. Ed. Peter F. Sugar and Donald W. Treadgold. Seattle, 1974.

Watrous, Jerome A., ed. *Memoirs of Milwaukee County*. 2 vols. Madison, 1909.

Wytrwal, Joseph A. *America's Polish Heritage*. Detroit, 1961.

B. *Articles*

Blegen, Theodore C. "The Competition of the Northwestern States for Immigrants," *Wisconsin Magazine of History, 3* (September 1919), 3–29.

Carroon, Robert G. "Foundations of Milwaukee's Polish Community," Milwaukee County Historical Society, *Historical Messenger, 26* (September 1970), 88–96.

Cooper, Jerry M. "The Wisconsin National Guard in the Milwaukee Riots of 1886," *Wisconsin Magazine of History, 55* (Autumn 1971), 31–48.

Greeley, Andrew M. "Catholicism in America: Two Hundred Years and Counting," *The Critic, 34* (Summer 1976), 14–47, 54–70.

Gregory, John G. "Foreign Immigration to Wisconsin," *Wisconsin State Historical Society Proceedings* (1901), pp. 137–43.

Haiman, Mieczysław. "J. E. Ks. Biskup Paweł P. Rhode, Jego Życie i Czyny," *Przegląd Katolicki,* 9 (March–April 1934), 11, 14, 16, 18–27.

Kuzniewski, Anthony J. "Boot Straps and Book Learning: Reflections on the Education of Polish Americans," *Polish American Studies,* 32 (Autumn 1975), 5–26.

Miller, Frank H. "The Polanders in Wisconsin," Parkman Club *Publications,* 10 (1896), 239–46.

Piekoszewski, Jan. "Kościół i Polonia w Stanach Zjednoczonych Ameryki," in Hieronim Kubiak and Andrzej Pilch, eds., *Stan i Potrzeby Badań nad Zbiorwościami Polonijnymi* (Wrocław, 1976), pp. 375–96.

Sanford, Albert Hart. "The Polish People of Portage County," Wisconsin State Historical Society *Proceedings* (1907), pp. 259–88.

Siekaniec, Ladislaus. "The Poles in the Diocese of Superior, Wisconsin," *Polish American Studies,* 15 (January–June 1958), 10–17.

Swastek, Joseph. "Kardynał Ledóchowski," *Sodalis,* 38 (March 1957), 68–70.

Syski, Aleksander. "Wódz Duchowy Wychodźtwa Polskiego w Ameryce, J. E. Ks. Biskup Rhode, na Tle Wspomień Osobistych," *Przegląd Katolicki,* 9 (March–April 1934), 31–32, 34, 36–40.

Tomkiewicz, John W. "Polanders in Wisconsin," Wisconsin State Historical Society *Proceedings* (1901), pp. 148–52.

Whyte, William F. "The Bennett Law Campaign," *Wisconsin Magazine of History,* 10 (June 1927), 363–90.

Wyman, Roger E. "Wisconsin Ethnic Groups and the Election of 1890," *Wisconsin Magazine of History,* 51 (Summer 1968), 269–93.

C. *Jubilee Books*

Album Jubileuszowy: Srebrny Jubileusz Kapłaństwa Ks. Prob. F. N. Kaczmarczyka, 1929–1954. N.p., 1954.

Betley, Anthony, and Piontek, Cyril. *Diamond Jubilee of the Founding of St. Casimir's Congregation at Northeim (Newton), Wisconsin.* N.p., 1943.

Borun, Thaddeus, ed. *We, the Milwaukee Poles.* Milwaukee, 1946.

Fifty Years: A Memoir on the Fiftieth Anniversary of the Mother of Good Counsel Province of the Congregation of the Sisters of St. Felix. Chicago, 1960.

Klukowski, Constantine. *History of St. Stanislaus, Bishop and Martyr, Church Hofa Park, Wisconsin, Written on the Occasion of the Diamond Jubilee of the Parish, 1883–1958.* Pulaski, Wisconsin, 1958.

Księga Pamiątkowa "33" Polskiego Narodowego Katolickiego Kościoła. Scranton, Pennsylvania, 1930.

Masalewicz, Edward A. *History of St. Hedwig's Congregation, Thorp, Wisconsin, Commemorating the Diamond Anniversary, 1891–1966.* N.p., 1966.

The Memorial Volume: A History of the Third Plenary Council of Baltimore, November 9–December 7, 1884. Baltimore, 1885.

Pamiątka: 25-Letnej Rocznicy Założenia Parafii Świętego Piotra. Stevens Point, Wisconsin, 1901.

Pamiętnik Jubileuszowy Zgromadzenia Sióstr Świętego Józefa Trzeciego Zakonu Świętego Franciszka, 1901–1951. N.p., 1951.

Pamiętnik Srebrnego Jubileuszu Kolegjum św. Bonawentury w Mount Pleasant-Sturtevant, Wisconsin, 1901–1926. Pulaski, Wisconsin, 1926.

Po Drodze Życia: Wydanie Jubileuszowe na Pamiątkę 25-Lecia Powstania Polsko-Narodowego Katolickiego Kościoła w Ameryce, 1897–1922. Scranton, Pennsylvania [1922].

The Roman Catholic Church, Assumption of the Blessed Virgin Mary Parish, Pulaski, Wisconsin, Diocese of Green Bay: 75 Years Since Established, 1888–1963. Pulaski, Wisconsin, 1963.

Souvenir Album of the Golden Jubilee of the Dedication of St. Josaphat's Basilica, 1901–1951. Milwaukee, 1951.

Sprawozdanie z Finansowego Zarządu za Rok 1930 Parafii Św. Rodziny w Cudahy, Wisconsin. Milwaukee, 1931.

Złoty Jubileusz Parafji Św. Jacka, 1934. Milwaukee, 1934.

Życiorys Przew. Ks. Edwarda Kozłowskiego, Proboszcza parafii św. Stanisława K. w Bay City, Michigan: Program 25-letniego Jubileuszu Jego Kapłaństwa. N.p., 1912.

D. *Dissertation*

Kuzniewski, Anthony J., Jr. "Faith and Fatherland: An Intellectual History of the Polish Immigrant Community in Wisconsin, 1838–1918." Unpublished Ph. D. dissertation, Harvard University, 1973.

Index

Abbelen, Rev. Peter, 10
  Abbelen Memorial, 10
Agliardi, Cardinal Antonio, 53
Ahlstrom, Sydney, 2
Alban, Wisconsin, 20, 100
Altoona, Pennsylvania, 87
American Courier (Milwaukee), 121
American Ecclesiastical Review, 46
American Federation of Polish Catholic
    Laymen, 106, 108, 117
  condemned in pastoral letter of 1912,
    95–97
  evolution to insurance company,
    115–16
  legislation sought in Madison, 103
  origins, 83–85, 88
  response to pastoral letter, 97–103
Americanism, result of World War I, 6,
    119, 123
"Americanist" Controversy
  concept condemned by Leo XIII, 11
  description, 2
  issue in church war, 113–14
Antigo, Wisconsin, 67
Antonucci, Msgr. Joseph, 52, 53, 56, 58,
    73
Ashland, Wisconsin, 24
Austria, 12
  see also Galicia; Poland, Austrian Par-
    tition

Baltimore, Third Plenary Council of, 7,
    80
  cited in school controversy, 37
Barzynski, Rev. Vincent, 33, 44
Bay City, Michigan, 103

Bayonne, New Jersey, 76
Bennett Law, 30, 124
Berlin, Wisconsin, 56
Bethman-Hollweg, Chancellor Theobald
    von, 82
Bismarck, Chancellor Otto von, 12
  pressures Poles in Germany, 14–15
  see also Poland, German Partition;
    Kulturkampf
Bonzano, Archbishop John, 99
Bończak, Rev. Francis, 114–15
Borodziej, Łucja, 16
Bójnowski, Msgr. Lucyan, 3
Breslau (Wrocław), Diocese of, 15
Brown County, Wisconsin, 21
Buczek, Daniel, 3, 4
Buffalo, New York, 31, 47, 49, 50, 55,
    79, 84

Cahensley, Peter Paul, 2, 113, 126
  and Lucerne Memorial, 10–11
  reactions to his proposals, 32–33
  supported by W. Kruszka, 47
Catholic Church
  government, 1–6, 80–81
  and immigrants, 1–6, 8–12, 45–47
  and Polish-American Catholics, 1–6,
    40–45, 47–49, 62–63, 69, 70, 76,
    106, 113, 125–26
  and Polish Catholics, 13–17
  see also Goral, Boleslaus; Katzer,
    Frederick; Kozlowski, Edward;
    Kruszka, Michael and Wenceslaus;
    Messmer, Sebastian; Pastoral Letter;
    Polish-American Catholics; Polish
    Church War

Catholic Citizen (Milwaukee), 49, 56
Catholic Universe (Cleveland), 46
Celichowski, Rev. Bronislaus, 63
Central Committee of Polish Parishioners
  in America, 98–99
Cerretti, Archbishop Bonaventure, 91, 94
Chicago, Illinois, 31, 32, 50, 68, 75, 84,
  93, 97, 107
  Polish immigrants, 19
  Resurrectionist parishes, 44
Church War. *See* Polish Church War
Cleveland, Ohio, 76, 85
Committee of National Defense, 116
  see also World War I
Congregation of the Consistory, 104
Congregation for the Propagation of the
  Faith, 7–8, 50, 52–53
  opposes Polish auxiliary for Mil-
    waukee, 48–49
  receives protests on Kruszka's mission,
    53–54
  receives Symon's report, 57–58
  see also Ledóchowski, Cardinal Miec-
    zyslaus
Conventual Franciscans. *See* Francis-
  cans, Conventual
Corrigan, Archbishop Michael, 11
Croke, William J. D., 56
  analysis of Symon mission, 58
Cyborowski, Martin, 63, 101
Czerwinski, Ignatius, 58, 102
  animosity towards M. Kruszka, 40
  organizer of PAA, 33
  role in PES controversy, 38
  sues *Kuryer*, 110
Czerwinski, Roman, 22, 30

De Lai, Cardinal Cajetan, 104
Detroit, Michigan, 84, 92–94, 97, 111
Dillingham Committee, 19, 20
Dinder, Archbishop Julius, 15, 16
Dombrowski, Rev. Joseph, 24–25, 27
"Don't Pay" campaign, 82, 83, 96, 102
  see also American Federation of Polish
    Catholic Laymen; Kruszka,
    Michael; *Kuryer Polski*

Duluth, Minnesota, 76
Dziennik Chicagoski (Chicago), 49, 65,
  92
  critique of W. Kruszka on Polish-
    Americanism, 44, 45
Dziennik Milwaucki (Milwaukee)
  demise, 58–59
  on W. Kruszka, 44
  origins, 40
  rivalry with *Kuryer,* 40
Dziennik Narodowy
  connections with W. Kruszka, 94
  condemned by Chicago clergy, 90, 94
  condemned in pastoral letter of 1912,
    96
  lawsuits against, 110–111
  sold by M. Kruszka, 114
Dziennik Polski (Milwaukee), 29

Eis, Bishop Frederick
  language decree controversy, 44–45,
    107
  signs pastoral letter of 1912, 95
Eldorado, Wisconsin, 42
Ellis, John Tracy, 2

Falconio, Archbishop Diomede
  involvement in W. Kruszka complaint
    against Goral, 72, 75, 76–77, 88
Fałkowice, Poland, 16
Faribault and Stillwater Plans, 11
Farley, Cardinal John, 97
Federation, the. *See* American Federation
  of Polish Catholic Laymen
Federation Life Insurance of America,
  115
  see also American Federation of Polish
    Catholic Laymen
Felician Sisters, 25
Fiori, Dom Sisto, 56, 57
Flasch, Bishop Kilian, 10, 11
"Fourth Partition" of Poland, 44, 116
Fox, Bishop Joseph, 67, 94, 107
  and pastoral letter of 1912, 95, 96
Fox, Paul, 4

Franciscans (O. F. M.)
  arrival in Pulaski, 21
  see also Manel, Rev. Francis;
    Miesięcznik Franciszkański;
    Pulaski, Wisconsin
Franciscans, Conventual, 79–80
  see also St. Josaphat Parish
Franciscan Sisters, 50
Freeman's Journal (New York City),
  45–46, 49
Free Press (Milwaukee), 84, 93, 97, 104,
  117
Frydrychowicz, Rev. Jan, 25
Fudzinski, Rev. Hyacinth, 79–80

Galicia, 32
  see also Poland, Austrian Partition
Garvey, Bishop E. A., 87
Gazeta Wisconsinska (Milwaukee), 29
German-American Catholics, 9
German extraction, bishops of
  attacked by M. Kruszka, 71, 82
  attacked by W. Kruszka, 62, 67, 81–82
  challenged by second Polish-American
    Congress, 47–48
  dispute with Irish-American bishops,
    2–3
  judged in light of Kruszka mission, 55
  leadership over Wisconsin Catholi-
    cism, 5, 7–12, 81–82, 125
Germany, 12
  defended by Messmer, 117–18
  Kuryer banned, 82, 110
  see also Poland, German Partition
Gibbons, Cardinal James, 8, 11, 57, 59
  assessment of Milwaukee's Poles, 33
  connection with Kruszka's mission to
    Rome, 50, 53
  intervenes in Heiss succession struggle,
    10
  warns against nationalism in the
    Church, 11
Głos Polek (Milwaukee), 23
Goral, Rev. Boleslaus, 65, 70, 88, 89,
  99, 103, 104, 107, 110
  biographical data, 65

on bishop issue, 120–21
and Catholic cemetery in Milwaukee,
  101, 102
in church war, analysis of role, 127
dependence on Messmer, 75, 87–88,
  89
as diocesan consultor, 87–88
on federation, 84
against Koudelka appointment,
  85–86
M. Kruszka's characterization, 70–71
and W. Kruszka's ecclesiastical complaint 72–77
and W. Kruszka's expulsion from Detroit convention, 93
and *Nowiny's* establishment, 65–67
pastor of St. Vincent Parish, 73–74
  see also Kruszka, Michael and Wences-
    laus; Messmer, Sebastian; *Nowiny
    Polskie*
Gordon, Rev. Francis, 65
Gotti, Cardinal Girolamo, 49
  and Kruszka mission, 52–53, 54
  and Symon mission, 56
Grand Rapids, Michigan, 97, 103
Greeley, Andrew, 4, 5
Green Bay, Diocese of, 6, 8, 11, 64, 67,
  70, 83, 96, 99, 107, 108
  effects of pastoral letter of 1912 on,
    100, 102
Green Bay, Wisconsin, 20, 21, 23–24, 27
Greene, Victor, 4, 5
Gregory XVI, 13
Grenbowski, Rev. Thomas, 25
Grunwald, Battle of
  commemorated in Milwaukee, 81–82
Grutza, Rev. Wilhelm
  erection of St. Josaphat Basilica, 41–42
  Katolik publisher, 40
  W. Kruszka's evaluation of, 42
  PES goals condemned, 38
Gulski, Rev. Hyacinth, 26, 40, 56, 57,
  59, 78, 128
  analysis of influence, 87–88
  death, 87
  on federation, 84
  on Koudelka appointment, 85–86

leadership of Milwaukee's Polish community, 28, 32, 35, 87
suggested as auxiliary bishop in Milwaukee, 48–49
Gwiazda Polarna (Stevens Point), 21, 100

"Hakatism"
allegation used in church war, 67, 68
description, 15
see also Poland, German Partition
Handbook for Catholic Parishioners of the Archdiocese of Milwaukee 8, 78
Harrison, President Benjamin, 49
Hay, John, 50
Heiss, Archbishop Michael, 9–10, 26–27, 28
Henni, Archbishop John Martin, 8–9, 26
Herald (Milwaukee), 59
Herberg, Will, 2
Hergenroether, Cardinal Joseph, 9
Hoan, Mayor Daniel W., 122
Hodur, Bishop Francis, 55, 114–15
Hof, John J., 21
Hofa Park, Wisconsin, 21
Hudson, Winthrop, 2

Ireland, Archbishop John, 11
on Abbelen Memorial, 10
Irish-American Catholics
bishops attacked by W. Kruszka, 62, 67
challenged by second Polish-American Congress, 47–48
dispute with German-American Catholics, 2–3, 125
judged in light of Kruszka mission, 55

Jesuits. *See* Society of Jesus
"Józefinki". *See* St. Joseph, Sisters of

Kaminski, Stefan, 50
Katolik (Milwaukee), 40, 42
Katzer, Archbishop Frederick, 12, 28, 50, 60, 80, 125, 126

appointed archbishop of Milwaukee, 10–11
bishop of Green Bay, 10
dispute with W. Kruszka, 42–43
efforts to secure Polish bishop for Milwaukee, 48–49
on PES controversy, 38
on Testem Benevolentiae, 11
Keane, Bishop John
against Abbelen Memorial, 10
responds to petition of second Polish-American Congress, 48
Kelly, Msgr. ("Vox Urbis"), 55–56
Kenosha, Wisconsin, 20, 24, 86, 94
Kenrick, Archbishop Peter, 10
Kleczka, Congressman John, 122
Knights of the Cross. *See* Teutonic Knights
Knights of Labor, 29
Kopp, Archbishop George, 15
Kościuszko Guard (Company K, Wisconsin National Guard), 23, 34, 36 in labor riots of May, 1886, 29
Koudelka, Bishop Joseph M., 88, 89, 91
appointment to Milwaukee, 85
opposition to appointment of, 85–86, 127
transferred to Superior, 103
Kozlowski, Bishop Anthony, 50
Kozlowski, Bishop Edward, 31, 76, 126
activities in Milwaukee, 106–7, 108
appointed auxiliary bishop in Milwaukee, 103–4
death, 118
evaluation by Messmer, 119–20
installation of, 104–6
support for Polish-American bishops, 106–7
war relief efforts, 116
Krakow, Wisconsin, 21, 83
Kruszka, Joseph, 31, 32, 35
association with PES, 36
Kruszka, Michael, 32, 50, 63, 73, 87, 95, 114, 123
assaulted by *Nowiny* manager, 102–3
and Catholic Church: adopts utilitarian view of Church, 41; attacks on bishops, 62–63, 110; "Don't Pay"

campaign, 82; loss of clerical support, 68–69, 90, 93, 108; opposition to Church analyzed, 88, 89, 108; on parochial schools, 79; reaction to pastoral letter of 1912, 97–102, 121; role in church war evaluated, 126–28; support of Polish-American bishops, 6
death, 122
early leader in Wisconsin's Polish community, 28–31
and federation, 83–85, 88
and Hyacinth Gulski, 32–35
on Josaphat debt, 41, 63
journalistic career: beginnings, 28–29; competition with *Dziennik Milwaucki,* 40–41, 58–59; effectiveness analyzed, 59, 126–27; ownership of *Dziennik Narodowy,* 90, 94, 114; "Polish Americans," 98; "The Polish Church War," 98
and W. Kruszka, 31–32, 71, 77–78
lawsuit involvements, 109–14
and Messmer, 70–72, 74–75, 80–81, 86, 88, 108, 117–18, 126
in PES controversy, 37–39
political career, 30–31, 39–40
and World War I, 116, 121–22
see also Dziennik Narodowy; Kruszka, Wenceslaus; *Kuryer Polski;* Kuryer Publishing Co.; Messmer, Sebastian; *Nowiny Polskie;* Rhode, Bishop Paul
Kruszka, Rev. Simon, 28, 64
Kruszka, Rev. Wenceslaus, 32, 50, 58, 63, 65, 67, 70, 95, 97, 102, 107, 115, 120, 121
accused of violating celibacy, 61
American hierarchy criticized, 59, 81–82, 120
against bilingual catechisms, 78
biographical data, 31–32, 35
Catholic cemetery administration criticized, 101
ecclesiastical suit against Goral, 72–77
expulsion from Detroit conference, 92–94, 104

history of Poles in America prepared, 1–2, 43–44
and Katzer, 42–43
Kenosha address controversy, 86–87, 88, 89, 91, 94–95
on Koudelka appointment, 85–86, 87, 88
and Kozlowski, 104, 106
M. Kruszka's defense, 71
Kuryer's policies criticized, 77–78
language decrees of Messmer and Eis defended, 44–45
leadership evaluated, 126, 127–28
and Messmer, 60–61, 64–65, 91, 108, 120; analysis of relationship, 88, 89, 120, 126; criticism of Messmer on Josaphat debt, 80–81
mission to Rome: chosen as delegate, 47; mission in Europe, 52–55; preparation for mission, 49–50; reactions to mission, 55–56
Nowiny criticized, 74, 76, 81
papal promise used as rationale, 69, 86–87, 89, 96, 128
on pastoral letter of 1912, 99–100, 102
on Polish-American bishop question, 4, 6, 45–47, 78, 86–87, 88, 91, 94–95, 120
at Polish-American Congress of 1901, 47–48
at Polish-American Congress of 1904, 56
priestly faculties denied, 67, 99–100
Ripon "exile" protested, 60–61, 67
series "Sprawy Narodowe i Kościelne" described, 61–62, 63, 64
silenced by Messmer, 67–69
writings: *Historya Polska w Ameryce* (The Polish History in America), 43–44, 64–65; *Neapol, Wesuwiusz, i Pompeji,* 42; "Polyglot Bishops for Polyglot Dioceses," *(Freeman's Journal,* 1901), 45–46; *Rzym,* 32, 41; *Supplices Preces,* 52–53; *The Unbeliever before the Tribunal of Reason,* 42
see also Goral, Rev. Boleslaus; Katzer, Frederick; Kruszka, Michael;

Kuryer Polski; Messmer, Sebastian; *Nowiny Polskie;* Polish-Americanism; Polish Church War
Krytyka (Milwaukee), 28–29
Kubiak, Hieronim, 4
Kulturkampf, 5–6, 7, 15–17, 28, 32
  rhetoric used in church war, 62, 67, 78, 81–82, 97, 125
Kuryer Polski (Milwaukee), 19, 22, 23, 27, 28, 40, 43, 45, 49, 57, 68, 70, 71, 73, 74, 75, 84, 85, 91, 94, 97, 99, 101, 106, 126
  banned in German Empire, 82, 110
  Catholic opposition, 82–83, 87, 90, 93
  and *Dziennik Milwaucki,* 58–59
  establishment and early policies, 29–32, 34–35
  expansion, 58–59, 98
  against German- and Irish-American bishops in the U.S., 67
  on independent bishops, 50, 115
  on Kozlowski appointment, 104
  and W. Kruszka, 32, 61–62, 63, 64, 77–78, 92
  on language decrees of Messmer and Eis, 44
  lawsuits against, 110
  against Messmer on Josaphat debt, 80
  and PAA, 33, 82
  and pastoral letter of 1912: background, 92, 95; condemnation, 96; effects of the letter, 100, 102–3, 108, 121; suit against Wisconsin bishops, 111–14
  PES supported, 36–39
  on Rhode, 76, 107
  on Symon mission, 56
  and World War I, 116, 117–18, 121–22
  see also Kruszka Michael and Wenceslaus; Kuryer Publishing Co.; Messmer, Sebastian; *Nowiny Polskie,* Pastoral Letter of 1912
Kuryer Publishing Co.
  expanded, 98
  organized, 40–41
  successor to M. Kruszka chosen as head, 122–23

suit against Wisconsin Province bishops, 111–14
Kuryer Publishing Co. v Messmer et al., 111–14

LaBoule, Rev. Joseph, 72
La Crosse, Diocese of, 8, 11
Ledóchowski, Cardinal Mieczyslaus, 14
  in *Kulturkampf,* 15
  Propaganda head, 33
  refuses request for Polish auxiliary in Milwaukee, 48–49
Leo XIII, 10, 11, 50, 53
Lex, Rev. Anthony, 61
Lucerne Memorial. *See* Cahensly, Peter Paul
Lwów Exposition (1894), 34

Mahany, Rowland B., 49–50, 52–53
Manel, Rev. Francis, 82, 90
Manistee, Michigan, 31
Manitowoc, Wisconsin, 23, 27, 31
Marathon County, Wisconsin, 20
Marquette, Diocese of, 8, 99
Martinelli, Cardinal Sebastiano, 42, 44
Masuria, Poland, 16, 17
Melcher, Bishop Joseph, 24–25
Messmer Archbishop Sebastian G., 11, 55, 58, 77, 92, 93, 107, 109
  on Americanism, 118, 119
  church war activities evaluated, 126–28
  counteroffensive in church war: actions taken, 90–91, 93–97, 101–2, 103–5, 106, 107; analysis of actions, 107–8, 126; position at outset, 87–88, 89, 90
  efforts to win allegiance of Milwaukee's Poles, 63, 70, 78, 89
  and Goral, 75, 87–88, 89, 127
  Josaphat debt issue, 79–80, 126
  and "Józefinki" origins, 50
  Kozlowski appointment, 103–6, 119
  M. Kruszka's attacks, 70–72, 80–81, 86, 88, 117–18
  and W. Kruszka: disputes, 60–61, 64–65, 67, 80–81, 91, 108, 120; in

ecclesiastical suit against Goral, 72, 74, 76–77; exacts loyalty oath after Kenosha speech, 91, 94–95; on Kruszka's exclusion from Detroit convention, 93–94
language decree controversy, 44–45, 107
litigation with Kuryer Publishing Co., 111–12, 113
and *Nowiny Polskie,* 65–66, 74–75
and pastoral letter of 1912, 95–97
Poland Corner schism, 25
on Polish-American bishops: belief that Polish lay people do not desire national bishops, 55, 60, 119–20; resistance to appointment of Polish-American bishops, 59–60, 118–20; willingness to seek Polish-American auxiliary, 73
on Polish-American clannishness, 102, 118, 119, 126
and Resurrectionist controversy, 64–65
Rhode's appointment to Green Bay, 107–8
and World War I, 117–18
see also Goral, Boleslaus; Kruszka, Michael and Wenceslaus; *Kuryer Polski;* Milwaukee, Archdiocese of; *Nowiny Polskie;* Polish Church War
Miąso, Józef, 4
Mickiewicz, Adam, 82
Miesięcznik Franciszkański (Pulaski), 21, 76, 95
Milwaukee, Wisconsin, 5, 6, 8, 11, 18, 36, 41, 42, 50, 52, 56, 58, 60, 61, 63, 65, 72, 73, 74, 76, 77, 79, 80, 83, 84, 85, 87, 93, 94, 97, 98, 99, 101, 102, 103, 105, 114–15, 116, 117, 118, 121, 123
Board of School Directors, controversy over Polish instruction, 36–39
election of Polish-American candidates, 30, 59, 122
M. Kruszka mourned, 122
number of Polish immigrants, 19–20
Polish settlements described and analyzed, 22–23, 25–35

Symon visit, 57
Milwaukee, Archdiocese of, 5–6, 8–9, 48–50, 73, 78, 85, 91, 95, 99, 109, 111, 120
Moeller, Archbishop Henry, 62

National Council, 116
see also World War I, relief efforts by Polish-Americans
Neuman, Casimir, 31, 35, 126
New Britain, Connecticut, 3
Niezorawski, Frank, 37
Norwegian Immigrants, 20
Nowiny Polskie (Milwaukee), 23, 68, 71, 78, 80, 85, 87, 91, 95, 110, 114, 116, 117, 118, 122, 126
apostolic delegate criticizes, 77
and "Don't Pay" campaign, 82
establishment, 65–67
and Goral, 65–66, 70, 72–73, 75
on independent Polish Catholics, 115
on Kozlowski appointment, 103, 104, 106
W. Kruszka attacked, 76–77, 81, 90, 93, 100
Messmer's backing, 74–75, 88, 111
PAA organ, 82
and pastoral letter of 1912, 100, 102–3, 121
promoted in parochial schools, 79
see also Goral, Boleslaus; Kruszka, Michael and Wenceslaus; *Kuryer Polski;* Messmer, Sebastian

Oconto County, Wisconsin, 21
Old Catholics, 27
Orędownik Językowy (Milwaukee), 65
Original Quartz Hill Gold Mine, 41
Oshkosh, Wisconsin, 83
Ostmarkverein, 15
see also Poland, German Partition
Owocki, Casimir, 36

PAA. *See* Polish Association of America
Paderewski, Jan, 116–17

Pastoral Letter of 1912
  analysis, 108
  effects, 97–103, 109
  implementation, 97
  lawsuit, 111–14
  origins and content, 95–96
  see also Fox, Joseph; Kruszka,
    Michael and Wenceslaus; *Kuryer
    Polski;* Messmer, Sebastian; *Nowiny
    Polskie*
Peoria, Diocese of, 97, 99
PES. *See* Polish Educational Society
Philip, Governor Emmanuel, 122
Pitass, Rev. John, 48, 55, 67
  and Kruszka's mission to Rome, 49–50
  at second Polish-American Congress,
    47
Pius X
  blesses *Nowiny,* 66
  promise given to W. Kruszka, 54
  receives W. Kruszka, 53
  and Symon mission, 56–58
Pociecha, Rev. Jan, 64
Polak, Rev. Jan, 20
Poland
  Austrian Partition, 17
  emigration from, 19–20, 22
  German Partition, 31: economic and
    political pressure against Poles, 15,
    Kulturkampf described, 14–16; rise
    of Polish national consciousness, 14,
    16–17
  during nineteenth century, 12–17, 24
  relief collections during World War I,
    116–17
  restoration, 121–22
  Russian Partition, 17
Poland Corner, Wisconsin, 20–21; 24–25
Polish-American Catholics
  analyzed, 114, 127
  critical reaction to church war, 108
  effects on American Catholic history,
    3–6
  forced Americanization opposed by
    Kozlowski, 107
  Messmer's assessment, 59, 80
  studied by Symon, 56–68

Polish-American Congresses, 78
  second, 47–50
  third, 56
Polish-Americanism
  evolution of concept, 50–51
  W. Kruszka's definition debated,
    43–44, 45
Polish Church War
  brief description, 2, 5–6, 109
  evaluation, 124–28
  see also Catholic Church; Goral,
    Boleslaus; Gulski, Hyacinth; Koz-
    lowski, Edward; Kruszka, Michael
    and Wenceslaus; *Kuryer Polski;*
    Messmer, Sebastian; *Nowiny
    Polskie;* Polish-American Catholics
Polish Association of America (PAA)
  Federationists excluded, 101
  Nowiny supported, 82
  origins, 33, 35, 63
Polish Educational Society (PES), 36–39
Polish immigrants
  differences according to partition of
    origin, 5
  in Wisconsin, 18–35
Polish National Alliance, 23, 29, 117
  association with PES, 36
Polish National Catholic Church, 55, 117
  establishment in Wisconsin, 107,
    114–15
Polish National Cemetery (Milwaukee),
    99, 101–2
Polish Priests' Association, 106, 121
Polish Roman Catholic Union, 23, 29,
    44, 92, 110
  assistance to W. Kruszka's mission to
    Rome, 50
  opposition from Milwaukee, 33, 35
Polish schismatic movements in the
    United States, 3
  concern from Polish Roman Catholics,
    47–48
  establishments in Wisconsin, 114–15
  and W. Kruszka, 60, 68
  reconciliation through Paul Rhode, 76
  "Red Church" at Poland Corner,
    24–25

see also Polish National Catholic
Church

"Polish School Sisters of St. Joseph" (Sisters of St. Joseph of the Third Order
of St. Francis). *See* St. Joseph, Sisters of

Polish Women's Alliance, 23

Polonia (Chicago), 81

Polonia Committee, 116, 117
see also World War I

Polonia, Wisconsin, 27, 100
origins described, 24–25

Pomerania, 14, 16
see also Poland, German Partition

Portage County, Wisconsin, 20–21, 76

Poznan-Gniezno, Archdiocese of, 14–15

Poznania, 5, 14, 17
see also Poland, German Partition

Princeton, Wisconsin, 41

"Propaganda, The". *See* Congregation
for the Propagation of the Faith

Przegląd Emigracyjny (Lwów), 31

Przegląd Kościelny, 106–07

Przyjaciel Ludu (Milwaukee), 23

Pulaski, Wisconsin, 21, 56, 76, 82, 115

Quigley, Archbishop James, 47, 49, 126
declines to enforce pastoral letter of
1912 in Chicago, 97, 107
and Rhode appointment, 5, 75

Racine, Wisconsin, 20, 24

Rainer, Rev. Joseph, 86

Resurrection, Congregation of the ("Resurrectionists"), 92, 111
founded, 13
Messmer *imprimatur* controversy,
64–65
on Polish-Americanism, 44
suit against *Dziennik Narodowy,*
110–11

Rhode, Bishop Paul, 103, 104, 118–19,
126
appointed bishop in Chicago, 5, 75–76
condemns "bad press," 87, 90, 92, 94

cooperation with Messmer, 89
Green Bay assignment, 107–08
and W. Kruszka: assistance in securing
Milwaukee pastorate, 77; Kruszka's
expulsion from Detroit convention,
92–94; requests Kruszka to drop
complaint against Goral, 76, 88
and *Kuryer Polski,* 76, 107
suit against *Dziennik Narodowy,* 111
see also Green Bay, Diocese of;
Kruszka, Wenceslaus; Messmer,
Sebastian

Richter, Bishop Henry, 10

Ripon, Wisconsin, 42, 43, 55, 60–61, 67,
70

Rodowicz, Rev. John, 26–27

Rolnik (Stevens Point), 21, 76, 122

Roosevelt, President Theodore, 50
statement to Symon, 57

Rose, Mayor David, 39–40, 57

Rossi, Peter, 4

Russia, 12
see also Poland, Russian Partition

St. Adalbert's Cemetery (Milwaukee),
101–2

St. Adalbert Parish, 77, 81, 91, 102, 106,
120
see also Kruszka, Wenceslaus

St. Adalbert Parish (South Milwaukee),
102

St. Casimir Parish, 61

St. Hedwig Parish, 26–27, 28, 63, 102

St. Hyacinth Parish, 26

St. Josaphat Parish, 38
basilica erected, 41–42
debt issue, 41–42, 62–63, 79–81, 120,
126, 127
parish high school attacked, 38–39

St. Joseph, Sisters of . . . of Third Order
of St. Francis, 50

St. Louis, Missouri, 76

St. Paul, Archdiocese of, 8

St. Stanislaus Parish, 25–26, 104

St. Vincent Parish, 73, 84
see also Goral, Boleslaus

Sts. Cyril and Methodius Parish, 38
Sanford, Albert, 20
Schinner, Bishop Augustine, 57, 103
Schrembs, Bishop Joseph, 103
Schwebach, Bishop James, 11
Scranton, Pennsylvania, 68
Semenenko, Peter, 13
Sentinel, The (Milwaukee), 26, 61, 74, 105
Shawano County, Wisconsin, 21
Sienkiewicz, Henryk, 62
 Krzyżacy (The Knights of the Cross), 62
Silesia, Lower, 14, 16, 17
 see also Poland, German Partition
Slomka, Jan, 13, 17
Slupecki, Edwin, 37, 39
Słowacki, Julius, 13
Słowo (Milwaukee), 31
Smith, Rev. Richard, 72–73
Sobieski, Wisconsin, 21
Society of Jesus (Jesuits), 32, 70
Society of Polish Priests in the United States, 28, 53
South Milwaukee, Wisconsin, 115
Spalding, Bishop John Lancaster, 10, 49, 54
Springvale, Wisconsin, 42
Stevens Point, Wisconsin, 27, 50, 56, 76, 97, 100
 Polish settlement, 20–21
Still, Bayrd, 19
Stillwater Plan. *See* Faribault and Stillwater Plans
Straż (Scranton), 114, 115
Superior, Wisconsin, 20, 24
Superior, Diocese of, 57, 103, 108
Svampa, Cardinal Domenico, 53
Symon, Archbishop Francis, 56–58, 64, 68
Sztuczko, Rev. Casimir, 53, 55, 78
Szukalski, Rev. John, 38, 56, 104

Tarasiewicz, Rev. Aegidius, 52
Testem Benevolentiae, 11–12
 reaction of W. Kruszka, 45

Teutonic Knights
 anti-German epithet in church war, 62, 67, 81
 novel of H. Sienkiewicz (*Krzyżacy*), 62
 see also Kulturkampf, rhetoric used in church war
Thomas, Florian, 3
Thorp, Wisconsin, 27
Toledo, Ohio, 31, 97, 103
Traudt, Rev. Bernard, 74, 107, 117
Trempeleau County, Wisconsin, 21
Trobec, Bishop James, 46, 54
Trusteeship, lay
 elimination of, in Roman Catholic Church: nationally, 7; in Wisconsin, 8
 federation goal, 90
 issue in church war, 98–99, 102
Trzeciakowski, Lech, 16–17
Tygodnik Anonsowy (Milwaukee), 28
Tygodniowy Kuryer Polski (Milwaukee), 29

Vilatte, Bishop Rene, 27
"Vox Urbis." *See* Msgr. Kelly

Wachtl, Karol, 4
West Prussia, 5, 14, 17, 28
 see also Poland, German Partition
Wiarus (Winona), 32, 40
Wild, Thaddeus, 36
Wilson, President Woodrow, 116
Winona, Minnesota, 97
Wisconsin, 5–6, 8–9, 11, 12, 36, 58, 76, 82, 84, 100, 114, 116, 117, 122, 124–25, 127, 128
 Polish immigrants, 18–27, 34–35, 43, 50–51, 89, 90, 124–28
 Symon's visit, 57
Wisconsin Supreme Court, 112
World War I, 6, 23, 120, 124
 effect on church war, 109
 and German-American Catholics, 2–3
 and M. Kruszka, 121–22

and Messmer, 117–18
relief efforts by Polish-Americans, 116–17
Wrocław, Poland, Archdiocese of. *See* Breslau, Archdiocese of

Zeininger, Rev. Augustine, 38
Zgoda (Milwaukee), 23
Znaniecki, William, 3
Zwierzchowski, Stanislaus, 116, 122–23
Źródło (Milwaukee), 42